MW01120214

Criminal Justice
Recent Scholarship

Edited by
Marilyn McShane and Frank P. Williams III

A Series from LFB Scholarly

Juvenile Homicide
Fatal Assault or Lethal Intent?

Raquel Maria Warley

LFB Scholarly Publishing LLC
El Paso 2011

Library of Congress Cataloging-in-Publication Data

Warley, Raquel Maria, 1969-
  Juvenile homicide : fatal assault or lethal intent? / Raquel Maria
Warley.
      p. cm.
  Includes bibliographical references and index.
  ISBN 978-1-59332-480-3 (hardcover : alk. paper)
  1. Juvenile homicide--United States. 2. Violence in adolescence--
United States. I. Title.
  HV9067.H6W37 2011
  364.1520835'0973--dc23
                          2011020659

ISBN 978-1-59332-480-3

Printed on acid-free 250-year-life paper.

Manufactured in the United States of America.

Table of Contents

List of Tables

List of Figures

Acknowledgments

I would like to express the deepest appreciation to Michael Smith, Irwin Epstein, Bernadette Hadden, Andrea Savage, Susan Crimmins, and Karin Elliot Brown for their guidance and support throughout this endeavor. Thanks to the National Institute on Drug Abuse (NIDA) for generously funding the Learning About Violence Among Adolescents (LAVIDA) project. Without their financial support, neither the original nor the present research would have been possible. Likewise, I am thankful to the youth who participated in the study. Their contribution made this inquiry feasible; moreover, their candor has added to the knowledge-base and will hopefully be used to save lives!

I am thankful to the wonderful men in my life—Jeffrey Warley, Jason Warley, Robert Miree, and Donald Law.

Special thanks to Cecil Whitmore, Sr.; your insight and input has enhanced my perspective, particularly concerning the adaptive nature of gang violence. I also give thanks to my mother, Regina Warley; and extend my deepest appreciation to Michelle Hood and Geraldine Law for nurturing me through the toughest years of my life. Finally, this book, as well as my life, is dedicated to my daughter, Royale Ashli Warley, whom I love so much!

CHAPTER 1:
Juvenile Homicide: A Definition of the Problem

INTRODUCTION

The killing of one human being by another is an egregious offense against society and public law. Be that as it may, youthful homicide offending is an obvious violation of propriety. The American conception of childhood is opposed to the notion of children engaging in such aberrant and forceful behavior. Still, juveniles in this country commit hundreds of homicides each year (Horowitz, 2000; Fox and Zawitz, 2007; Benekos and Merlo, 2008, 2010). Over the past few decades this phenomenon has become a major public concern, and recent school shootings in California, Colorado, Georgia, Arkansas, and Mississippi have solidified public fear (Lane, Cunningham, and Ellen, 2004; McGee, Carter, Williams and Taylor, 2005; Brennan and Moore, 2009).

Certainly, teen murder is not a monolithic event. There are different types of adolescent homicide, namely, mass murder, such as those by school shootings; familicide; thrill killing; acts of murder motivated by cultural hate; and urban street homicide. In addition, the correlates of juvenile murder are likely determined by the type of homicide (Lennings, 2004; Allen and Lo, 2010). That is, the demo- graphic, predisposing, and situational characteristics of lethal school violence are distinct from those involved when young people kill their family members. Likewise, the correlates of drive-by murders and common street homicide in inner cities differ from those associated with homicides that result from hate crimes or thrill killings.

Notwithstanding the variations, urban street killing is by far the most commonly occurring type of juvenile (and adult) homicide in the

1

United States (Anderson, 1997; Blumstein and Cork, 1996; Blumstein, 1995b; Cook and Laub, 1998; Harries, 1997; Prothrow-Stith, 1991; Center for Disease Control and Prevention [CDC], 2007; Molnar et al., 2009). Inasmuch as trends consistently indicate that most victims and perpetrators of homicide are male[1] (Bureau of Justice Statistics, 2007; Harries, 1997; Meithe and Regoeczi, 2004; Wolfgang, 1958; Yonas, O'Campo, Burke, Peak, and Gielen, 2005), many homicide scholars presume that these events may be related to male honor contests (e.g. Daly and Wilson, 1988, 2001; Harries, 1997; Levi, 1980; Luckenbill, 1977; Meithe and Regoeczi, 2004; Polk, 1993; Wilkinson and Fagan, 1996; Wilson and Daly, 1985; Wolfgang, 1958; Brezina, Agnew, Cullen, and Wrtie, 2004; Piquero and Sealock, 2010; Wilkinson, McBryde, Williams, Bloom, and Bell, 2009; Brennan and Moore, 2009). In these situations, lethal violence results from discreet conflicts between two or more males, followed by physical confrontations (Jacob, 2004; Rich and Grey, 2005; Kubrin and Weitzer, 2003; Stewart, Schreck and Brunson, 2008; Stretesky and Pogrebin, 2007).

Studies also have documented that potential outcomes from these assaultive encounters range from no injury to death (Kleck and McElrath, 1991; Brennan and Moore, 2009; Rich and Grey, 2005). Ipso facto, acknowledging the similarities between homicide and aggravated assault is necessary to developing a full understanding of youthful homicide offending. Conceptualizing these events as different points on a continuum of potential outcomes for violent encounters suggests a more refined understanding of the relationship between antecedent variables and deadly events. Despite this awareness, there is a lack of empirical observations of and substantive literature on both the relationship between masculinity and juvenile lethality, as well as the situational factors that determine death from assault in violent encounters involving juvenile male perpetrators.

Juvenilization of Lethal Violence

As evidenced by arrest data collected by the Federal Bureau of Investigations, long term trends and patterns in youthful homicide in the United Sates remained stable from 1976 through 1987 (Fox and Zawitz, 2007). Beginning in 1987, however, and up to the time of 1994, there was an epidemic outbreak of lethal violence among adoles-cents (Blumstein, 1995a, 1995b; Cook and Laub, 1998, 2002; Fagan, Zimring, and Kim, 1998; Swisher and Latzman, 2008; Spano and

Boland, 2010). During this period, homicide arrest rates dramatically increased for persons under age 18, from 17 arrestsper 100,000 persons nationwide to 31 per 100,000 (Fox and Zawitz, 2007). More strikingly, though, the proliferation of juvenile murder was attended by a much smaller increase for the 18 to 24 age cohort and a decline in homicide arrest rates for the 25 and older cohort (Blumstein 1995a, 1995b; Blumstein and Rosenfeld, 1999; Cook and Laub, 1998, 2002; Miethe and Recogeczi, 2004; Fox and Zawitz, 2007).

Historically, increases in the size of the juvenile population have been a strong predictor of both youth and overall crime (Smith and Feiler, 1995). Heide (1999), however, rejects the idea that changes in the juvenile population led to the proliferation of lethal violence among adolescents from the late 1980s to the early 1990s, since this population was actually declining during the epidemic period. Still, in spite of the population decline for this cohort, Smith and Feiler (1995) discovered that arrest rates for juveniles during the aforementioned time period, far exceeded any rates generated by the juvenile cohort of the baby boom generation.

There were other important demographic differences and changes during the epidemic period. Firstly, the outbreak of juvenile homicide offending was concentrated among males. Male juvenile arrest rates went from 7.6 offenders per 100,000 persons nationwide in 1984 to 16.8 per 100,000 by 1993 (Heide, 1996). Secondly, African Americans experienced significant increases in homicide arrest rates. African American juvenile arrest rates went from 45.2 offenders per 100,000 persons nationwide in 1984 to 62.3 per 100,000 in 1993 (Heide, 1996). Finally, guns contributed greatly to the dramatic increase in juvenile homicide offending rates. During this epidemic period, gun homicides increased 229% among the 10 to 17 age cohort, with no change in nongun homicides for this group (Blumstein 1995b; Blumstein and Cork, 1996; Blumstein and Rosenfeld, 1999; Cook and Laub, 2002; Zimring, 1997, 1998).

Since 1994, juvenile homicide arrest rates have dropped precipitously (Blumstein, 1995a; Blumstein and Rosenfeld, 1999; Butts and Travis, 2002; Gonzalez, 2001; Heide, 1999; Herrenkohl et al., 2001; Shumaker and McKee, 2001; FBI, 2007; CDC, 2007; Benekos and Merlo, 2008, 2010). The Bureau of Justice Statistics (2007) indicated that juvenile homicide offending went from 4,593 incidents in 1994 to 1,672 by the year 2005. In spite of the drop in incidence and prevalence, juvenile arrest rates for murder have increased since 2005 (Benekos and Merlo, 2010; Swisher and Latzman, 2008. Moreover, the juvenile homicide rate in the United States is among the highest of other industrialized nations (Hagan and Foster, 2001; Kuhn, Nile, O'Brien, Withers, and Hargarten, 1999; Staub, 1996). An investigation by Hagan and Foster (2001), for instance, showed that the homicide rate for juveniles in this country is six times that of Canada's.

Fatal Assault or Specific Intent to Kill

The rapid growth and decline, as well as the general incidence and prevalence of fatal violence among juveniles have been attributed to two conditions in particular. First and foremost, juvenile homicide rates have been linked to gun availability, weapon carrying, and firearm use (Blumstein, 1995b; Blumstein and Cork, 1996; Blumstein and Rosenfeld, 1999; Cook and Laub, 2002; Zimring, 1997, 1998; Vaugh et. al, 1996; Gonzalez, 2001; Kahn et. al, 1998; Lizotte and Sheppard, 2001; Sheley and Wright, 1993; Black and Hausman, 2008; Wilkinson et al., 2009; Brennan and Moore, 2009; Spano and Bolland, 2010, Nielsen, Martinez, and Rosenfeld, 2005). Access to handguns place juveniles at greater risk for homicidal behavior inasmuch as it encourages higher risk criminal offending, inspires arms races among rival gang members and drug traffickers, facilitates violent behavior in poorly controlled children, and intensifies routine conflicts and fist fights (Cornell, 1993; Gonzelez, 2001; Canada, 1996; Stretesky and Pogrebin, 2007; Nielsen et al., 2005; Yonas et al., 2007; Allen and Lo, 2010).

Levels of gun violence in the United States, however, are not evenly distributed. For certain, sex is a risk marker for both firearm offending and victimization (Black and Hausman, 2008; Wilkinson et al., 2009 Brennan and Moore, 2009). It is common knowledge that most of the people who are killed or physically injured by guns are male. It is also generally known that males are more likely than females to use guns in acts of violence and other predatory crimes. The concentration of gun violence in the African American community has also remained an empirical fact. For almost four decades, homicides involving firearms have been the leading cause of death for African American adolescents in this country (Fox and Zawitz, 2007). In fact, the Nation Center for Injury Prevention and Control (2008) posited that young Black males are 18 times more likely than the general population to fall victim to gun homicide. This population is also more likely, on average, to use handguns in the course of violent attacks or other predatory crimes (Harries, 1997; Black and Hausman, 2008; Allen and Lo, 2010; Nielsen et al., 2005). In their thesis, *Guns, youth violence, and social identity*, Fagan and Wilkinson (1998) argued that youth gun violence has become more prevalent and more concentrated demographically and spatially among African American adolescents in urban communities.

Gun ownership, carrying, and use are related to a range of delinquent and criminal behaviors. Gun possession is common among young males involved in drug trafficking, robbery, and other criminal endeavors (Brennan and Moore, 2009). Still, the reasons for gun possession among teens are varied and complex. Scholars in the field of violence insist that possession of weaponry goes beyond crime-oriented ownership for many disadvantaged youths (Anderson, 1994, 1998; Fagan and Wilkinson, 1998; Vaughan et. al, 1996; Wilkinson and Fagan, 1996; Black and Hausman, 2008; Harcourt, 2006; Stretesky, Pogrepin, Unnithan and Vendor, 2007; Wilkinson et al., 2009; Spano, Rivera, and Bolland, 2010). In high crime neighborhoods possession of a firearm also serves a tactical purpose for survival. Many researchers have convincing data indicating that juveniles primarily carry guns for personal safety and protection reasons (Blumstein, 1995; Boyum and Kleinman, 2003; Sheley and Wright, 1993; Vaughan et. al, 1996; Brennan and Moore, 2009; Khoury-Kassabri, Astor, and Benbenishty, 2007; Spano and Bollan, 2010). Perceptions and experiences of vulnerability in their immediate social worlds lead youth to risky actions, like gun ownership, carrying, and use.

Research also reveals that firearms have an aesthetic value for many inner city adolescent males. In particular, ethnographic studies by Wilkinson and Fagan (1996), Anderson (1997), and Oliver (2001) indicate that guns afford disadvantaged youth feelings of worth and bring them status in their communities (see also: Wilkinson et al., 2009; Stretesky and Pogrebin, 2007). Regardless of the circumstances, however, gun ownership in general and gun carrying in particular are obvious preconditions for their use in homicide and other violent crime.

Blumstein's diffusion theory (1995a, 1995b), which is currently the most popular explanation in social science for the dramatic increase in juvenile homicide rates between the mid-1980s and the early 1990s (see Blumstein and Cork, 1996; Blumstein and Rosenfeld, 1999; Heide,

1997; O'Brien et al., 1999; Prothrow-Stith, 1991),[2] makes reference to the impact of gun availability, ownership, and carrying on the juvenilization of lethal violence. Other scholars are of the same opinion and, like Blumstein, they postulate that in typical circumstances juvenile recklessness translates the presence of a gun into homicide (Fagan and Wilkinson, 1998; Hagan and Foster, 2001; Hardwick and Rowton-Lee, 1996; Massey, 2005; Wilkinson and Fagan, 1996; Black and Hausman, 2008; Wilkinson et al., 2009; Felson, Deane, and Armstrong, 2007). This theory is compatible with the general notion that homicide is fundamentally nothing more than a fatal assault—that is, a physical attack that escalated beyond the projected course of action (e.g. Wolfgang, 1958; Harries, 1997; Block, 1977; Block and Block, 1991; Luckenbill, 1977; Brookman, 2003, Kleck and McElrath, 1991; Weaver et al., 2004; Polk, 1998). This speculation, however, is in opposition to the other assumed cause of the growth in youthful homicide: offender lethality (Bennette, DiIulio, and Water, 1996).

While many homicide theorists suppose that murder is commonly a result of chance and not the intention to kill, other students of homicide believe that a large number of killings are done by design (Felson and Messner, 1996; Felson and Steadman, 1983; Miethe and Regoeczi, 2004; Nielsen et al., 2005). It is argued that the presence of lethal intent increases the likelihood of death from assault. Proponents of the lethal intent thesis proclaim that weapon choice generally mediates the relationship between offenders' specific intent to kill their victims and the outcome of assaultive encounters. They admit it is probable that people who wish to kill their victims will use more lethal weapons, namely firearms, to accomplish the task. When a firearm is not available, however, they maintain that people who intend to kill their victims will compensate by using more force and/or targeting more vital areas of the body to achieve their destructive goal. Nevertheless, fatal outcome is primarily a function of the offender's specific intent to do lethal harm.

Both propositions are plausible. Moreover, the weapon instrumentality effect hypothesis and the lethal intent thesis are both open to dispute since lethal intent is not well-researched in general (Brennan and Moore, 2009; Nielsen et al., 2005), and the intervening and interactive effects of offenders' intent, weapon instrumentality, and severity of outcome in assaultive violence have not been assessed in particular (Brennan and Moore, 2009). In the juvenile homicide literature, this discourse is almost entirely absent. In the general/adult literature, the significance of lethal intent as a determinant of death from assault and the relationship among intent, weapon, and outcome is certainly minimized. In the vast majority of tests of weapon instrumentality, as well as studies of gun density and homicide rates, the matter of offenders' intent is ignored. Where intent is considered, it is usually included as a confounding variable. In the few research models where offenders' intent has been measured and analyzed, there are critical methodological flaws concerning conceptualization, operational definitions, the unit of analysis, and statistical strategies. Moreover, to the extent that gun homicide is largely a male activity (Bailey, 2000; Polk, 1999; Wolfgang, 1958; Harries, 1997; Meithe and Regoeczi, 2004; Black and Hausman, 2008; Wilkinson et al., 2009), the lack of empirical observations into firearms, offenders' specific intent to do harm, and death from assault as related conditions in practices of male violence is another deficiency in the state of knowledge.

POLICY AND PRACTICE IMPLICATIONS

The estimated number of murders involving juvenile offenders fell 65% between 1994 and 2005 (Fox and Zawitz, 2007). Still, adolescents are involved in hundreds of murders each year in the United States (Swisher and Latzman, 2008; Benekos and Merlo, 2008; Merlo and Benekos, 2010). The economic and social costs of juvenile homicide are excessive. Lethal violence by adolescents affects the social functioning of individuals, groups, and communities; as well as their capacity to meet their needs, to self-actualize, to realize their value, and to perform their function in society. Above and beyond this are the public expenditures for medical care, legal defense, law enforcement, and incarceration, in addition to the larger cost to society in terms of productivity losses for homicide victims and institutionalized offenders (see Payne and Button, 2009; Welsh, Loeber, Stevens, Stouthamer-Loeber, Cohen, and Farrington, 2008).

Policy makers, largely attribute the rapid growth and decline, as well as the general incidence and prevalence of lethal violence among juveniles to patterns of firearm availability and use, to a cohort of juvenile "super-predators" (Bennett et al., 1996), and to a lenient and ill-equipped juvenile justice system. Inasmuch as policy and programming are established on theory about root causes, it is not surprising that public policy has been fashioned on gun control and the retribution and punishment approach.

Evaluating Gun Violence: Supply and Demand

Violence among youth in this country has been the subject of discourse for more than two decades. Inasmuch as firearms are involved in a substantial proportion of homicides involving juvenile perpetrators (Zimring, 1996; Fagan and Wilkinson, 1998; Meithe and Regoeczi, 2004; Kubrin and Hertig, 2003; Bailey, 2000; Brennan and Moore, 2009; Black and Hausman, 2008; Wilkinson et al., 2009; Spano and Bolland, 2010; Nielsen et al., 2005), gun violence in particular has been the focus of public concern. In response to growing perceptions of an increase in gun possession and gun violence by young people, nearly every state in the union has adopted youth violence prevention and intervention programs to reduce juvenile gun violence. The decisions and actions behind most of these policies and practices, however, have largely been influenced by criminology and the criminal justice system—as opposed to the fields of sociology and forensic social work.

As determined by legal instruction, gun violence prevention and intervention efforts have two overarching objectives: 1) control the sale and distribution of firearms to individuals under the age of consent and 2) prevent and deter juveniles from seeking to acquire and use guns. Policies and programs that attempt to disrupt the flow of firearms to adolescents represent a supply side approach to reducing juvenile gun assault. Demand side strategies, on the other hand, endeavor to deter gun acquisition and criminal intent among youth. Together, these regulatory and enforcement actions attempt to reduce the availability of guns to youth and, hence, the use of firearms in juvenile criminal offending.

Currently, there are many initiatives at the federal, state, and city levels that seek to restrict systematic trafficking of firearms to criminals and juveniles (Braga and Pierce; 2005; Piquero, 2005). Neighborhood-based prevention and intervention programs, such as Operation Ceasefire in Boston (Braga and Pierce, 2005), the Kansas City Gun Project (Sherman and Rogan, 1995), the Oakland Gun Tracing Project (Calhoun, Dodge, Journel, Zahnd, 2005), and Operation Gun Stop in New York City (Golden and Almo, 2004), are the essence of supply side welfare policies. These protection-focused strategies use policing approaches as the framework for uncovering complex mechanisms and various sources of illegal firearm distribution, as well as for developing interventions to disrupt gun trade and seize firearms before they are used in violent crimes. However, on the whole, empirical research indicates that supply side efforts do little to alter gun violence in general and homicide in particular among youth (Piquero, 2005; Braga and Pierce, 2005).

Demand side theory and strategies in the reduction of violence is concerned with motivations for juvenile gun possession and use. More specifically, the demand for guns is intimately related to notions of criminal intent and offender lethality. To this extent, demand side precepts, as determined by legal instruction, include accountability and punishment-based sanctions, such as mandatory penalties for firearm possession and sentence enhancement for gun crimes, including life in prison without the possibility of parole and capital punishment for juvenile homicide offenders as young as 12-years-old (Benekos and Merlo, 2008, 2010; Stewart et al., 2008; Piquero and Steinberg, 2009).

Judicial punishment is meant to dissuade youngsters from possessing firearms and engaging in gun violence by making criminal penalties severe enough that the costs outweigh the benefits gained by the offense (i.e. rational choice theory). However, this philosophy ignores the fact that children and adolescents tend to act without thought or reason. Consequently, they do not take notice of the possibility (or probability) of punishment until they are caught. These policies also do not account for the fact that in marginalized communities young men may not fear prison, due to a foreshortened life expectancy and/or the status that comes with "doing a bid" (i.e. prison time). More importantly, current demand-side strategies do not address structural conditions that create, perpetuate, and facilitate youth gun violence in socially disadvantaged communities. Ipso facto, legal deterrence does not work for many young people.

Moreover, the retribution approach alone is not likely to solve the problem since it does not address root causes of gun possession and use among juveniles. If the institutional arrangements and community values and norms that strongly increase the probability of gun possession and violent behavior among certain groups of juvenile boys are not disrupted, this social problem can not and will not be abated in any noticeable way (Stewart et al., 2008; Yonas et al., 2007; Matjasko, Needham, Grunden, and Farb, 2010; Duke, Borowsky, Pettingel, McMorris, 2009; Piquero and Steinberg, 2009; Parker and

Reckdenwald, 2008; Piquero and Brame, 2009; Allen and Lo, 20010). In fact, there is currently a lack of evidence to support the effectiveness of enhanced sentencing policies in reducing juvenile homicide. Overall, it appears to be reactive social policy: someone is killed then we punish, rehabilitate or treat the offender.

Risk-Focused Prevention: A New Demand Side Approach

Although gun control and stringent sentencing policies for adolescent homicide offenders are worthwhile in some regard, in the context of reducing juvenile homicide they are largely inadequate prevention strategies. Most forms of legal intervention are tertiary in nature. These frameworks are used to intercede where problems already exist. Services are rendered to individuals, families, and/or communities, usually in the form of "corrections", for unresolved circumstances or deficiencies in personal development. Ostensibly, legal deterrence is not meant to prevent young people from killing by taking steps to eliminate or minimize contributory factors before the event occurs.

In consideration of human security and the greater good of society, it is time to adopt prevention and protection strategies over punishment and deterrence as national goals. This proactive policy alternative is based on the point of view that it is more advantageous to prevent the destruction of human life by means of prior action than it is to punish or constrain the offender once he has killed another person. In other words, the goal of public and social policy should be to protect citizens from juvenile homicide by preventing at-risk youth from killing at the outset.

To be effective, risk-focused prevention must be rooted in sound theory and evidence-based practice. The aim is to generate or ascertain theory that identifies a set of potential risk factors for juvenile homicide offending, is amendable to research, and provides a plausible explanation for the association between predictor variables and youthful lethality. Factors that are shown to predict or impede violence among adolescents and offer an intervention possibility can be used as the basis for program designs and interventions that successfully deal with at-risk behaviors and facilitative conditions. This strategy constitutes a social action model. This approach requires social welfare researchers and practitioners to work together to design, implement, and evaluate risk-focused prevention/intervention programs that promote positive youth development and reduce the incidence and prevalence of assaultive violence among juveniles.

A MANDATE FOR FORENSIC SOCIAL WORK

There are many social work practice theories and program models that systematically address what are known to be root causes of youthful violence, namely social and economic deprivation, community disorganization, and personal development deficits. The profession has traditionally used community-based programming and grass roots organizing established on the theory that positive gains in personal and social responsibility, as well as educational aspiration, academic achievement, and employment training will reduce adolescent violence. On the condition that there is adequate funding for programs and services, social work knowledge, techniques, and skills can certainly permit purposeful action in the reduction of fatal violence among young males. However, juvenile homicide theorizing, research, and policy has operated within the purview of criminology. Although social work generally concerns issues of interpersonal violence, customarily interfaces with youth in all systems, and has expertise in the area of juvenile homicide, the profession has been conspicuously absent in defining the problem of homicidal aggression among youth, as well as generating knowledge that would lend to a greater understanding of murderous behavior in adolescents and the conditions that tend to produce it. Moreover, the profession has been remiss in publicly pronouncing solutions that have the potential to effectively address this grave social problem.

In fact, a search of Social Work Abstracts and Dissertation Abstracts Online suggests there is disinclination in the field to take on this problem, both empirically and practically. The lack of discourse means there is a shortage of social work knowledge in regard to this phenomenon and interventive models that may successfully prevent youthful lethality. This is unfortunate. Given social work's emphasis on positive youth development, human ecology (i.e. the person-in-environment perspective), and its many primary and secondary prevention models, practitioners can readily comprehend and direct attention to the structural, cultural, and situational determinants of fatal violence. To the extent that this is true, these practitioners are particularly qualified to develop study in the area of homicide, to shape the policy agenda around youthful lethality, and to handle the practicalities of service organization and delivery to at-risk client systems. Given present knowledge about the intersections of masculinity, social class, race/ethnicity, and violence, social work interventions that promote positive male identity development in boys and young men in inner cities are more likely than suppression and punishment strategies to be successful in reducing juvenile homicide (Payne and Button, 2009; Black and Hausman; Matjasko et al., 2010; Wilkinson et al., 2009; Yonas et al., 2007; Allen and Lo, 2010).

INTERVENTIONS IN MALE IDENTITY DEVELOPMENT

In disadvantaged communities, illegal gun trade is rampant (Spano and Bolland, 2010; Wilkinson et al., 2009; Brennan and Moore, 2009; Black and Hausman, 2008). Therefore, firearms are readily available to children and adolescents, and the rules and norms of disorganized neighborhoods impact decisions to carry and use guns (Anderson, 1997; Wilkinson and Fagan, 1996; Fagan and Wilkinson, 1998; Cook and Laub, 2002; Oliver, 2001; Stewart et al., 2008; Yonas et al., 2007 Spano et al., 2010; Rich and Grey, 2005). Gun ownership and gun play among young males in socially and economically disadvantaged communities in particular are connected to social identity and respect (Fagan and Wilkinson, 1998; Oliver, 2001; Brezina et al., 2004; Rich and Grey, 2005; Yonas et al., 2005; Black and Hausman, 2008; Wilkinson et al., 2009; Brennan and Moore, 2009; Taylor, Esbensen, Brick, and Freng, 2010; Blokland, 2008; Allen and Lo, 2010). There is a high expectation of gun violence in these environments. Moreover, firearms and violence are part of a street code that permits or prescribes such behavior for self protection, to defend perceived threats to manhood, and to enhance status and credibility (Anderson, 1997, 1998). These factors speak to the demand for firearms, which has a measurable impact on juvenile gun violence and homicide.

In the realm of firearms and gun violence, policy analysts and criminologists suggest that demand reduction strategies support supply side interventions (Piquero, 2005; Braga and Pierce, 2005; Brennan and Moore, 2009). Whether death is a consequence of technology (i.e. the weapon used) or criminal intent, ascertaining why juvenile males carry guns and why they use them to resolve conflict is important information for planning effective primary and secondary prevention initiatives (Spano and Bolland, 2010). Risk-focused, evidence-based social policy and service delivery established around matters of sex, race/ethnicity, and neighborhood context can surely be included in the framework of demand side prevention of juvenile homicide. Programs designed to promote healthy male identity for disadvantaged youth by establishing prosocial norms, developing positive values and ideals, and creating real opportunities for advancement, have actual potential to achieve preventive effects and social betterment. This sort of organization is within the purview of the social work and social welfare professions.

PURPOSE OF THE PRESENT STUDY

The present research is grounded in a body of knowledge encompassing theoretical and empirical work from several fields of study. In the same way, the findings of this investigation have implications for practice, research, and education in social work, as well as criminology, public health, and pedagogy. Using a non-experimental comparison group method involving available data concerning adjudicated juvenile homicide and aggravated assault cases, this study examined distal and proximal pathways to lethal violence for adolescent male offenders. The overall goal of this work was to develop an understanding of the processual nature of youthful violence and juvenile homicide. The plan was to progress the research problem to a new level of analysis and offer a different set of principles to explain adolescent killing. To this extent, strategic planning vis-à-vis youthful murder will not rely on gun control and stricter sentencing policies. When this occurs, national policy and the administrative response to it will entail a new dimension of risk-focused prevention that can better serve at-risk youth, families and communities, as well as better protect society.

The study utilizes two research strategies. The main objective was to document situational factors under which assaultive transactions involving juvenile male perpetrators end in the death of the victim. For this purpose, a correlational approach was employed to examine the association between incident characteristics, namely offenders' specific intent to do harm, type of weapon involved, motive, offenders' perception of victim-precipitation, social audience effects, and systemic drug-relatedness (i.e. drug trafficking).

Inasmuch as the purpose of the study was to also provide a strong theoretical base for problem-oriented program planning in the area of youth violence, the framework for the investigation integrates principles of strain/anomie, social disorganization, symbolic interactionism, and the subculture of violence theories. Therefore, providing information with respect to variables that describe the structural and cultural position of the study participants is necessary. Prior to the principle analysis, descriptive research was used to delineate distal characteristics that dispose adolescent males to violent interactions. In this segment of the analysis, the relationship between structural-cultural variables and severity of outcome are also investigated. Structural-cultural variables include offenders' race/ethnicity, neighborhood violence, neighborhood drug trafficking, availability of guns in neighborhood, association with violent peers, gun ownership, gun carrying, gun use, and involvement in drug trafficking.

In the second portion of the study, it was hypothesized that aggravated assault and homicide offenses involving juvenile male perpetrators would not differ by structural-cultural factors (see Figure 1). These crimes typically include at-risk youth who are disposed to serious aggression as a result of inequalities, socialization, chronic strain, and opportunities for violence that originate in their environment (Piquero and Sealock, 2010; Agnew, 2006; Kaufman, Rebellon, Thaxton, and Agnew, 2008; Perez, Jennings, Gover, 2008; Jennings, Piquero, Gover, and Perez, 2009; Jang, 2007). However, aggravated assaults and homicides for this cohort, were expected to differ according to situational risk factors. According to the notion of "face" and "honor" that underlie the paradigm of compulsory masculinity, how the event ends and/or how the offender decides to act in the event (i.e. with lethal intent or not) is potentially a function of the intensity of the conflict and the magnitude of the threat to one's manhood. Firearms, illegal drug trade, and the presence of third parties are likely to intensify conflict and raise identity stakes for youthful male offenders who reside in communities characterized by concentrated disadvantage.

Figure 1. Compulsory Masculinity: Distal and Proximal Risks for Assaultive and Lethal Violence

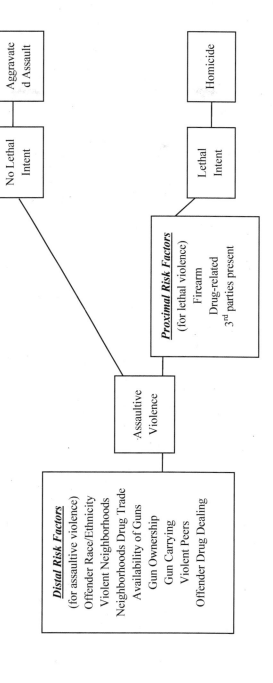

CHAPTER 2:

Juvenile Homicide: Structural and Cultural Risk Factors

DYNAMIC CONTEXTUALISM: AN INTEGRATED THEORY OF JUVENILE HOMICIDE

In his composition on the preparatory steps to the advanced study of violence, Toch (1980) stated that "we can understand a person's violent behavior better when we know the context in which it occurred and the stimuli that precipitated it" (p. 663). Studying the context of violence requires an examination of distal and proximal circumstances that converge to inspire assaultive and predatory behavior. By inference, effective prevention of juvenile homicide necessitates the identification of a distinct set of developmental risks and immediate situational influences that lead to murderous behaviors in teenagers.

The overarching theoretical framework for this study integrates three kinds of explanations that have been put forth to account for juvenile violence. This is a dynamic contextual theory of how structural, cultural, and situational factors converge to produce a social context in which the occurrence of lethal violence is possible. Specifically, this theory is intended to define how structural and cultural conditions translate into values, norms, role orientations, and lifestyles among certain adolescent males that facilitate violent encounters. Moreover, this research study is devised to explain how some assaultive encounters involving juvenile male perpetrators eventuate in lethal outcomes.

Integration and elaboration of theory is indispensable in the theory building process (Akers, 1994). Propositional integration is established on the notion that various frameworks are supplemental and complementary rather than contradictory (Oberwitter, 2004). Notwithstanding, the current model is inspired by the desire to more firmly link theory to the reality of juvenile homicide in the United States. Altogether, this orientation is an amalgamation of anomie and strain, social disorganization, social learning, and cultural deviance theories. In addition, it includes symbolic interactionism and the criminal lethality perspective. Otherwise, this paradigm is known as the compulsory masculinity thesis.

The author caveats this discussion with the following declarations: First, this document encompasses empirical and theoretical literature on predisposing and situational effects that are not necessary specific to adolescent homicide, but, nonetheless, contributes to an understanding of this social phenomenon. Second, this essay does not include an exhaustive discussion on the long-term risk factors and situational conditions that effect assaultive violence in general. Rather, the aim here is to review specific bodies of work that significantly contribute to knowledge regarding the etiology of homicidal aggression in males and among adolescent males in particular.

Risk Factors

Risk factors are conditions that increase one's chance for homicidal offending. Essentially, these are background and life situations that predispose young people to lethal violence. These factors are not necessarily causes in the actual sense of the word. Rather, they are precursors or antecedents of homicidal behavior. In truth, there is no single determinant of lethal aggression. Homicide researchers maintain that the accumulation of risk factors is more important than individual risk factors in determining murderous conduct (Gonzalez, 2001; Freeman and Hemenway, 2000; Hardwick and Rowton-Lee, 1996; Herrenkohl et al., 2000; Huizinga, Loeber, Thornberry, and Cothern, 2000; Felson et al., 2007). Substantively, the etiology of juvenile homicide is mediated by a combination of neurological, psychological, sociological, structural, environmental, behavioral, and situational risk factors.

In the juvenile literature, risk factors are generally grouped into five generic domains: individual, family, peer, school, and community. Some of these domains become more or less important as the person matures, while the influence of others persists throughout the life span. No single risk factor is powerful enough to predict with certainty which youth will become violent or homicidal. In fact, most young persons who are identified as "at-risk", because of a single factor or set of risk factors, never come to be violent, let alone murderous (Farrington, 1997; Huizinga et al., 2000; Lipsey and Derzon, 1998; Rutter, 1985; Werner and Smith, 1982, 1992). Moreover, risk factors can only be used to predict violence in groups with certain characteristics; they are unable to predict violent behavior for individuals.

Social science has documented a number of factors that put children and adolescents at-risk for violence, including homicide. Ewing (1990) implicated four variables in particular in the rise of juvenile homicide in the United States. In 1996, Heide followed suite with a compilation of fourteen factors. In the aggregate, these elements include growth in the juvenile population, child abuse and neglect, absence of positive male role models, crisis in leadership, witnessing violence, the accessibility of guns, teen alcohol and illicit drug abuse, poverty and lack of resources, low self-esteem, low-frustration tolerance, impaired judgment and despair.

Nevertheless, two matters remain at issue. First, previous research provides mixed findings about whether risk factors vary by race. Some research shows that risk factors are equally valid predictors of violence regardless of race or ethnicity (Williams, Ayers, Abbott, Hawkins, and Catalano, 1991; Williams, Stiffman, and O'Neal, 1998; Brezina et al., 2004), while others suggest that risk factors for violence differ across racial groups (Harrer and Steffensmeire, 1992; Salts, Lindholm, Goddard, and Duncan, 1995; Stewart et al., 2008; Unnevers, 2008; Wilkinson et al., 2009). In addition, research has yet to resolve whether risk factors differ by sex or if there are sex differences in coping mechanisms for stress, frustration, fear, and anxiety, all of which can facilitate violence in general and lethal assault in particular. The rather meager literature on sex differences regarding risk factors for violent and homicidal behavior among juveniles seems inconclusive. In any event, risk factors have the potential to disrupt healthy child and adolescent development, particularly if not addressed early.

Developmental Pathways

The idea of development is critical in the study of juvenile homicide, insofar as disruptions in the social, psychological, and emotional growth of children and adolescents can produce criminality and other antisocial behavior. These long-term or distal effects can help to predict, with caution, which youths are more likely to be homicidal, given similar situational opportunities to kill. Pre-homicidal experiences and behaviors can contribute to lethal violence in at least two ways: directly through propensity and personality characteristics or indirectly by putting offenders in contact with dangerous people, places, and situations (Harries, 1997; Stretesky and Pogrebin, 2007; Felson et al., 2007).

In developmental studies, temporal priority—that is to say, the timing of risk factors and the onset of antisocial behavior—is important. For that reason, longitudinal methods, which involve repeated contact with the same juveniles over a substantial period of time and development, are generally state-of-the-art for identifying background risk factors. Hence, longitudinal initiatives rather than cross-sectional studies are preferable for the identification of biological, sociological, psychological, and environmental factors that contribute to or cause homicidal violence in teens. However, because murder is rare, especially among juveniles, prospective designs are problematic in the investigation of adolescent homicide. Consequently, most studies of murder involving children employ retrospective designs.

Since the 1930s[3] social scientists have used research to learn more about juvenile homicide in the hopes of predicting and controlling this phenomenon. As a result of their efforts, it is understood that homicide is largely a male activity (Baily, 2000; Polk, 1999; Stewart et al., 2008; Yonas et al., 2005). It is also known that the risk of an adolescent committing a homicide increases if he:

- Has a history of delinquent or violent behavior, substance abuse, or poor educational attainment (Blumstein and Cork, 1996; Cork, 1999; Darby, Wesley, Kashani, Hartke, and Reid, 1998; Henry, Avshalom, Moffitt, and Silva, 1996; Horowitz, 2000).

- Has neurological or psychological problems that impair thinking, feeling, or impulse regulation (Bender, 1959; Denno, 1990; Farrington, 1995; Henry et al., 1996; Kandel and Mednick, 1991; Lewis et al., 1985; Lewis, Shanok, Grant, and Ritvo, 1983; Miller and Looney, 1974; Myer and Scott, 1998; Russell, 1979; Sendi and Blomgren, 1975).

- Has access to a weapon, particularly a firearm (Blumstein and Cork, 1996; Cork, 1999; Black and Hausman, 2008; Wilkinson et al., 2009).

- Resides in a chaotic or violent household or community (Crespi and Rigazio-DiGilio, 1996; Darby et al., 1998; King, 1975; Lewis et al., 1988; Russell, 1985; Sorrell, 1977; 1980; Zagar, Arbit, Sylvies, Busch, and Hughes, 1990; Stewart et al., 2008; Yonas et al., 2007; Spano et al., 2010).

- Associates with violent peers (Brewer, Damphousse, Adkinson, 1998; Crimmins, Brownstein, Spunt, Ryder, and Warley, 1998; Farrington, 1998; Wilkinson et al., 2009; Brennan and Moore, 2009; Stretesky and Pogrebin, 2007).

Risk factors included in this thesis were selected in consideration of the theoretical orientation for the study, as well as the availability of measures within the dataset used for this inquiry.

STRUCTURAL CONSIDERATIONS

Structuralists postulate that human nature is corrupted by society insofar as structural arrangements inhibit the development of individuals by impeding self-actualization (Gil, 1996). It is generally assumed that the effects of inequality cause people to devise adaptive responses to their problems; deviance and crime are two ways of doing so (Massey, 2005; Ousey, 1999; Kubrin and Hertig, 2003; Stretesky and Pogrebin, 2007; Stewart et al., 2008; Swisher and Latzman, 2008). Anomie is a structural explanation of crime and delinquency. It was formulated as a general theory of deviance. Although it does not particularly concern criminality, anomie is well-suited to an explanation of the matter. Emile Durkheim created the term anomie to describe a state of normlessness and distrust that resulted from rapid social change and the weakening of social ties (Giddens, 1972). He hypothesized that the lack of social regulation in modern society caused higher rates of suicide.

Merton's (1968) strain perspective is the most popular criminological theory of anomie. He reconceptualized Durkheim's ideas to suggest that the social structure exerts pressure upon certain groups in society to engage in non-conforming behavior. This explanation is used to understand variations in crime rates across society and social groups within society. It has been instrumental in explicating the concentration of crime by age, sex, race, and socioeconomic class. Moreover, the assumptions that underlie anomie and strain theory have implications for socioeconomic class, race/ethnicity, and sex as these variables are collectively related to masculine violence among juveniles.

Implications of Socioeconomic Status

Macrosociological studies have consistently shown that poverty is positively associated with homicide rates in the United States (e.g. Blau and Blau, 1982; Messner, 1982; Messner and Tardiff, 1986; Smith and Parker, 1980; Martinez, 1997; Kovandzic, Vieratis, and Yeisley, 1998; Massey, 2005). Poverty is not presumed to be a direct cause of antisocial behavior in children and adolescents; rather, the supposition is that poverty creates the conditions that lead to it (Harries, 1997; Oliver, 2001; Prothrow-Stith, 1991; Nielsen et al., 2005; Parker and Reckdenwald, 2008; Stewart et al., 2008; Spano et al., 2010). Economic and social deprivation caused by discrimination undermines normal childhood development by decreasing needed resources and increasing stressors and exposure to pathological conditions that impede healthy social maturation (Spano et al., 2010; Brandt, Ward, Powes, and Fisher, 2005; Volsin, 2007).

Although the large majority of poor youth avoid criminal behavior in general and homicide in particular, socioeconomic status predicts delinquency and youth violence (Farrington, 1998; Hawkins, Herrenkohl, Farrington, Brewer, Catalano, Harachi, and Cothern, 2000). Class differences appear to be even more distinct for serious violence (Salts, Lindhom, Goddard, and Duncan, 1995; Hawkins, Laub, Lauritisen, and Cothern, 2000; Fagan, Piper, and Moore, 1986; Heimer, 1997; Matjasko et al., 2010). Empirical observations consistently show that homicide offenders, for instance, are disproportionately drawn from the ranks of the poor (Channing Bete Company, 2004; Hawkins, 1990; Wolfgang, 1958; Williams, 1984; Messner and Tardiff, 1986).

Implications of Race/Ethnicity

Race/ethnicity is a major vector of social and economic inequalities in the United States (Massey, 2005; Avakame, 1997; Hawkins, 1983; Wilson, 1997; Unnever, 2008; Stewart et al., 2008; Taylor et al., 2010). It is also the offender attribute most studied, and a significant predictor of homicide (Meithe and Regoeczi, 2004; Allen and Lo, 2010). High rates of homicide among Blacks is well-documented (see Brearly, 1932; Wolfgang, 1958; Porkorny, 1977; Hawkins, 1985; Lee and

Ousey, 2005; Juvenile Justice Bulletin, 2000; Hawkins et al., 2000; Stewart et al., 2008; Yonas et al., 2007; Wilkinson et al., 2009; Rich and Grey, 2005; Piquero and Brame, 2008). As cited in Wolfgang (1959), for example, in 1939 Emil Frankel found that "the extent to which Negros are present in the general population of the counties, to that extent is the general homicide rate affected" (p. 40). This observation became the rationale for "percent Black" as a control variable in aggregate studies of homicide rates.

The determination of what is considered homicide, however, has been historically arbitrary and inconsistent (Miethe and Regoeczi, 2004). Case in point, lynching of Blacks was not defined as a homicide for a long time in American history. Perloft (2000) estimates that between 1882 and 1968 alone, at least 3,500 Blacks were lynched by White individuals in front of witnesses and no arrests were made. Meanwhile, Blacks have traditionally been more likely than Whites to be arrested, charged, and convicted of private killing (Piquero and Brame, 2008; Piquero and Sealock, 2010).

Notwithstanding, Blacks disproportionately contribute to criminal homicide relative to their proportion in the general population. Moreover, the racial gap in rates of homicide for the juvenile population widened dramatically between 1986 and 1994. During this period, homicide rates for White youth aged 14 to 17 doubled from 7.0 to 15.6 per 100,000 persons. Meanwhile, homicide rates for Black youth in the same age group tripled from 44.3 to 139.6 per 100,000 persons. Handgun murder in particular was most prevalent among Black adolescents during the epidemic; the incidence of gun homicide for this cohort increased over 200% between 1986 and 1994 (Blumstein and Rosenfeld, 1999).

Research indicates that Blacks have a disproportionately higher rate of homicide offending even among other marginalized ethnic groups (Massey, 2005; Hawkins, 1993; Nielsen et al., 2005; Allen and Lo, 2010). This has been attributed to hypersegregation among Blacks (Shihadeh and Maume, 1997; Ousey, 1999; Hawkins, 1990). That is to say, Blacks are more spatially segregated than any other group of people, and the concentration of Blacks relative to Whites and others is a significant determinant of Black homicide rates (Taylor et al., 2010; Brezina et al., 2004; Wilkinson et al., 2009). Other studies have indicated that Hispanics also have a high rate of homicide offending (e.g. Sommer and Baskins, 1990; Martinez and Lee, 1999; Piquero and

Brame, 2008); however, this community has largely been ignored in the research on juvenile homicide.

It should be noted that race specific studies tend to be methodologically flawed. The most critical limitation being that they generally lump groups of people together. Dichotomizing the race variable into White/Black or White/Non-White and not examining patterns of homicide within race and ethnic groups potentially masks variations in homicide offending. Statements that might be true, on average, might not be representative of all subgroups within the aggregate (Hawkins, 1990). Furthermore, many race-based studies at both the aggregate and the case level employ mysterious recording methods for the offender race/ethnicity variable. To the extent that there is no indication of how or which ethnic groups comprise the race dichotomy, evidence of racial and ethnic differences in homicide offending should be accepted with caution.

Implications of Sex

Merton (1968) was a structural functionalist; he presumed that most members of society are socialized into a common system of values. These culturally defined goals transcend class and race/ethnicity. In the American value system, money is central. Money is highly regarded for the materials and merchandise that it can buy, the social prestige it provides, and the personal worth that it represents. For that reason, economic and social inequalities are expected to cause strain among the lower strata of society. Merton maintained, however, that the pressure to be wealthy or financially independent is not evenly distributed among sex. If socioeconomics was the major determinant, females would be expected to commit more crimes than males. After all, females are socially and economically deprived relative to males.

According to Merton (1968), the masculine role intrinsically carries elements of strain. Money, power, success, and bravado constitute the social construction of masculinity; yet, opportunities to fulfill prototypes and idealized examples of manhood are largely ascribed on the basis of particularistic group membership. Sex stratification and blocked opportunities result in a compensatory process where toughness and the acquisition of money and material goods by any means necessary are admired, and even obligatory (Swisher and Latzman, 2008; Stretesky and Pogrebin, 2007; Yonas et al., 2007; Allen and Lo, 2010). Inasmuch as, young males are particularly concerned with their masculinity, life situations related to class and race/ethnicity can generate problems in masculine identity development for adolescent boys. Alpha-male alternatives, including violence, may become a resource for juveniles who lack other means for accomplishing gender (Messerschmidt, 1993; Oliver, 2001; Polk, 1999; Brezina et al., 2004; Taylor et al., 2010).

Masculinity is an important construct for understanding violence in general and homicide in particular (Daly and Wilson, 2001, 1988; Wilson and Daly, 1985; Wolfgang, 1958; Mears, Ploeger and Marr, 1998; Duxbury, 1980; Oliver, 2001; Meithe and Regoeczi, 2004; Harries, 1997; Allen and Lo, 2010). Several studies have devoted attention specifically to the intersection between masculinity and violence (see Messerchmidt, 1993, 1997, 2000 Jefferson, 1997; Hern, 1998; Collier, 1998; Polk, 1994, 1997; Brookman, 2003; Krienert, 2003; Allen and Lo, 2010). The vast majority of research supports the masculinization of violence thesis regardless of whether masculinity or sex is a specific focus of study. A trend analysis by the Bureau of Justice Statistics (2004), for instance, found that males are 10 times more likely than females to commit murder.

Structural pressures alone, however, are not enough to explain the intersection between masculinity and violence. The specific cultural adaptations and pathologies concerning stereotypical behavioral features of masculinity that develop as a result of inequalities and strain in certain communities must also be considered.

CULTURAL CONSIDERATIONS

It is postulated that anomie results in social disorganization. Social disorganization theory proposes that structural inequalities create neighborhoods plagued by poverty and social deprivation. In the adaptation process that arises as a consequence of economic and social inequalities, specific behavioral and interactional patterns develop among inhabitants of disorganized localities. It has been presumed that the conditions, experiences, values, and norms associated with these social patterns lead to crime and delinquency among residents in these "differently organized" ghettos.[4]

Social disorganization theory departs from the criminological tradition of biological inferiority and personal degeneracy. Proponents of this hypothesis are environmental determinists; they focus on the physical features of neighborhoods that create and sustain crime and delinquency. This paradigm has its origins in the study of ecology, which is the examination of the relationship between organisms and their environment. The theory was first developed by sociologists at the University of Chicago in the Institute for Juvenile Research in the 1920s (Akers, 1994). Park and Burgess were the first to do an ecological analysis of crime causation that focused on social area characteristics instead of offender attributes (Akers, 1994). Shaw and McKay (1969) borrowed from Park and Burgess' work to examine the relationship between social area and crime rates among juveniles (Gottfredson, McNeil, and Gottfredson, 1991; Akers, 1994). From then until now, much intelligence regarding the characteristics of disorganized communities and neighborhood effects on criminogenic outcomes has been gathered.

Neighborhood Effects[5]

Empirical and theoretical literature indicate that communities characterized by social disorganization include physical decay, high rates of out-of-wedlock births and one-parent/female-headed households, illiteracy, persistent unemployment, drug addiction, crime, and mental illness (see Wilson, 1987; Wilson and Sampson, 1995; Sampson, 1997; Peterson and Krivo, 1999; Lee and Ousey, 2005; Stewart et al., 2008). Children in socially disorganized areas are exposed to these social pathologies, which increase their risk of violent offending and other antisocial behavior (Herrenkohl et al., 2000; Blau and Blau, 1982; Lee and Ousey, 2005; Spano et al., 2010; Volsin, 2007).

Social disorganization theory is not concerned with individual family economics status as much as it is with area socioeconomics. It finds explanation for moral poverty in the process of ghettoization and segregation of unwanted people. Proponents of this theory implicate hypersegregation and the concentration of poverty in the establishment of an urban underclass and a population of truly disadvantaged citizens (Marks, 1991; Sampson, 1997; Lee and Ousey, 2005, Wilson and Sampson, 1995; Spano et al., 2010; Matjasko et al., 2010). Involuntary confinement to socially disorganized areas is proclaimed to be the result of income inequalities and other structural arrangements that impede residential and social mobility for certain segments of society.

Residential segregation among Blacks and Whites is an enduring feature of American life, irrespective of social class. Even though class segregation commonly signifies racial segregation in this country, the proportion of the poor who live in disadvantaged ghettos vary dramatically by race (Massey, 2005; Piquero and Sealock, 2010; Allen and Lo, 2010). There is overwhelming evidence to support the claim that Blacks are more likely to live in extremely impoverished areas than Whites (Fagan et al. 1996; Kubrin and Hertig, 2003; Massey, 2004; Messner and Tardiff, 1986; Miethe and Regoeczi, 2004; Ousey, 1999; Prothrow-Stith, 1991; Shihadeh and Maume, 1997; Brezina et al., 2004; Taylor et al., 2010; Swisher and Latzman, 2008; Felson et al., 2007). Specifically, in 1992, Sommers and Baskin used disaggregate data to examine the extent of violent offending by sex, race, and age characteristics. In addition to the main findings of the study, these data revealed that 65% of the Black population of New York City lived in disadvantaged neighborhoods compared to 22% of the Hispanic population and 13% of the White population. Sociologist Robert Sampson (1997) conducted a meta-analysis that also indicated that poor Blacks and poor Whites live in very different kinds of neighborhoods. His work suggested that 70% of poor Whites live in non-poor neighborhoods versus 16% of poor Blacks. Moreover, results showed that less than seven percent of poor Whites reside in extremely poor areas compared to 38% of poor Blacks. Research by many others provides evidence of this differential as well (see Denton and Massey, 1988, Lee and Ousey, 2005, Massey and Denton, 1993, Massey, Gross, and Eggers, 1991, Sampson and Wilson, 1995, and Wilson, Aponte, Kirschenman and Wacquant, 1988).

Intriguingly, Massey (2004) discovered that nearly one-half (48%) of all metropolitan Blacks, regardless of income level, live under conditions of hypersegregation and concentrated disadvantage. By that very fact, Blacks are exposed to far higher rates of social disorder and violence than any other social group (Massey, 2004; Massey and Fischer, 1999; Nielsen et al., 2005; Allen and Lo, 2010). To this point, he remarked:

> As segregation concentrates poverty, it also concentrates anything that is correlated with poverty to create a uniquely disadvantaged social environment ... Because crime is also associated with poverty, segregation likewise ends up concentrating social disorder and violence, yielding an usually

hostile and threatening environment to which…African Americans must adapt (p. 17).

In economically and socially disadvantaged communities, residents have the greatest risk of homicide offending and victimization (Avakame, 1997; Kubrin and Hertig, 2003; Stewart et al., 2008; Spano et al., 2010; Brennan and Moore, 2009; Parker and Reckdenwald, 2008; Piquero and Sealock, 2010); yet, these effects also appear to vary by race. For instance, using a sample of U.S. cities to determine the effects of residential segregation on race-specific homicide victimization rates, Peterson and Krivo (1999) concluded, in agreement with Parker and McCall's (1997) study of race-specific homicide offending rates, that residential segregation and concentrated disadvantage has a stronger effect on African American homicide than they do on White homicide rates. These findings, and others like it (see Sampson et al., 2002; Sampson, 2003; Felson et al., 2007; Stewart et al., 2008; Piquero and Brame, 2008; Swisher and Latzman, 2008; Nielsen et al., 2005), seem to corroborate the contention that differential spatial distribution of White and Black neighborhoods explain racial disparities in homicide offending and victimization rates.

Neighborhood effects also vary by child's age and sex (Pebley and Sastry, 2003; Matjasko et al., 2010). Adolescents and male children are more susceptible to neighborhood context than are young children, preteens, and female juveniles. In any case, ambient hazards, such as poverty, substance use, and drug trafficking are correlated with delinquent and violent behavior in youths. Several studies show that youngsters living in high crime neighborhoods are more likely than their counterparts in low-crime neighborhoods to engage in delinquent and violent activities.

Researchers studying children in poor urban communities have suggested that neighborhood characteristics play a major role in influencing juvenile development. Brooks-Gunn, Duncan, Klebanov, and Sealand (1993) postulated that neighborhood effects are even more powerful than family factors in predicting adolescent outcomes. Likewise, Pebley and Sastry (2003) observed that youth violence vary significantly by neighborhood income level and less by other characteristics such as female-headship and family socioeconomic status. Moreover, neighborhood effects appear to be more closely associated with delinquency rates than with any other type of child and adolescent outcome (Sampson, Morenoff, and Gannon-Rowley, 2002). With regard to violent behavior, Prothrow-Stith (1991) is of a similar opinion; she maintained that neighborhood characteristics are culpably involved in the epidemic of violence among young lower-class males. In her insightful narrative on masculine youth violence and the social context in which it occurs, she and her co-author, Michaele Weissman, even argued that "where a young man lives may be the single most important factor in predicting violence" (p. 65).

Farrington's (1998) systematic review of major longitudinal studies of youth violence suggested that boys living in high crime neighborhoods are more violent than those living in low crime communities. Similarly, in a study to ascertain whether social areas exert contextual effect on the behavior of inhabitants, Gottfredson, McNeil, and Gottfredson (1991) found that community disorganization is positively related to interpersonal violence among adolescent males. However, in this investigation, only two percent of the variance in individual delinquency was accounted for by area factors. On the other hand, research by Williams and his partners (1998) failed to demonstrate that neighborhood characteristics predict violent behavior in adolescents at all.

With respect to juvenile homicide, though, Van Horn (1992) found that homicidal youths are more likely than non-homicidal, violent youths to come from "dangerous" neighborhoods. In the same way, another evaluation of 90 young murderers revealed that most juvenile killers are from lower class areas where violence is common (Heide, 1999). Research by Sorrell (1980) and Busch and his colleagues (1990) also provide evidence to this effect. More than a decade later, the correlation between youth violence and neighborhood disadvantage continues to be an empirical rule (Stewart et al., 2008; Brezina et al., 2004; Wilkinson et al., 2009; Anderson and Meier, 2004; Nielsen, 2005; Felson et al., 2007).

On the whole, conventional wisdom does suggest that homicide offenders are likely to live in economically and socially disadvantaged communities (Harries, 1997; Martinez and Lee, 1999; Short, 1997; Wolfgang, 1958). Scholars tend to show that neighborhood characteristics influence violent behavior in adolescents through community norms and values that are favorable toward drug use, drug trafficking, firearm use and availability, and violence as a means of conflict resolution (Blunstein, 1995b; Fagan and Wilkinson, 1998;

Fraser, 1996; Harries, 1997; Oliver, 2001; Kubrin and Weitzer, 2003; Stewart et al., 2008; Swisher and Latzman, 2008; Rich and Grey, 2005; Ronel, 2010; Nielsen et al., 2005; Allen and Lo, 2010; Felson et al., 2007). Violence in poor communities is promoted through conditions and codes that encourage it, and, moreover, through the absence of mechanisms to discourage violent behavior. Children are socialized into delinquent subcultures by adults and delinquent peer groups in the neighborhood, which are often unsupervised due to the high prevalence of single-parent households (Sampson, 1987a) and the lack of structured activities (Lee and Ousey, 2005; Oliver, 2001) in these communities. The dearth of suitable male role models and father figures in these neighborhoods, to influence and guide adolescent males appropriately have a big impact on gender identity and role behavior in young boys (Parker and Reckdenwald, 2008; Yonas et al., 2007; Allen and Lo, 2010). Rites of passage for teenage males in many poor communities relate closely to the enculturation of ghetto specific manhood roles, namely, the tough guy, the hustler, and the player (Oliver, 2001). Overall, enculturation and the persistence of hypermasculine behavior are products of structural strain and cultural adaptation, in addition to the social learning process as it propagates cultural transmission and is involved in experiencing and witnessing social actions characterized by compulsory masculinity (Oliver, 2001; Anderson, 1997; Allen and Lo, 2010).

Enculturation and ghettoization owing to the hypersegregation of Blacks has been used to explain high levels of both offending and victimization among this population (Massey, 2005; Setwart et al., 2008). Research consistently shows that people of color, particularly African Americans[6] and Hispanics, are increasingly perpetrators and victims of homicide (Brewer et al., 1998; Martinez, 1997; Maxson, Klien, and Sternheimer, 2000; Miethe and Regoeczi, 2004; Ousey, 1999). In fact, homicide is the leading cause of death among young Black males between the ages of 15 and 24 in the United States (Fox and Zawitz, 2007; Yonas et al., 2007; Wilkinson et al., 2009; Rich and Grey, 2005; Piquero and Brame, 2008). Homicide victimization rates are consistently higher for this population than they are for any other race or sex group (Felson and Steadman, 1983; Kuhn et al., 1999; Oliver, 2001; Weaver et al., 2004; Wilson and Daly, 1985). Even when compared to their White counterparts, young Black males in this country are six times more likely to be the victim of homicide (Wilson,

1997). Furthermore, young Black males are particularly at-risk of falling victim to gun violence (Wilkinson et al., 2009; Nielsen et al., 2005). In fact, Black and Hausman (2008) estimate that this cohort is 18 times more likely than the general population to die from homicide by firearm.

Although the vast majority of lethal assaults involve victims and offenders of the same race[7] (Block and Block, 1991; Decker, 1993; Martinez, 1997; Porkorny, 1965), analysis of homicide trends in the United States indicates a preponderance of Black-on-Black cases among intra-racial homicides (Block and Block, 1991; Decker, 1993; Kuhn et al., 1999; Martinez, 1997; Miethe and Regoeczi, 2004; Porkorny, 1965; Wolfgang, 1958). Specifically, an investigation of firearm related murders in Milwaukee from 1991 through 1997 involving adolescents and young adults as victims and offenders (Kuhn et al., 1999) revealed that 96% of the intra-racial homicides consisted of Black-on-Black violence as compared to 69% for events involving Whites as both victim and offender; the difference in percentages were significant at p < .001. Decker (1993) also found that Black-on-Black violence is the modal category for intra-racial homicides, accounting for 83% of all the cases in his study. Again, this phenomenon has been attributed to residential segregation and diminished opportunities for interracial social interaction among Blacks (Massey, 2005).

In fact, Black-on-Black crime in general and masculine violence in particular is purportedly indicative of the underclass phenomenon. Social disorganization and the poverty of social networks and valued roles, not economic deprivation as such, are the distinguishing attributes of the underclass and the truly disadvantaged. Isolation and separation from elemental economic and social institutions of mainstream society beget a unique system of values that dominate the beliefs and lives of members of the underclass. Perceptions of opportunity and history of victimization in impoverished communities result in code-based beliefs that support survival as well as adaptation to status insecurity (Brezina et al., 2004; Allen and Lo, 2010). In relation to masculine violence, these focal concerns emphasize toughness and criminal enterprise to acquire money and material goods. Again, this value system is assumed to be a collective solution to the problem of economic and social inequalities that obstruct the progress of healthy masculine identity development. Ultimately, neighborhood violence is promoted through conditions and codes engendered by the alpha-male subculture (Miller, 1958; Anderson, 1994, 1997; Oliver, 2001; Brezina et al., 2004; Stewart et al., 2008; Swisher and Latzman, 2008; Piquero and Sealock, 2010; Stretesky and Pogrebin, 2007). Consequently, social learning histories for boys in these communities provide the mindset and the knowledge that enables them to behave violently.

The foregoing proposition intersects social learning and subcultural theories of violence. Together, these explanations assert that certain groups or subcultures in society have values, attitudes, and dispositions that are conducive to crime and/or violent offending (Cohen, 1955; Miller, 1958; Luckenbill and Doyle, 1989). These norms are modeled and transmitted generation after generation through the enculturation process (Sutherland, 1924, 1937; Burgess and Akers, 1966; Allen and Lo, 2010; Anderson, 1994, 1997; Oliver, 2001).

In the main, sociologists and criminologists working in the tradition of the subculture of violence have researched a wide range of cultural subgroups using a variety of research methods. For example, the theory has been used to study and explain violence among youth (e.g. Felson, Liska, South, and McNulty, 1994; Baron, 1994), the poor (e.g. Miller, 1958; Blau and Blau, 1982), Blacks (e.g. Erlanger, 1974; Cao, Adams, and Jensen, 1997), men (Miller, 1966; Benedict, 1998), and by area of residence (e.g. Hackney, 1969; Anderson, 1997; Gastil, 1971). Empirical tests of the Black subculture of violence thesis are especially limited by operational measures of the independent variable. To determine how the subculture of violence affects crime rates, macro- level studies use the variable percent Black in area. Although this demographic characteristic often predicts violent crime rates, it does not adequately indicate that subcultural beliefs among Blacks are responsible for that phenomenon. Attitudinal measures of approval of violence are more appropriate; nevertheless, in many case-level investigations, attitude measures of approval of violence are based on self-reported responses to hypothetical situations.

Furthermore, case-level, race-based research in this tradition does not present neither consistent nor coherent evidence of a Black subculture of violence. For example, using national-level data to test the hypothesis that violent values are widespread among African American males, Cao and company (1997) found that White males are more likely than Black males to express violent tendencies in defensive encounters. According to their findings, however, there were no significant differences between Black and White males with respect to offensive situations. In an earlier case-level evaluation of the Black subculture of violence theory, Ball-Rokeach (1973) found that White respondents were more approving of violence to settle disputes, but Black respondents were more likely than Whites to actually engage in fighting.

Peer Risk Factors

Another construct of enduring interest in the cultural deviance-social learning theorem is peer group effects on juvenile delinquency and violence. Peer relations are a normal part of the juvenile subculture, and extremely important to adolescent social development. Children in socially disorganized communities are often socialized into delinquency by unsupervised peer groups in the neighborhood. Generally, by adolescence, peer effects take precedence over family risk factors in determining youth violence (Jang and Smith, 1997; Matjasko et al., 2010). In fact, peer relations is the single most important predictor of delinquency and violent behavior by adolescents (Empy and Stafford, 1991; Mears, Ploeger, and Marr, 1998; Warr, 1993; Wilkinson et al., 2009). Salts and her associates (1995) found that the amount of time spent with friends was a reliable predictor of violent behavior, especially when those friends engaged in antisocial activities. Likewise, Baron and Harnagel's (1998) investigation revealed that youth who reported having more delinquent peers also indicated greater participation in violence. The literature suggests, however, that there are sex-based differences concerning exposure to delinquent peers and the effect of peer pressure on individual violent behavior. In 1998, the *Journal of Research in Crime and Delinquency* printed a study on sex differences in peer influence and the moral evaluation of behavior (Mears et al., 1998). The research was designed to determine if male and female adolescents differ in their exposure to delinquent peers. Data for this investigation were drawn from wave III of the National Youth Survey, which included a national probability sample of respondents aged 13 to 19 years. The findings of this study indicated that male adolescents are more likely to have delinquent friends and are more susceptible to peer influences than their female counterparts.

Peer pressure and delinquent behavior among adolescent males is not only a matter of parental supervision and lack of structured activities; it also concerns impression management and stereotypical ideas about masculinity (Stretesky and Pogrebin, 2007). In social situations, particularly in the presence of other males, adolescent boys are often compelled to draw on behavioral norms associated with maleness (Brezina et al., 2004; Rich and Grey, 2005; Yonas et al., 2005; Matjasko, 2010). To the extent that masculinity is expressed and enacted within a social system that is stratified by race and class, poor young males (of color) draw on norms of toughness and risk taking to obtain money, self-respect, and status in their communities (Anderson, 1994, 1997; Oliver, 2001; Yonas et al., 2007; Yonas et al., 2005; Stretesky and Pogrebin, 2007; Allen and Lo, 2010). These young men generally have few positive outlets to assert their masculinity and fewer resources to shore up their self-image.

Young males with high dispositions to risk taking, commonly have peers who are actively involved in risk taking behavior as well, including heavy drinking and other substance use, unlawful activities, and interpersonal violence. In other words, attachment to antisocial peers encourages and/or reinforces externalizing behaviors, such as aggression, delinquency, and hypermasculinity in adolescent males. In the juvenile violence literature, discourse regarding the effects of peer group affiliation on individual violent behavior essentially moves in two different directions. One argument assumes that "bad company corrupts" good kids. That is to suggest that deviant peers lead youths with no prior history of violence to engage in violent behavior. The other argument stipulates that "birds of a feather flock together"; to wit, similar people find each other. According to this hypothesis, delinquent peer groups merely foster violent behavior in children and adolescents who are already violent. Little evidence has been offered to establish the truth of either contention (see Wilkinson et al., 2009; Stretesky and Pogrebin, 2007).

Even if these explanations make the importance of youth networks in predicting individual delinquency and violence by adolescents seem straightforward, there is a higher degree of complexity to understanding these situations. Youth associate with delinquent peer groups for a variety of reasons, including economic opportunities, social status, sense of belonging, and protection (Brewer, Damphousse, and Adkinson, 1998; Decker, 1993; Fagan, Piper, and Moore, 1986; Prothrow-Stith, 1991; Brennan and Moore, 2009; Yonas et al. 2005; Stretesky and Pogrebin, 2007). Proximity to subcultures of delinquency increases one's chance of associating with deviant peer groups, since children and adolescents are disposed to forming friendships with and mimicking those whom they encounter often. Moreover, deviant peer groups provide opportunities for learning and engaging in antisocial behavior, including violence (Duxbury, 1980; Heimer, 1997; Mears et al., 1998; Nielsen et al., 2005; Wilkinson et al., 2009; Brennan and Moore, 2009). To this extent, deviant peer relations carry with it the implications of intentionality or purposiveness, opportunities for social learning, and the liability of environmental circumstances and reference group orientation, comparable to any other facet of cultural causation. Be that as it may, it is understood that gang membership increases the risk of violence above and beyond the risk posed by delinquent friends (Brewer et al., 1998; Thornberry, Krohn, Lizzotte, and Chard-Wierschem, 1993; Brennan and Moore, 2009; Wilkinson et al., 2009; Stretesky and Pogrebin, 2007).

In the strict sense, gangs are relatively rare in most parts of the United States (Prothrow-Stith, 1991; Short, 1998). However, these deviant youth collectives have proliferated rapidly since the 1980s (Carter, 1998; Howell, Krisberg, Hawkins, and Wilson, 1995; Huff, 1998). It is estimated that there is currently over 25,000 gangs with almost one million active gang members across all 50 states of the union (Egley, 2000; Huff, 1998; Moore and Terret, 1998). Ordinarily, gang members range in age from 14 to 24 (Huff, 1998), and come from underclass and working class families.

The typical qualities of gang formation and gang structure include being organized; having an identifiable leadership; having identifiers, such as a group name, symbols, and group colors; being strongly tied to turf or territory; associating continuously; having a specific purpose or ideological beliefs; and engaging in deviant and illegal activities (Goldstein, 1991). Traditionally, gang members have engaged in one-on-one and group fist fights, alcohol and drug use, vandalism, and other petty crimes. These qualities, however, no longer characterize the formation, structure, or functioning of contemporary youth gangs (Spergel, 1995; Starbuck, Howell, and Lindquist, 2001). For one, modern youth gangs are a lot less organized (Decker, Byum, and Weisel, 1998; Decker and Curry, 2000; Sanders, 1994); generally, there is no leadership, hierarchy, allegiance, identifiers, or rules of conduct. Contemporary youth gangs are also a lot less territory-oriented, and their members tend to be younger than they were traditionally.

Moreover, there are more females and Caucasians, as well as a larger proportion of middle-class "bangers" in present-day youth gangs. Contemporary gang activity also involves more rampant substance use, drug trafficking, and violent behaviors, particularly aggravated assault and homicide (Goldstein, 1991; Nielsen et al., 2005).

Gang researchers have yet to engage in any rigorous study into the gang-homicide link, but where delinquency and violence has been considered with respect to gang membership, some important conclusions have emerged. For instance, a small self-report study (N=50) by von Dorn and Williams (2003) involving juvenile detainees at a secure facility in the Midwest found that adolescents in gangs are more likely to progress from nonviolent to violent offending compared to adolescents who are not in gangs. Another self-report study of non-institutionalized youth (Hill, Howell, Hawkins, and Battin-Pearson, 1999) found that adolescents involved in gangs are more likely than non-gang members to be involved in serious violence. This study also discovered that gang members were twice as likely to carry a gun and three times more likely to engage in drug trafficking than non-gang members in the sample. Other researchers have identified similar patterns in their self-report evaluations (Lizotte and Sheppard, 2001; Lizzotte, Howard, Krohn and Thornberry, 1997; Nielsen et al., 2005).

Research by Chaiken (2000), however, denies the truth of gang membership incurring the danger of unusual delinquency and violence. Her examination of a random sample of male adolescents aged 13 to 17 years living in one of three high-crime neighborhoods in Washington, D.C., revealed that boys in gangs "committed essentially the same number of assaults and other crimes in the weeks immediately before the interview, as did nongang members" (p. 6). Chaiken's observation, however, is questionable on at least two grounds. Firstly, the period during which involvement in delinquency and crime was assessed (i.e. "in the weeks immediately before the interview") seem too brief in time to ascertain the true relationship between patterns of delinquency and gang membership. Secondly, the nature and scope of delinquent activities asked about in this study were not adequately outlined and described in the research report; consequently, the reader does not have the ability to either judge the seriousness of the criminal behavior being related to gang membership nor to compare the findings to other studies.

Still, the nexus between juvenile homicide and gang membership is inconclusive. In a comparative analysis of adjudicated murder offenders aged 10 to 17 years and a matched sample of children and adolescents adjudicated for nonviolent offenses, Busch et al. (1990) found that youth who commit homicide are more likely to be involved in gangs. Carter (1998), however, found no difference between juvenile homicide and non-homicide offenders in terms of gang membership, as did Van Horn (1992), who ascertained that most of the violent youth in her study did not participate in gangs.

Even if gang activity and gang-related homicide are relatively uncommon in most parts of the country, fear of gang violence prevails owing to the group nature of juvenile offending (Austin, 1980; Cook and Laub, 1998; Sampson, 1987b; Short, 1998; Zimring, 1984; Wilkinson et al., 2009). To say nothing of movies and "gangsta" rap lyrics that contribute to the emulation of gang culture, including drug trafficking.

Drug Trafficking

The rise in youth murder rates has been linked to developments in the crack-cocaine market (Blumstein, 1995a, 1995b; Blumstein and Cork, 1996; Cork, 1999; O'Brien and Stockard, 1999). More specifically, the increase in lethal violence has been related to the recruitment of juveniles into the illegal drug trade and the subsequent distribution and diffusion of guns among adolescents. Crack-cocaine was first introduced in large cities like New York, Los Angeles, and Miami between 1983 and 1985. Prior to this time, cocaine was sold in powered form at prices that limited consumption primarily to middle and upper class individuals. The most important feature of crack was its low cost, which significantly expanded the consumer market for cocaine to a poorer clientele. The other important feature was its pharmacology, namely its rapid drug-induced stimulation, short-lived high, and addictiveness. Both innovations increased the volume of business in crack markets, and more dealers were recruited to meet the demands. Juveniles were a convenient source of labor for the drug trade because they were less vulnerable to adult criminal penalties, more likely to escape detection and prosecution, more reliable than adult workers since they tended to be non-users of crack, more daring and willing to take risks, and they could be compensated less than adults.

Moreover, the drug trade was, and still is, an attractive opportunity for many young, disadvantaged males who feel they have no opportunities for themselves in the legitimate economy (Fagan and Wilkinson, 1998; ONDP, 2000; Yonas et al., 2007; Stretesky and Pogrebin, 2007; Allen and Lo, 2010). Although the illicit drug trade is controlled by organized adult crime and youth serve in a more ancillary capacity as street level dealers, runners, steerers, transporters, and lookouts, trafficking provide juveniles with income and material comfort, as well as status, acceptance, and respect in their neighborhoods. Altogether, this gives many young marginalized males ample incentive to bear the risks and costs associated with drug dealing.

Unfortunately, in many poor communities drug dealers are the only visible sign of material success. Although most of the residents in these neighborhoods are hard working, they struggle to get ahead and are often kept in ignoble and abject conditions. Meanwhile, drug dealers in these communities seem to prosper. "Excesses of consumption by successful dealers embroil others, including young people who envy the material artifacts of their success—cars, gold chains, flashy clothing, attractive and fancily dressed women" (Short, 1998, p. 24). Drug trafficking has become the norm for a growing number of young people in underprivileged communities who see and sense that legitimate opportunities are few and far between, and generally not yielding to efforts at financial and material betterment. These youths are particularly susceptible to the enticement of drug trafficking, and likely to be socialized into the drug trade by peers, older relatives and adults in their neighborhoods.

For all the money, material, women, respect, and fear that this lifestyle can furnish, it is a fertile context for violence (Yonas et al., 2007; Yonas et al., 2005). Drug dealers are commonly targets for robbery and drug turf war. Since they cannot expect protection from the law or civil remedies if victimized or wronged, they must be self-appointed doers of justice. Inasmuch as this is true, guns are a standard tool of the drug trade (Blumstein and Cork, 1996; Cork, 1999; Decker, Pennel, and Caldwell, 1997; Fagan and Wilkinson, 1998; Stretesky and Pogrebin, 2007; Allen and Lo, 2010). Verily, the recruitment of juveniles into drug markets increased their access to firearms. In fact, research indicates that the drug business is a critical context for gun possession among adolescents (Chaiken, 2000; Lizotte and Sheppard, 2001; Lizotte, Howard, Krohn, and Thornberry, 1997; Sheley and Wright, 1993). Unquestionably, the influx of juveniles in the drug trade and the increased availability of guns, as well as the increasing number of open street markets are all important factors in the growth of drug market violence.

The violence associated with drug trafficking does not only affect those engaged in the trade (Anderson, 1994, 1997, 1998; Brezina et al., 2004; Swisher and Latzman, 2008; Rich and Grey, 2005; Nielsen et al., 2005). Innocent residents are indiscriminately victimized due to conflict between those who deal drugs or are otherwise involved or interested in narcotraffic. Drug market violence contributes greatly to the deterioration of neighborhoods and communities. Residents in visible, high intensity drug trafficking areas normally live in fear of violence. In these neighborhoods social engagement, active involve-ment in the community and collective efficacy are foiled. Moreover, violence becomes a way of life for children and adolescents in these communities. To survive they internalize a code of violence, which requires them to adopt violent strategies for self-preservation (Anderson, 1994, 1997, 1998). This upward spiral causes the overall level of violence in these neighborhoods to rise. African American communities in particular are often centers of street level distribution (Ensminger, Anthony, and McCord, 1997). The burden of illegal drug trade is especially a moral and social problem in these neighborhoods where wealth distribution is most treacherous.

Ordinarily, drug trafficking is a lifestyle hazard; it increases opportunities for violence[8] and exposure to dangerous people, places, and situations. Juvenile participants are not invulnerable to the activities, circumstances, and conditions which surround the drug business. In truth, drug trafficking predicts their involvement in violent behavior (Hawkins et al., 1998; Herrenkohl et al., 2000; Thornberry, Huizinga, and Loeber, 1995; Yonas et al., 2005; Allen and Lo, 2010), including homicide (McLaughlin, Daniel, and Joost, 1999; Fagan and Wilkinson, 1998; Van Horn, 1992). The relationship between drug trafficking and juvenile violence, however, is poorly understood. It is not fully known whether homicidal aggression naturally flows from conditions surrounding the drug business or the aptness of youths involved in drug markets to kill other human beings. This matter was the subject of discourse in Boyum and Klienman's (2003) article, *Breaking the drug-crime link*:

It is not clear how much of the violence among drug dealers is attributable to the drug trade itself, as opposed to the personal propensities of the individuals employed in it, or the economic, social, and cultural conditions of drug-plagued communities. Violent drug dealers tend to live and work in poor, inner-city neighborhoods, where violence is common independent of the drug business. (p.23)

And yet, they also took notice of the fact that:

A willingness to engage in violence is part of the implicit job description of a drug dealer in many markets. And the Darwinian logic of criminal enterprise suggests that surviving dealers are those who are best able to use violence, intimidation, and corruption to protect their positions. (p 23)

By that very fact, drug trafficking and gun carrying are co-occurring phenomena. Moreover, the presence of a firearm is a significant risk factor for lethal violence.

Gun Possession

The primary reason for the rise in juvenile homicide rates in the United States has been access to firearms. Although juveniles cannot purchase guns from federally licensed firearm dealers, they essentially have unrestricted access to them through the gray and black gun markets.[9] In their 1996 investigation, Vaughan and his partners also evaluated how juveniles obtained weapons. Sixty-five percent of their participants reported that they borrowed, stole, found, or had a weapon given to them. Although this study did not specifically assess how youths obtained guns, it has been revealed that many juveniles get possession of firearms in a similar manner (Cook and Ludwig, 1997; Decker et al., 1997; Wright , Rossi and Daly, 1983; Wilkinson et al., 2009).

Then again, Zimring (1998) maintained that the black market is how most illegal populations, including juveniles, obtain guns. Ostensibly, firearms are unrestricted and cost relatively little money in the unregulated retail market—making guns even more accessible to adolescents. A conversation between Heide (1999) and one juvenile murderer in her study illustrated just how obtainable guns are to young people in some communities.

Heide: Okay. How about guns? Were they easily accessible?

1002: [Laugh] Guns, most people had them. I'd go down the street and get me a soda with a gun.

Heide: So you could get guns?

1002: Yeah.

Heide: How much would a gun cost you?

1002: Depends on what kind you're gonna get…You're talking about a hot gun?

Heide: Yeah. Something you could get on the street.

1002: If a junkie selling it, you could probably get it for about $25. If it's a good gun, it ain't no dude who smoke reefer or nothing, you know, he will probably charge you about $30 to $40. The most I'd ever seen a person sell a gun for would be $120.

In other narratives for youth whom she assessed, there is the recurrent idea of firearms being on offer to juveniles in the black market for relatively little money.

Firearm density is an important risk factor in determining homicide rates. In 1991, McDowall published a macro study that examined the influence of firearm availability on Detroit's homicide rates from 1951 to 1986. Using the Index of Gun Density[10] to measure firearm availability, his hypothesis that firearm density is positively correlated with homicide rates was borne out. Moreover, his findings were consistent with the argument that non-Whites[11] and young people are over-represented when it comes to gun violence. Results suggested that homicide rates in Detroit increased with the proportion of the city's population that was non-White and the proportion of the population between the ages of 15 and 24 years.

Access to handguns place juvenile at greater risk for homicidal behavior inasmuch as it encourages higher risk criminal offending, inspires arms races among rival gang members and drug traffickers, facilitates violent behavior in poorly controlled children, and intensifies routine conflicts and fist fights (Cornell, 1993; Gonzalez, 2001; Brennan and Moore, 2009; Allen and Lo, 2010). Still, easy accessibility alone does not explain the negative impact that firearms in general have on our society. It is the glamorization of violence and the overly macho glorification of guns in movies, music, and video games that presents a special problem in this country. Even if the masculization of violence in not exclusive to the United States, easy access to guns and the glamorization of violence evidently is. Therefore, it is hardly surprising that firearm homicide rates among children in this country are as much as 16 times higher than among children in other developed nations (Kuhn, Nile, O'Brien, Withers, and Hargarten, 1999).

The problem of gun carrying by adolescents in the United States is related to lifestyle patterns, including peer affiliations (Black and Hausman, 2008; Wilkinson et al., 2009; Brennan and Moore, 2009; Yonas et al., 2007; Yonas et al., 2005; Stretesky and Pogrebin, 2007; Allen and Lo, 2010; Nielsen et al., 2005). Vaughan and partners (1996) discovered in their investigation that the probability of a junior high school youth carrying a gun increased sixteen-fold if he or she had a friend who carried a gun. Similarly, a secondary analysis of data from the Rochester Youth Development Study, designed to ascertain patterns of gun carrying among young urban males (Lizotte et al., 1997), revealed that being in a gang and having peers who own guns for protection increases the odds six- to eight-fold that an adolescent owns or carries a gun. In an evaluation of gun use by male juveniles for the Office of Juvenile Justice and Delinquency Prevention (OJJDP),[12] Lizotte and Sheppard (2001) also found gun carrying to be strongly related to gang membership and having friends who owned guns. The strong connection between gun carrying and gang membership, in particular, is consistent with many other studies (see Bjerregaard and Lizotte, 1995; Block and Block, 1993; Decker and Van Winkle, 1996; Miller, 1992; Sheley and Wright, 1993; Wilkinson et al., 2009). However, Lizotte and Sheppard found that drug dealing was more strongly related to gun carrying than peer affiliation. In their study, the odds of carrying a gun increased as much as thirty-five-fold for youths involved in drug trafficking.

As salient as neighborhood effects, peer risk factors, drug trafficking, and gun availability may be in the production of homicide, lethal violence is only partially explained by predisposing risk factors. Even youth who are disposed to violence do not act on these tendencies in all times and places (Farrington, 1998). Violence is highly contextualized, and background factors do not adequately explain lethal outcomes in some situational context more than others.

Similarly Situated Males: The Situational Nature of Male-to-Male Violence

SITUATIONAL CONTINGENCIES

The theory of criminal lethality postulates that the circumstances in which an action is located, namely the immediate goals of the action, the means of the action, and the conditions of the action determines whether a violent crime eventuates in death (Luckenbill, 1977; Pittman and Handy, 1964; Williams and Flewelling, 1988; Wolfgang, 1958; Zimring, 1972). While most theoretical discussions and empirical investigations emphasize the correlation between individual, cultural, and structural characteristics and homicidal behavior, the criminal lethality thesis examines situational variables that are potentially related to fatal outcomes in illicit interactions. By that very fact, this theory assumes that homicide is essentially a function of events that occur immediate to, during, and subsequent to violent encounters, as opposed to being the inevitable consequence of individual, structural and/or cultural antecedents.

Wolfgang (1958) was the first to publicly allude to the processual nature of violent encounters and the crucialness of alternative variables in affecting death from assault. Specifically, he asserted that "...quick communication, rapid transportation, and medical technological advances...may mean that many cases of physical assault are kept in the column of aggravated assault statistics and are thereby prevented from being listed as criminal homicide" (p. 119). His conclusions, however, were anecdotal and not based on objectively verifiable measurements; but, violence and medical scholars eventually substantiated his claims (e.g. Doerner, 1983, 1988; Giacopassi, Sparger, and Stein, 1992; Hanke and Gundlach, 1995; Harris, Thomas, Fisher, and Hirsch, 2002; Richardson, 2003; Zimring, 1972). Much discourse and empirical research on homicide since then has emphasized the situational and interactional dynamics of fatal assault. To this extent, many theorists and social scientists have discussed and documented situated transactions and conditions that potentially initiate and/or escalate violent interactions and determine death from violent assaults (see for example, Anderson, 1997; Athens 1985; Brookman, 2003; Deibert and Miethe, 2003; Luckenbill, 1977; Oliver, 2001; Polk, 1994; Wilson and Daly, 1985). In the cultural context of hypermasculinity, opportunities for violent interaction are abundant. Encounters are created when similarly situated males are in physical proximity and confronted with social conflict. Under these circumstances both parties are motivated and suitable targets for status enhancement (Oliver, 2001; Anderson, 1997; Wilkinson et al., 2009; Brennan and Moore, 2009; Stretesky and Pogrebin, 2007; Ronel, 2010). Whether intentional or inadvertent, events are liable to culminate in the use of force to settle disputes. The state of knowledge suggests that ultimately the violence may serve any function, including social control (Katz, 1988; Felson, 1993; Brennan and Moore, 2009; Stretesky and Pogrebin, 2007; Athen, 2005), justice or revenge (Katz, 1988; Brookman, 2003), domination and conquest (Polk 1994, 1998; Oliver, 1994); identity and reputation (Goffman, 1983; Luckenbill, 1977; Polk 1994; Wilkinson and Fagan 1996, 2001; Nielsen et al., 2005; Stewart et al., 2008; Taylor et al., 2010; Anderson and Meier, 2004; Athens, 2005; Allen and Lo, 2010); or survival and self-preservation (Anderson 1997; Canada, 1996; Oliver, 2001; Wilkinson and Fagan, 1996, 2001; Felson and Messner, 1996; Brezina et al., 2004; Swisher and Latzman, 2008; Rich and Grey, 2005).

The criminal lethality perspective has generally been applicable to the category of homicide that eventuates in the commission or attempted commission of another unlawful act, such as physical assault. In that capacity, this paradigm covers many different types of situated transactions that end with the death of the victim. Symbolic interactionism, however, has been integrated into the idea of criminal lethality and used to specifically account for elements of male violence that reflect honor contest homicide (e.g. Luckenbill, 1977; Oliver, 2001). In this sociological perspective, thoughts, other mental events, cultural considerations, and choices are placed at the core of human social action (Turner, 2003). Symbolic interactionists emphasize the concepts of self, identity, and role. Proponents argue that people develop feelings and attitudes towards themselves based on tangible and intangible objects they view as part of their being and crucial to their identity (i.e. the material self). Moreover, these theorists assert that human beings develop feelings about the self based on association with other people (i.e. the social self). According to the premises of the social self (James, 1900) and the looking glass self (Cooley, 1902), as cited by Turner (2003), one's relationship to others depends on being a certain kind of individual. Particularly when identity is established on cultural definitions and expectations, commitment to a set of behavioral and/or personal characteristics may be allied to self-esteem. Eventually pride in oneself becomes dependent on the successful execution of that role.

Erving Goffman's (1967) theory of impression management and violent criminal behavior has been the most influential symbolic interactionism theory in the study of male-to-male perpetrated violence (see Luckenbill, 1977; Felson and Steadman, 1983; Felson and Messner, 1996; Polk, 1994; Oliver, 2001; Felson, 1982; Anderson 1997; Deibert and Miethe, 2003). He created the term character contest to explain individual action, as well as transactions between two or more parties, in the production of violence. He surmised that violent encounters are generally situated transactions that involved the joint contribution of offenders and victims. In these collective transactions, character is at the heart of conflict inasmuch as one but usually both parties are willing to resort to violence in an effort to establish or save face at the other's expense.

Pioneers in this type of thought and research (i.e. Goffman, 1967; Luckenbill, 1977) assumed that character contests applied irrespective of sex. Researchers and theorists in this field of specialization, however, eventually connected the notion of tactical impression management and presentation of the self to masculinity and male-to-male perpetrated violence (see Ingram, 1993; Prothrow-Stith, 1991; Kennedy and Baron, 1993; Baron, Kennedy, and Forde, 2001); Wilson and Daly, 1985; Daly and Wilson, 1988; Polk, 1993, 1994, 1997, 2000; Oliver, 2001; Krienert, 2003; Messerchmidt 1993; 1997; 2000). Scientific inquiry into this phenomenon generally demonstrates that marginalized males place great emphasis on a strong sense of the masculine self. The personification of this identity is managed through dress, language, bravado, and other exaggerated symbols and props that represent masculinity. Case in point, a retrospective study of 704 incarcerated offenders in Lincoln, Nebraska (Krienert, 2003) revealed that masculinity by itself is not a significant predictor of violent offending. However, according to other findings of the study, men with few acceptable outlets to assert their masculinity are more likely than offenders with other means for masculine expression to engage in violent crime. In spite of this understanding, there has been a dearth of studious attention given to both situational risk factors for and male-to-male dynamics in juvenile perpetrated violence.

SITUATED TRANSACTIONS AND COERCIVE POWER IN THE PRODUCTION OF FATAL VIOLENCE

Background risk factors genuinely dispose minors to violent behavior. In urban communities, assaultive encounters generally occur between youthful males who are inclined to serious aggression as a result of inequalities, socialization, chronic strain, and opportunities for violence that originate in their environment (Stewart et al., 2008; Taylor et al., 2010; Piquero and Brame, 2008; Piquero and Sealock, 2010; Allen and Lo, 2010). However, because crimes of violence are highly contextualized, situational risk factors are absolutely essential to understanding how the potential for violence becomes an actuality. Moreover, these contingencies are crucial to an explanation of homicide since they have significant power in determining outcome from violent action.

The criminal lethality perspective has practical use in the study of juvenile homicide, insofar as it gives attention to process in conjunction with outcome. From this standpoint, certain details surrounding hostile and threatening events increase the odds of violent encounters resulting in death. On the whole, precipitating characteristics can affect the nature, development, and condition of acrimonious encounters. Each by itself or in totality, situational contingencies have the power to trigger aggressive or destructive behavior, raise the level of hostility, and influence the form of violence.

The circumstances presumed most likely to affect the course of assaultive events are related to: 1) the immediate goals of the action (i.e. offenders' specific intent to do harm), 2: the means of the action (i.e. the type of weapon involved), 3) the conditions of the action (e.g.

drug-relatedness), and 4) the facilitating nature of the location (e.g. the presence of third parties).[13]

The Facilitating Nature of Location: Social Audience Effects

In the existing literature, social audience and physical setting are often equivalent in connotation. Homicides that are situated in residential premises or other private settings are not available to spectators or third party influence in the same way as those events that occur in public venues. However, the overwhelming majority of research shows that homicides typically happen away from home in public settings where young males "hang out", such as street corners, clubs, bars, playgrounds, and alleys (Decker, 1993; Deibert and Miethe, 2003; Felson and Steadman, 1983; Gonzalez, 2001; Porkorny, 1965; Wolfgang, 1958, Polk, 1999; Oliver, 2001).

Contrary to popular opinion, murder frequently happens in view of spectators. Research indicates that an audience is present in approximately 70% of criminal homicides (Felson and Steadman, 1983; Luckenbill, 1977; Zahn and Sagi, 1987). In point of fact, the social audience can exert influence on hostile encounters, including the outcome of violent incidents, by defining the situation for the victim and/or the offender, participating in or instigating attacks,[14] mediating conflicts,[15] or doing nothing, which suggests approval or tolerance of violence (Decker, 1995; Deibert and Miethe, 2003; Felson, 1982; Felson and Steadman, 1983; Oliver, 2001). Furthermore, the very presence of a social audience is often germane to the development and escalation of social conflict, as it raises the identity costs of backing down (Daly and Wilson, 1988, 2001; Felson, 1982; Polk, 1997a, 1999; Brennan and Moore, 2009; Wilkinson et al., 2009; Stretesky and Pogrebin, 2007). As one student of homicide has said:

Those present at such interactions play a role in the violence by translating emotions into actions. Challenges to personal identity assume greater importance in the presence of others because of the premium placed on maintaining an identity on the street (Decker, 1995, p. 441).

Oliver's (2001) work corroborated the importance of spectators and self-image concerns in threatening and hostile encounters: While only two respondents admitted that they were trying to look good in front of the crowd, many admitted that they understood that it was important to act in a way that would deter others from attempting to take advantage of them in the future (p. 122). He used the following data strip from his study to illuminate this point:

> *Willie B. 5:* He was in my face. This kind of made me think that 'I can't let this man treat me like this in front of all these people'. That's the first thing I thought about…I don't want to look bad in front of other people. I don't want people picking on me. If they see him do it, then they want to do it. Then my life is ruined, because I won't have no respect from nobody. Everybody will be disrespecting me. (p. 122).

Many researchers have documented social audience effects in the escalation of disputes (e.g. Decker, 1995; Felson, 1983; Oliver, 2001; Felson, Ribner, and Siegel, 1994; Luckenbill, 1977; Tedeschi and Felson, 1994; Yonas et al., 2005; Wilkinson et al., 2009; Swisher and Latzman, 2008; Anderson and Meier, 2004; Ronel, 2010; Athens, 2005). Using a probability sample of 245 individuals aged 18 to 65 in New York State, Felson (1982) used Goffman's theory of impression management to derive hypotheses about the escalation of aggression and violence in his sample. Together with other tentative conclusions, Felson assumed that conflicts are likely to be more severe in the presence of third parties; this prediction was borne out by observation. Results showed that the presence of third parties increased the odds of a verbal dispute occurring one and one-half times, and the odds of physical violence two-fold. Moreover, both Felson and Steadman (1983) and Polk (1994, 1999) ascertained that assault often escalated to homicide when an audience was on hand. Still, there is conflicting evidence regarding third party effects in determining death from assault. For instance, in defiance of the foregoing conclusions, Felson and his partners (1984) identified no differences between homicide and assault in regard to the presence or actions of third parties. Inasmuch as varying observational procedures and methodological limitations do not readily explain the discrepant findings, more research into the social audience as a situational risk factor in predicting the severity of outcome for assaultive encounters involving juvenile perpetrators is required.

The Conditions of the Action: Drug Trafficking

Ordinarily, drug trafficking is a lifestyle hazard as it increases opportunities and exposure to dangerous people, places, and situations. Since the 1980s, the drug business has been a major source of adolescent homicide (Prothrow-Stith, 1991; Sheley and Wright, 1995; Miethe and Regoeczi, 2004; Blumstein, 1995; Blumstein and Cork, 1996; Cork, 1999; O'Brien and Stockard, 1999). Drug dealers, especially junior entrepreneurs, are commonly targets for violence. Inasmuch as this is true, guns are a standard tool of the trade (Blumstein and Cork, 1996; Cork, 1999; Decker, Pennel, and Caldwell, 1997; Fagan and Wilkinson, 1998; Miethe and Regoeczi, 2004: Yonas et al., 2007; Stretesky and Pogrebin, 2007; Allen and Lo, 2010) and a willingness to engage in violence is part of the job description (Boyum and Klienman, 2003).

Violence associated with the illicit drug market is varied and complex. To a usual extent these include rivalry between dealers; robbery involving traffickers; punishment by bosses or suppliers for dishonest accountancy, not making due on drug consignments, unfaithful allegiance, and failure to pay drug debts; in addition to other conflicts over drugs. Given these expectations, there is little evidence to suggest that homicide among juveniles is ordinarily drug-related in any way. Moreover, there is no information to speak of which indicates that homicide is more likely than its sibling offense, aggravated assault, to be related to the illegal trade of drugs.

Perchance the true incidence of drug-related juvenile homicide is located in circumstances that are not outwardly related to drug trade, but all the same associated with drug-market violence. One factor might be, as Blumstein (1995) suggested, the gun diffusion process and the probability of guns being present at the scene of drug crimes. Possession of a gun in hostile confrontation, particularly among males, increases the likelihood of aggressive behavior and the escalation of violence, which in turn increase the likelihood of the event ending in death. Furthermore, as others have suggested (e.g. Boyjm and Klienman, 2003), the relationship between violence and drug-trafficking may be explained by the personal propensity of individuals who are apt to become involved in the business of illicit drug trade, and/or the cultural mandate to use lethal violence to resolve disputes that is peculiar to this type of employment. Other possible connections may be derived from impression management theory and notions of honor and character. Given the enhanced status that is bestowed upon dealers in disorganized neighborhoods, they are suitable targets for violence by others who wish to advance their position in the street. In these settings, drug dealers are also motivated offenders for the reason that they are likely to be sensitive and responsive to maintaining their personal advantage in the community by use of violence.

While it is known that drug trafficking among urban adolescents is a serious problem (Miethe and Regoeci, 2004; Harries, 1997; Allen and Lo, 2010; Black and Hausman, 2008), little empirical attention has been given to the nature of illegal drug trade in the etiology of homicide. The present investigation is a preliminary effort to better understand the nexus between illegal drug trade and youth perpetrated violence.

The Means of Action: Firearms and the Instrumentality Effect

Guns are facilitating hardware in fatal violence simply because they are more lethal than any other weapon. However, some scholars speculate that firearms are also facilitative because they permit attacks from a distance and by weaker persons. Kleck (1991), for example, acknowledged that "guns provide a more impersonal, emotionally remote, even antiseptic way of attacking others, and could allow some attackers to bypass their inhibitions against close contact with their victims" (p. 221). Moreover, Wolfgang (1958) suggested that "the small physical size of the offender relative to that of the potential victim, or the offender's physical repugnance to engaging in direct physical assault by cutting or stabbing his adversary, may mean that in the absence of a firearm no homicide occurs" (p.79). Likewise, Hiede (1997) emphasized that many of the young killers in her study did not have the physical ability or emotional detachment to use other weapons to commit their crimes.

Whatever the reasons, the preponderance of the evidence supports the weapon instrumentality thesis. For example, Shumaker and McKee (2001) discovered in a comparative analysis of juvenile males charged with murder and juvenile males charged with other violent felony offenses, that homicidal youths were more likely than non-homicidal, violent youths to have used a gun in their instant offense. Research by Wells and Horney (2002) evaluated over 2,000 violent and hostile events described by 704 newly incarcerated males in a Midwestern state correctional facility to assess the role of weapons in violent and potentially violent encounters. They calculated that gun attacks are associated with a fourteen-fold increase in the odds of serious injury occurring. Similarly, Weaver and his partners (2004) determined from their quantitative secondary analysis of official record data that when a gun is used in violent attacks, victims are 12 times more likely to die.

Even though firearms pose a serious threat to human life, not every incident involving a shooting iron ends in death. Kleck and McElrath (1991), for one, found that the presence of a gun in hostile and potentially violent encounters actually reduces the probability of assault. Moreover, when a firearm is used in a violent attack, they also ascertained that injury is less likely for lack of hitting the target, which has a greater chance of happening with a gun than it does with any other assault weapon. Still, their evidence confirmed that when injured, wounds are more likely to be fatal if inflicted with a firearm. Yet, according to the National Center for Injury Prevention and Control (2008) there are tens of thousands of nonfatal shootings each year in the United States.

Research on weapon instrumentality indicates that victim characteristics such as age, race, and sex have indirect effects on whether a victim is killed during a violent encounter through weapon choice. Seemingly these characteristics influence the decision to use a weapon (Weaver et al., 2004), especially a gun (Cook and Laub, 2002; Felson, and Messner, 1996; Harries, 1997) in threatening encounters. It is purported that youths, males, and Black people are more likely to be attacked with a gun because of their perceived dangerousness. In other words, to be young and male, particularly for Blacks, is to be deemed able and/or likely to do harm. To all appearances, this thought even resonates with members of the defined population group.[16] The process of perceived dangerousness is ostensibly fostered and internalized by a history of disproportionate violent offending, as well as cultural stereotypes that demonize this band of people.

One of the biggest limitations in studies of weapon choice as a determinant of outcome from assault has been the lack of ability or means to discriminate between weapon instrumentality effect and specific intent to kill. Up to now, this kind of investigation has not been done because research on instrumentality effect typically employs aggregated data, which does not allow for exploration of the independent effects of weapon choice. Insofar as offenders' specific intent to kill is an essential risk factor in lethal violence, either in itself or through other situational contingencies such as weapon choice, additional and more adequate research into this phenomenon is required.

The Immediate Goals of the Action: Specific Intent to Do Harm

Criminal intent is a cognitive function. It refers to perception, reasoning, and, most of all, decision making at the time of or prior to a crime. In that capacity, intent, lethal or otherwise, is a condition that determines the course of a situation or has some bearing on it. In fact, in both criminal justice and social science, the assessment of intentionality is customarily based on objective measures surrounding a violent encounter. Moreover, where offenders' intent has been empirically investigated in the literature, it has in essence been considered as a situational risk factor or regarded in conjunction with the immediate circumstances of assaultive violence (see Wolfgang, 1958; Luckenbill, 1977; Felson and Messner, 1996; Phillip and Maume, 2007; Wells and Horney, 2002; Kleck and McElrath, 1991; Weaver et al., 2004).

In most respects, intentionality is a legal concern. It is meant to distinguish between murder with premeditation or malice aforethought and unlawful killing without expressed or implied intent to do injury for matters of prosecution. In a court of law, first degree homicide suggests premeditated, deliberate killing of one human being by another. Second degree murder, on the other hand, is applied to deaths that occur as a result of malice aforethought or the desire to kill in the absence of premeditation. First and second degree homicide both intimate specific intent to kill. The charge of voluntary or involuntary manslaughter, however, indicates a lack of evil intent prior to killing. Specifically, the former signifies killing in the "heat of passion", while the latter connotes death as a result of reckless behavior. Finally, felony homicide, which is at times considered first degree murder or downgraded to voluntary manslaughter, is applied to killing as a result of another crime, such as robbery.

Many homicide scholars suppose that murder is commonly not the result of intention to kill (Block, 1977; Block and Block, 1991; Brookman, 2003; Doerner, 1983; Felson and Messer, 1996; Felson and Steadman, 1983; Hardwick and Rowton-Lee, 1996; Harries, 1997; Katz, 1988; Kleck and McElrath, 1991; Luckenbill, 1977; Polk, 1993, 1998; Porkorny, 1965; Schmideberg, 1973; Weaver et al., 2004;

Williams and Flewelling, 1988; Wilson, 1997; Wilson and Daly, 1985; Wolfgang, 1958; Zimring, 1972; Brennan and Moore, 2009). Rather, it is assumed that in typical circumstances, criminal homicide is committed spontaneously or in the heat of passion. Then again, other students of homicide believe that a large number of killings are done by design (e.g. Felson and Messner, 1996). These researchers theorize that the presence of a gun is the direct function of offenders' intent to do lethal harm; this hypothetical proposition is known as the weapon facilitation thesis. This theory assumes that firearms, because of their lethal properties, are the weapon of choice when an offender is determined to kill his victim (see Felson and Messner, 1996; Kleck and McElrath, 1991; Miethe and Regoeczi, 2004; Wells and Horney, 2002). Ipso facto, the presence and use of a gun and the offender's lethal intent are both situated risk factors vis-à-vis fatal outcome in assaultive encounters.

For this reason, advocates of the weapon facilitation thesis also argue that homicides will generally not be avoided with gun control. If firearms are not available, they maintain that offenders who wish to kill their victims will select other lethal weapons, strike more blows, or target more vital areas on the body to achieve their destructive goal. This particular assumption is known as the weapon compensation or weapon substitution thesis.[17]

Altogether, however, offenders' intent is believed to increase the chance of death from assault, either directly or as it is related to circumstances surrounding violent assault. To that extent, the discourse and empiricism concerning fatal violence delineates offenders' intent as a situational risk factor. With respect to lethal intent in particular, for example, Felson and Messner (1996) insisted that:

> A substantial portion of homicide offenders really do intend to kill their victims and not merely to injure them. The death of a victim, therefore, is not an incidental outcome that reflects extraneous considerations, but rather is an integral part of the incident that is likely to be systematically related to other features of the incident (p. 520).

Furthermore, they suggested that "the presence of lethal intent increases the likelihood of a killing even though the association between intent and actual outcome is not perfect" (p.523).

Motive for Action: Male Honor Contest Violence

Motive is another important situational feature of interpersonal violence. Knowing why a person kills another gives insight into the context of homicide which potentially has important practice and policy implications for reducing murder among juveniles. In the homicide and violence literature, the term motive has been variously defined. For instance, Wolfgang (1958) simply characterized motive as the inducement to kill, while Mills (1940) bounded the term in more experiential language—describing it as the factual features of a situation as seen or believed to be. Felson, Baccaglini, and Ribner (1985), on the other hand, had a skeptical attitude about motives of criminal violence; they pronounced motives to be excuses or justifications for felonious behavior. Still, Oliver (2001) used more eloquent logic in his characterization of motive. He maintained that the motive state is tantamount to "circumstances in which an individual evaluates a particular situation, attributes meaning to that situation, considers a variety of responses, and decides on a particular course of action" (p. 179).

Conceptions of motive in criminological research often subsume aspects of criminal intent (i.e. spontaneity vs. premeditation), yet these two variables should not be confused. While motive is that which inspires violent behavior, intent refers to the design, resolve, or determination with which that behavior is done. In criminal justice, consideration of motive is important insofar as it makes plausible offenders' intentions. In the scientific study of masculine violence, however, proof of motive should be deemed significant in its own right, since homicide manifests itself in a number of forms depending on the motivational driving force of perpetrators. Moreover, this phenomenon is worthy of special attention inasmuch as certain motives may incite lethal intent in violent offenders (Katz, 1988; Wilkinson et al., 2009).

The initial classification system of homicide motives in the adult literature was outlined by Wolfgang more than fifty years ago.[18] His investigation of 588 cases of murder which occurred in Philadelphia during the five-year period of 1948-1952, yielded 13 categories of homicide. The most frequent motive or circumstance was related to "altercations of relatively trivial origin". Other motives included: domestic quarrel, jealousy, altercation over money, robbery, revenge, self-defense, halting felon, escaping arrest, and concealing birth. Wolfgang's system was innovative at the time, but, in truth, it had some major limitations.

In 1973, Wolfgang, Block and Zimring sub-classified motives for homicide to differentiate between instrumental and expressive killings. Instrumental homicides are goal-oriented and planned for the purpose of gaining benefit. This category of motive includes economic compulsive and systemic drug-related murders, as well as other felony homicides not related to the use or distribution of drugs. Expressive homicides, on the other hand, are usually spontaneous acts of rage, anger, or frustration that start with arguments or confrontations.

The instrumental/expressive dichotomy has been used in several studies and theoretical compositions since Block and Zimring (see Block, 1977, 1981; Block and Block, 1991; Decker, 1993, 1996; Meithe and Drass, 1999; Riedel, 1987; Ronel, 2010; Athens, 2005). Although there are commonalities between these phenomena, criminological research overwhelmingly indicates that instrumental and expressive homicides are fundamentally and qualitatively different in their motivations and social context (Fritzon, 2000, Meithe and Drass, 1999; Meithe and Regoeczi, 2004; Salfati, 1999, 2000; Salfati and Canter, 1999; Salfati and Haratsis, 2001).

Despite the fact that these homicides rarely happen in pure form (Block and Block, 1991; Decker, 1993, 1996; Salfati and Haratsis, 2001), expressive killing is the most prevalent type of private murder (Bernard, 1990; Blumstein and Cork, 1996; Daly and Wilson, 1988; Fox and Zawitz, 2004; Salfati and Haratsis, 2001; Wilson and Daly, 1985; Wolfgang, 1958). In a study of macro-level data that employed qualitative comparative analysis to inspect the features of instrumental and expressive homicides, Meithe and Drass (1999) found that expressive motives exceeded instrumental motives almost four to one.

Meanwhile, Felson and Tedeschi (1995) firmly maintained that the instrumental/expressive classification of motive is lacking in validity, since all violence is essentially instrumental or goal-oriented. According to these authors, whether physical force is exerted to obtain money or sex, to restore justice, to define identity, to control the behavior of others, or to protect self, nonetheless, there is an end in view. By the very nature of this argument, interpersonal violence is derived from benefit irrespective of the various and sundry underlying causes and reasons.

The other major typology of homicide motive in the adult literature specifically constitutes the circumstances and characteristics of masculine homicide,[19] which is germane and central to systematic investigations of assaultive violence since "across time and culture, violent crime, particularly homicide, has been predominately committed by [males]" (Adler and Polk, 1997, p. 1; also see Bailey, 2000, Cook and Laub, 2002; Fox Zawitz, 2004; Krienert, 2003; Mear et al., 1998; Polk, 1993, 1994, 1998, 1997b). Evolutionary psychologists Martin Daly and Margo Wilson were the first students of homicide to develop a classification system specifically for masculine lethal violence. In a compelling analysis of anthropological and historical data from around the world, they used biosocial theory to facilitate a deeper understanding of homicides involving male victims and offenders (Daly and Wilson, 1988). According to Daly and Wilson, masculine homicidal violence is widely existent because males are more biologically predisposed than women to competitive risk taking (Daly and Wilson, 2001; Wilson and Daly, 1985), as well as guarding, defending, and controlling the sexual behavior and reputation of their partners. From this source, they classified masculine homicide into five types: murder in the context of sexual intimacy or family relations; confrontational homicides flowing out of disputes that escalate quickly to physical confrontation; revenge or retaliation homicides resulting from a perceived wrong or injustice; and killings originating from other crimes.

Polk (1994) substantiated Daly and Wilson's explanation and typology of masculine violence. Except for revenge killings, he identified and confirmed the taxonomic classification of masculine violence set fourth in their conceptual framework. In his detailed contextual analysis of 388 male-to-male homicides in Victoria, Australia between 1985 and 1989, one more motive emerged from scenarios of manful violence—that is, homicide as a form of conflict resolution. According to the interpersonal signification of homicide, most murders are a matter of conflict resolutions; in Polk's opinion, however, conflict resolution homicide is a phenomenon that follows situations where violence is employed as a way of settling long-standing personal disputes between victims and offenders. In this way, homicide victims contribute to the interaction that culminates in their death.

In truth, homicide is generally not a one-sided event. The typical homicide is the result of expressive confrontations in which both parties are active participants in the assaultive encounter (Curtis, 1974; Hannon, 2004; Polk, 1993; 1997a; Sobol, 1995, 1997; Voss and

Hepburn, 1968; Wikstrom, 1991; Wolfgang, 1958; Stretesky and Pogrebin, 2007; Brennan and Moore, 2009; Wilkinson et al., 2009; Spano and Bolland, 2010). The notion of victim-precipitation was first introduced by von Hertig in 1948. It is Wolfgang (1958), however, who is widely regarded as the originator of victim-precipitation theory in homicide. According to Wolfgang, "victim-precipitated cases are those in which the victim was the first to show and use a deadly weapon [or] to strike a blow in an altercation—in short, the first to commence interplay of resort to physical violence" (p. 252). As determined by this definition, 26% of the homicides in his Philadelphia sample were classified as victim-precipitated.

There is convincing evidence to support the existence of victim-precipitated homicide, particularly as it relates to s. Polk (1993) found that in one-half of the male-to-male homicides he studied, the ultimate victim of lethal violence instigated the event that led to his death. Felson and Messner (1983) examined 159 incidents of homicide and assault in New York State; the results of their investigation suggest that victims of homicide were more aggressive and more likely to engage in identity attacks, physical assaults, and verbal threats than victims of aggravated assaults. Furthermore, an evaluation of 157 criminal homicide cases that occurred in Buffalo, New York between 1992 and 1993 (Sobol, 1997) determined that two-thirds of victims contributed to their murder in some way. This research also indicated distinct race and sex differences in victim-precipitation. As demonstrated by this particular study, Blacks were more likely than Whites to facilitate their deaths. Additionally, males were more likely than females to contribute to their own demise. This information corroborates the general ideology of compulsory masculinity and male honor contest violence. To a greater extent, however, it furnishes support for the subculture of violence theory as it relates to marginalized males in disorganized communities.

Luckenbill's (1977) seminal efforts substantiate the intersection between these two premises, which are used to explain the most typical instance of male perpetrated violence. Luckenbill's conceptualization of victim-precipitation was subjective. He suggested that the role of the victim in his homicide is mainly based on the perception of the offender. Pivotal to this explanation of victim-precipitation is a set of assumptions about situational cues and the interpretive processes underlying individual decisions to engage in violent behavior (see also

Bernard, 1990; Fagan and Wilkinson, 1998; Miethe and Regoeczi, 2004; Oliver, 2001; Wilkinson et al., 2009; Yonas et al., 2007; Brezina et al., 2004; Rich and Grey, 2005; Brennan and Moore, 2009; Ronel, 2010). Per Luckenbill, "what the victim intends may be inconsequential" (p.17); what matters most in murderous episodes, he found, is how the offender interprets pre-homicide transactions. Whatever happens, the offender's typification of the situation is based on previous experiences, situational identity concerns, and one's expectations of physical injury or humiliation (see also Felson and Steadman, 1983; Krienert, 2003; Polk, 1999; Ronel, 2010). Interpretations of what is happening and what is likely to happen is a consequence of activity by the victim, as well as the survival or impression management needs of the offender. Luckenbill calculated that 63% of the cases of homicide in his study were victim initiated.

From his data, Luckenbill (1977) developed a five stage model of victim-precipitated homicide. He asserted that in typical circumstances, private killing is the consequence of a dynamic interaction involving a victim, an offender, and sometimes an audience. In the first stage, one party makes an "opening move"; that is, a verbal and/or physical gesture which is perceived by the other to be offensive or threatening. In the second stage of the encounter, that party makes a retaliatory move. Usually, this is a verbal or physical challenge aimed at restoring face. The third stage begins with the counter-retaliatory move, and by the fourth stage both parties are committed to battle. In the fifth stage, the battle ensues and a victim is left dead or dying (see Stretesky and Pogrebin, 2007 for an alternative model of moves and countermoves in the escalation of violence).

This interplay is evocative of the study and typology of male honor contest violence, which is derived from symbolic interactionism and structural-cultural conceptions of masculine violence as a function of race *x* class *x* sex stratification. The essences of male honor is contained in discourse on cultural intersectionality, social disorganization theory, and the subculture of violence thesis as it relates to disputatiousness and assaultive violence among young, poor, ethnic minority males in this country. Most of the research that has examined characteristics of male violence in relation to honor contests, however, has been carried out abroad. Furthermore, many of the investigations are based on qualitative research designs.

The major classification system for male-on-male slaying vis-à-vis honor contest violence is divided into two main categories. The first category, dispute-related homicide, includes three general classes: confrontational, homicide, conflict resolution killing, and revenge murder. The second category is murder resulting from the course of other crimes, more specifically, robbery homicide.

Dispute-related Homicides

Many male-perpetrated homicides occur between similarly situated males[20] who are known to each other to settle emerging[21] or long-standing[22] disputes.[23] A sizeable majority of dispute-related murders are confrontational homicides (Bernard, 1990; Daly and Wilson, 1988; Fox and Zawitz, 2004; Harries, 1997; Kuhn et al., 1999; Meithe and Regoeczi, 2004; Kubrin and Hertig, 2003; Luckenbill, 1977; Uniform Crime Reports, 2004; Wells and Horney, 2002; Wilson and Daly, 1985; Wolfgang, 1958, Polk, 1993, 1994, 1999; Spano and Bolland, 2010; Athens, 2005; Wilkinson et al., 2009), centering around some form of immediate character or honor contest between males. Confrontational homicides customarily begin with an intentional or unintentional, real or imagined offense that one male commits against another's social self. Again, Luckenbill's (1977) qualitative analysis of criminal homicide over a 10 year period (1963-1972), indicated that three basic types of situated transactions constitute "opening moves" in honor contest, confrontational violence. The initial actor issues a direct verbal expression, physical gesture, or nonverbal message that is perceived as personally offensive by the second player, or refuses to cooperate or comply with the request of that party. The second player reciprocates with a retaliatory move aimed at restoring face and demonstrating strong character. The encounter eventually escalates to homicide as both participants "attempt to establish or save face at the other's expense by standing steady in the face of adversity" (Luckenbill, 1977, p. 177). The following case example, taken from Polk's (1994) study, illustrates how confrontation involving honor and disrespect can escalate quickly to an event that result in death:

> Late on Saturday night, Anthony N. (age 19) was walking back with friends towards their home after attending a local 'Octoberfest'. They had enjoyed a pleasant evening of drinking at that event. In a small park, they met up with another

group, including Don B. (age 18) and Peter T. (age 18). One of the young women in Anthony's group was part of the triggering of the confrontation between the two groups when she asked if she could ride Peter's bike. He replied: 'You can have a ride, if I can ride you.' Insults and challenges began to flow back and forth between the two groups. At one point, Anthony is recorded as having said to Don: 'You're a bit young to be going to Octoberfest, aren't you? Don responded with: 'Don't call me a kid'.

The exchange escalated into pushing and shoving...Don then threw a punch at Anthony, and the fight was on. At first it was a general group scuffle...The main group conflict began to simmer down, but Anthony and Don sought each other out and continued their personal dispute. At first Don was armed with a broken pool cue, but Anthony was able to take it off of him. Peter handed Don a knife. Witnesses agree that at this point, Anthony kept repeating to Don: 'I'll kill you'. Don was able to come in close to Anthony, however, and slashed out with his knife, stabbing Anthony in the left thigh, right hand, and finally the left side of his chest...The two groups broke off the fight, each going their separate ways.

One of Anthony's friends asked if he was feeling all right, to which he replied: 'I think I have been stabbed'. The friends helped him to a nearby house and called an ambulance, but Anthony died before medical help arrived. Don had no idea of the seriousness of the injuries he had caused, and was said by his friends to be 'shocked' when he was informed the next day of Anthony's death (Case No. 3661-85, pp. 60-61).

Several other studies have documented the escalating nature of quarrels stemming from challenges to manhood or honor (see Anderson, 1997; Athens, 1985; Brookman, 2003; Felson, 1982; Levi, 1980; Savitz, Kumar, and Zahn, 1991). In particular, Deibert and Meithe's (2003) cross-sectional analysis of 185 incidents of dispute-related assaults in Las Vegas, Nevada revealed that two-thirds of homicides result from escalating character contests. Wilson and Daly (1985) researched homicide conflicts in the city of Detroit in 1972, and found that more than one-half of the 339 cases in their sample were attributed to "escalated showing-off disputes".

Another dispute-related type of murder is revenge homicide. In this instance, violence is a planned devise for achieving retribution. Even if destruction of human life is not intended, the shedding of blood resulting in murder is inflicted as punishment in return for a wrong committed against the offender or someone close to him. Sociologist Jack Katz (1988) referred to this phenomenon as "righteous slaughter", because its most prominent feature is that it arises from a sense of violation or injustice. Besides violence as sanction for failure to comply with street codes, physical retaliation is also used to transcend humiliation or preserve status and honor (Felson and Steadman, 1983; Brezina et al., 2004). In point of fact, from a sample of 337 narratives of retaliatory homicides taken from the St. Louis Metropolitan Police Department, Kubrin and Weitzer (2003) found "honor and disrespect play a prominent role in the production of retaliatory violence" in poor neighborhoods (p. 170).

Following are three illustrative synopses of revenge homicide. The first summary is an excerpt from Fiona Brookman's (2003) study of lethal violence among males in England and Wales:

The offender (JoJo, age 19) had learned that Kofi (the victim, age 30) had sold crack-cocaine to his sister. JoJo was incensed by the news and decided to seek revenge. He gathered three male friends, all of who armed themselves with baseball bats and knives. They searched for Kofi and eventually found him in a parked car with a friend. Kofi was dragged from the car onto the street where he was beaten and stabbed to death. Many witnessed the attack, which took place at around 5:00 PM on a Saturday (Case Code: F. 11/96, p. 45).

The next case, which is taken from Daly and Wilson's (1988) work, is similar to the first example, except that it is representative of exact retribution—that is, violence as a counter to violence.

The victim (a male, age 23) accused the offender (a male, age 17) of having broken into his home, and then gave the teenager a beating. The latter left, got a gun from a friend, returned and killed his assailant before several witnesses (Case 79, p. 177).

This event is particularly notable for its dramatic progression. The victim, believing the offender burglarized his home, retaliated first; the offender then delivered a return attack "equal" in kind to the offense suffered by him. Revenge of this kind may be related to neighborhood values and norms (i.e. "codes"), but mainly it is produced by the innate desire to inflict punishment in return for insult or injury.

The final illustration, which also comes from Daly and Wilson, is a typical example of humiliation in the causation of retaliatory violence:

> The victim (a male, age 19), the offender (a male, age 23), and others were drinking and bantering together at an acquaintance's home. The victim was a boxer, and was talking about his fights. The offender was carrying a night stick, which he placed between the victim's legs and then lifted the latter off the ground. The victim, embarrassed, had to ask to be let down, then accused the offender of tearing his pants and demanded that the offender pay for them. The latter laughed at this demand, and so did some of the other men in the room, whereupon the victim struck the offender, and both were asked to leave. The victim left first, and waited on the porch, where the offender maintains that he was again struck as he exited, whereupon he produced a gun and killed the teenage boxer (Case 121, p. 176).

The last class of dispute-related killing is conflict resolution homicide. In this type of violence, physical force is a strategy for ending ongoing conflict (Block and Block, 1991; Fagan and Wilkinson, 1998; Polk, 1994) or it arises spontaneously from "historical roots" between the victim and the offender (Luckenbill, 1977). Time is the main differentiation between the various modes of dispute-related murder (Polk, 1997a); whereas confrontational homicides follow a single interaction in which violence happens without delay, revenge and conflict resolution killings proceed behind interactions rooted in earlier exchanges. Even though revenge violence often follows a single interaction, time elapses between the original event and the counterattack. The opposition might quietly lie in wait for the victim, leave the scene briefly to retrieve a weapon, or plan the attack and implement it at a future point in time. Conflict resolution homicide, on the other hand, ensues after a number of pre-homicidal confrontations between the victim and the offender. Luckenbill (1977), having found that almost one-half of the homicides in his sample followed previous disputes, referred to these non-fatal conflicts as "rehearsals" for encounters that result in fatal violence at some other time and/or place (also see Oliver, 2001; Polk, 1994). Transituational conflicts involve at least two encounters in which the victim and the offender either argue or argue and fight (Oliver, 2001). It could take months, even years, and several hostile encounters before confrontation ends in death.

Here is an Australian example of conflict resolution homicide taken from Polk's (1994) work:

Gregory R. (age, 25) and Ken S. (age 24) had been close friends since primary school. Neither had regular full-time employment, and evidence suggests that they were well enmeshed in the local drug scene.

A recent rift had developed between them, arising out of a $600 loan Ken owned Gregory (Gregory had lent him the money as part of a drug deal, but Ken had used the money to buy drugs for himself). Ken also had reason to believe that Gregory had been informing on him to their motorcycle gang ('The Immortals').

Deciding to bring the matter to some sort of head, Ken obtained a gun and persuaded a friend to drive him around looking for Gregory. They tried a number of addresses, including a party where Gregory had been earlier. The two ultimately found Gregory back at home. Ken went up to the door carrying his gun. Gregory, apparently having been fore-warned that trouble was afoot, met Ken at the door holding a sawn-off shot gun in his hands. An argument ensued, leading to a struggle in which glass panels of the door were broken. Ken's gun fired, striking Gregory in the head and killing him instantly (Case No. 175-86, p. 114).

Irrespective of its form, dispute-related homicide is about males making their own justice. Perchance this is because traditional means of protection and conflict resolution are not available to them on account of street codes (Anderson, 1994, 1997; Fagan and Wilkinson, 1998; Wilkinson and Fagan, 1996), lack of faith in the police and judicial system (Anderson, 1998; Kubrin and Weitzer, 2003; Meithe and Regoeczi, 2004; Polk, 1994; Brezina et al., 2004; Swisher and Latzman, 2008; Rich and Grey, 2005) or involvement in activities not covered by police protection or the law (Polk, 1994; Stretesky and Pogrebin, 2007; Black and Hausman, 2008).

Homicide Originating from Other Crimes

Most homicide by adolescents occurs during the commission of other very serious crime (Lennings, 2004; Zimring, 1984). In fact, research by Brewer and associates (1998) involving descriptive and correlational research designs and the use of official record data and media documentation to investigate homicide involving juveniles in Houston, Texas between 1990-1994, found that adolescents are twice as likely as adults to be involved in felony homicide. In the law of murder, felony homicide is when the victim dies during the commission of a felony, namely arson, burglary, robbery, or rape. Polk (1994) referred to this phenomenon as a "double victim" crime, since "the victim in the initial crime becomes the victim in the homicide as well" (p. 93). In his study of Australian homicide, he noted that double victim violence is rather ordinary—one-half of male-perpetrated murders occurred during the course of another crime.

Robbery is the foremost collateral felony resulting in homicide (Cook, 1985; Polk, 1994; Wolfgang, 1958; Zimring, 1984; Kubrin and Hertig, 2003). Although the vast majority of robberies do not end in murder, research indicates that robbery and homicide are interrelated. For instance, McDowall (1991) found that robbery and homicide rates in Detroit were positively correlated in such a way that higher levels of robbery raise the risk of homicide. Generally, robbery-turn-homicide result from unintended or extraneous factors in the social context; for example, the troubled or anxious mind state of the offender, the victim's reaction, or the presence of a weapon.

Robbery is mainly a youthful crime (Cook and Laub, 1998; Wilkinson et al., 2009), and, consequently, robbery homicide is particularly prevalent among adolescents. While intent to kill is perceivably no more of a factor in robberies committed by youth, their lack of skill and experience, in addition to their failure to plan for a successful crime, results in robberies that are more likely to end in murder. In fact, Gonzalez (2001) found that almost one-half (48%) of juvenile murders occur during the commission of a robbery.

According to available evidence, robbery homicide is more male dominated than homicide in general (Daly and Wilson, 1988; Polk, 1994; Wolfgang, 1958; Wilkinson et al., 2009). Males are more likely to be victims and offenders in this type of homicide. Although females are just as often victims of robbery, men and adolescent boys are more often killed in these crimes for resisting or being noncompliant (Daly and Wilson, 1988; Polk 1994; Meithe and Regoeczi, 2004). Seemingly, robbery involving males is an arena for victims and/or offenders to act out scenarios of toughness, honor, status, competition, and risk-taking. Consider the following two examples of would-be robbery turned into character contest homicide, cited by Meithe and Regoeczi (2004):

> While returning home from a laundromat the 15-year-old male victim was accosted by three males. He was ordered to hand over his letterman's jacket. When he refused, he was stabbed fatally. Witnesses identified the killers. Two 18-year-old, Negro males were charged with murder. (Los Angeles, January 1973, p. 122).

> The suspect was walking with the witness when they saw the victim get out of an auto to use a pay phone. They passed by and when they got to a vacant lot the suspect said he wanted to go back for the victim's jacket. Witness #1 remained on the vacant lot. Witness #2 gave the suspect his gun and accompanied the suspect back to where the victim was on the phone. The suspect said 'what's up, Blood? Give me your jacket.' The victim responded 'get for real.' The suspect then shot the victim and he and the witnesses fled. Afterwards, witness #2 asked the suspect why he shot the victim. The suspect said he hated for people to think he was a joke. (St. Louis, case #91031, p. 186).

Certainly, homicide is a very complex phenomenon. To the extent that this is true, simplistic and singular theories neither fully explain nor adequately allow for effective solutions to the problem of juvenile perpetrated homicide. Consequently, this chapter attempted to offer an integrated, yet fairly parsimonious framework to account for juvenile lethality. This dynamic, contextual point of view defines how structural and cultural conditions translate into values, norms, role orientation, and lifestyles among certain adolescent males that facilitate violent encounters. With that general understanding, it is hypothesized that aggravated assaults and homicides involving juvenile male perpetrators are not differentiated by structural and cultural variables. As a rule, assault-related violence involve at-risk male youth who are disputatious mainly as a result of inequalities, socialization, and chronic strain that are counter to healthy masculine identity development. Moreover, the inclination to use physical force to resolve disputes is a consequence of abundant opportunities for violence, as well as the prevailing concern with personal safety and self-preservation in disorganized communities.

On the other hand, aggravated assaults and homicides are expected to differ according to situational risk factors. Foremost, these criminal events are hypothesized to differ according to the type of weapon involved and the offender's specific intent to kill his victim. In this regard, it is anticipated that intentionality will exert the most influence on severity of outcome either in itself or indirectly through the type of weapon involved. Offenders who wish to kill their victims will generally use a firearm because of its lethal properties (i.e. weapon facilitation). However, irrespective of the type of weapon involved, it is predicted that in cases where lethal intent is observed, events will end in the death of the victim (i.e. weapon compensation).

Moreover, in accordance with the notions of face or honor and coercive power in homicide transaction, it is assumed that the severity of outcome in general and offenders' intent in particular are functions of intensity of conflict and the magnitude of threat to manhood. In this analysis, firearms, drug trafficking, and the presence of third parties are indicators of intensity and magnitude. This decision is buttressed by the state of knowledge in the area of homicide and violence, which suggest that these situational factors affect the production of lethal violence.

Lethal Intent and the Weapon Instrumentality Effect

THE CRIMINAL LETHALITY PERSPECTIVE

Long ago, Merton (1968) advocated the use of "middle-range" theories and frameworks that delimited aspects of social phenomena in place of grand and all-inclusive perspectives. His advocacy supported the evolvement of more modest sociological paradigms and empirical studies that focused on structural and cultural mechanisms that could explain variations among differentiated groups in society. Still, social structures and cultural norms apart from individual factors and social interaction do not completely or adequately explain homicide as a social phenomenon. Since homicide is clearly a dynamic situation that can be modified in form or character according to various social actions and events, a more adequate approach takes into account micro-level social activities, particularly those immediate to the social situation; thence, the criminal lethality perspective.

The theory of criminal lethality postulates that the circumstances in which an action is located, namely the immediate goals of the action (i.e. intent and motive), the means of the action (i.e. weapons used, number of people involved), and the conditions of the action (i.e. drug/gang-relatedness, police and medical response, intervention by others, quality of trauma care) determines whether a violent crime eventuates in death (Luckenbill, 1977; Williams and Flewelling, 1988; Wolfgang, 1958; Zimring, 1972; Felson and Messner, 1996; Nielsen et al., 2005).

While most theoretical discussions and empirical investigations emphasize the correlation between individual, cultural, and structural characteristics and homicidal behavior, the criminal lethality thesis examines situational variables that are potentially related to fatal outcomes of violent interactions (Anderson and Meier, 2004). By that very fact, this theory assumes that homicide is essentially a function of events that occur immediate to, during, and subsequent to violent encounters, as opposed to being the inevitable consequence of structural and cultural antecedents.

Wolfgang (1958) was the first to publicly allude to the processual nature of violent encounters and the salience of alternative variables in affecting death from assault. Specifically, he asserted that "...quick communication, rapid transportation, and medical technological advances...may mean that many cases of physical assault are kept in the column of aggravated assault statistics and are thereby prevented from being listed as criminal homicide" (p. 119). His conclusions, however, were anecdotal and not based on objectively verifiable measurements; but, violence and medical scholars eventually substantiated his claims (e.g. Doerner, 1983, 1988; Giacopassi, Sparger, and Stein, 1992; Hanke and Gundlach, 1995; Harris, Thomas, Fisher, and Hirsch, 2002; Richardson, 2003; Zimring, 1972;).

Much discourse and empiricism on homicide since then has emphasized the situational and interactional dynamics of fatal assault. To this extent, many theorists and social scientists have discussed and documented situated transactions and conditions that potentially initiate and/or escalate violent interactions and determine death from violent assaults (e.g. Anderson, 1997; Athens, 1985; Brookman, 2003; Deibert and Miethe, 2003; Luckenbill, 1977; Oliver, 2001; Polk, 1994;Wilson and Daly, 1985; Phillip and Maume, 2007).

CRIMINAL LETHALITY AND FIREARM AVAILABILITY

Lethality has generally been a term designating the ability of guns to kill. In fact, access to firearms has been the primary explanation given for the most recent outbreak of juvenile homicide in the United States (e.g., Blumstein, 1995a). During the epidemic period of juvenile lethality, from 1985-1996, gun homicides among the 10 to 17 age cohort increased 229%, with no change in nongun homicides for this group (Blumstein 1995b; Blumstein and Cork, 1996; Blumstein and Rosenfeld, 1999; Cook and Laub, 2002; Zimring, 1997, 1998).

Nevertheless, gun violence is a symptom of a larger gun culture and the moral climate of American society. The Second Amendment to the Constitution—the right of private citizens to keep and bear arms— is a cultural endorsement for gun ownership. Perchance that is why

America is more heavily armed than any other industrialized nation (Weaver, Wittekind, Corzine, Corzine, and Jarvis, 2004; Wilson, 1997). It is estimated that over 250 million guns are in the hands of private citizens in the United States (Rojek, 1999; Weaver et al., 2004). Given that kind of density, juveniles have tremendous access to guns; and the number of youths who report that they carry firearms is significant. For example, Vaughan and colleagues (1996) studied weapon possession and use among 2,000 Hispanic students in three New York City junior high schools by method of anonymous, group administered questionnaires. Results revealed that one in five students carried a weapon. Of those students, almost one-third (28%) said that weapon was a gun. In addition, their study showed a sex differential by patterns of gun carrying; boys were three times as likely as girls to indicate that they carried a firearm.

Blumstein (1995) also sought to explain trends in weapon carrying among juveniles. He estimated that 10% of male high school students carry guns. He suggested that gun carrying is even more common among male teenagers who reside in high-crime neighborhoods (25%) and male juvenile offenders (80%). Similar patterns were discovered in other studies by Gonzalez (2001), Kann et al. (1998), Lizotte and Sheppard (2001), and Sheley and Wright (1993).

With regard to the social context of violence, criminologists and sociologists have realized that guns have an aesthetic value, serving as status symbols in certain communities and playing a crucial role in the initiation and escalation of violence (Prothrow-Stith, 1991; Anderson, 1994, 1997, 1998; Fagan and Wilkinson, 1998; Wilkinson et al., 2009; Stretesky and Pogrebin, 2007). All things considered, the idealization and proliferation of firearms in mainstream society has apparently paved the way for a gun-based male, youth subculture in inner city ghettos.

Blumstein (1995b) argued, though, that the growth of the crack-cocaine market in the United States during the 1980s and 1990s in particular stimulated increased availability and possession of guns among inner city juveniles. Youth involved in illegal drug markets were the first to acquire guns; accordingly, that motivated firearm ownership among juveniles residing in or connected to surrounding areas and networks (also see Blumstein and Cork, 1996; Felson et al., 2007; Black and Hausman, 2008; Wilkinson et al., 2009). This greater availability and diffusion of guns among youths, he insisted, was responsible for the juvenilization of lethal violence. Specifically, Blumstein noted that "translating the presence of guns into homicide is undoubtedly facilitated by the seeming recklessness with which juveniles are ready to use guns" (p.11).

Juveniles who own and/or carry guns for protection or status reasons tend to engage in an array of illegal activities (Lizotte et al., 1997; Lizotte and Sheppard, 2001; Brennan and Moore, 2009; Spano and Bolland, 2010). However, on most occasions, when a gun is at hand, it is assumed that there is no intent to wound or to kill. Rather, firearms are usually presented because they give a sense of power and allow young aggressors to scare, dominate, and get compliance from others (Stretesky and Pogrebin, 2007; Brennan and Moore, 2010. Ironically, a gun can thereby prevent or serve as a substitute for an actual attack. Kleck and McElrath (1991) presented an illuminating discussion on the violence-suppressing effects of guns. They speculated that guns give perpetrators an opportunity to achieve criminal, social, and emotional goals without killing their victims. To this extent, they surmised that firearms can actually suppress the escalation of violence and prevent lethal outcomes in hostile interactions.

By and large, though, research on juvenile violence fails to support Kleck and McElrath's (1991) suppression hypothesis. Most observations indicate that guns provoke violence (e.g. Bailey, 2000; Blumstein and Cork, 1996; Cook and Laub, 2002; Fagan and Wilkinson, 1998; Goldstein, 1991; Heide, 1997; Kubrin and Hertig, 2002; Wilson, 1997). Specifically, where juveniles are concerned, access to guns often escalates disputes into homicide (Anderson, 1994; Bailey, 2000; Canada, 1996; Fagan and Wilkinson, 1998; Heide, 1997; Kubrin and Hertig, 2003; Prothrow-Stith, 1991; Black and Hausman, 2008; Wilkinson et al., 2009; Brennan and Moore, 2009; Nielsen et al., 2005), and increases the risk of a death occurring during the commission of another crime (McDowall, 1991; Zimring, 1996).

For instance, robbery homicide is particularly prevalent among adolescents (Cook and Laub, 1998; Wilkinson et al., 2009). In fact, Gonzalez (2001) found that almost one-half (48%) of juvenile murders occurred during the commission of a robbery. It is conceivable that adolescents who commit robberies are more likely than those who engage in pure assaults to have a gun in their possession because firearms enable them to get compliance from their victims (see Kleck and McElrath, 1991). While intent to kill is perceivably no more of a factor in robberies committed by youths than it is in robberies involving adult perpetrators, their lack of skill and experience, in addition to their failure to plan for a successful crime, results in robberies that are more likely to end in murder.

LETHAL INTENT AND WEAPON FACILITATION

Since guns are the primary method of killing in the United States,[24] much empirical attention surrounding the criminal lethality perspective has been given to weapon choice as a determinant of death from assault (Brearley, 1929; Decker, 1993; De Portes and Parkhurst, 1935; Harries, 1997; Kuhn et al., 1999; Martinez, 1997; Weaver et al., 2004; Spano and Bolland, 2010; Nielsen et al., 2005; Brennan and Moore, 2009), also known as the "weapon instrumentality effect" (Cook, 1991; McDowall, 1991; Miethe and Regoeczi, 2004; Wright et al., 1983).

Franklin E. Zimring (1968, 1972), who coined the phrase "weapon instrumentality effect," was the first researcher to empirically evidence that weapon dangerousness had a significant independent effect on the death rate from assault. In 1967, in response to escalating homicide rates in Chicago during the mid-1960s, he conducted a comparative analysis of fatal and non-fatal assaults in that city. Assuming that the rise in homicide rates was connected to an increase in the availability of handguns and that firearms have a greater destructive potential than other types of weapons, including knives[25], he evaluated injurious outcomes from knife versus gun assaults. The results showed a significant difference in knife and firearm fatality rates, with guns being five times more lethal than knives.

Since Zimring's (1968, 1972) seminal work in this area, medical and public health researchers in particular have taken an interest in weapon instrumentality theory (Doerner, 1983; Hanke and Gundlach, 1995; Richardson, 2003). Harris, Thomas, Fisher, and Hirsch (2002), for example, examined the link between changes in the lethality of criminal assault in the United States from 1960-1999 and changes in weaponry. Using local medical data, they confirmed that trauma from gun shot wounds is by far the most likely of all criminally induced trauma to be lethal. Moreover, by analyzing national-level data of homicide and aggravated assaults known to the police, in addition to police, agency-based counts of aggravated assaults and homicide aggregated to the county-level, they determined, as did Zimring (1972,

1996), that changes in weaponry can influence the death rate from assault.

Nevertheless, a matter for dispute concerns lethal intent and weapon facilitation; that is, whether firearms are the weapon of choice when people are determined to kill (see Miethe and Regoeczi, 2004). Many homicide scholars suppose that murder is commonly not the result of intent to kill (Block and Block, 1991; Brookman, 2003; Doerner, 1983; Felson and Steadman, 1983; Hardwick and Rowton-Lee, 1996; Harries, 1997; Katz, 1988; Luckenbill, 1977; Polk, 1993, 1998; Porkorny, 1965; Schmideberg, 1973; Weaver et al., 2004; Williams and Flewelling, 1988; Wilson, 1997; Wilson and Daly, 1985; Wolfgang, 1958; Zimring, 1972). Rather, it is assumed that in typical circumstances, criminal homicide is committed spontaneously or in the heat of passion. As Block (1977) acknowledged long ago, "there are few well intentional homicides…most killings are the outcome of either aggravated assault or robbery which somehow progressed beyond the degree of harm intended by the offender" (p. 10). Even Zimring (1968, 1972) assumed that in the vast majority of homicides, the offender does not harbor the intent to kill. Fatal outcomes in injurious attacks, he believed, are dependent on the lethality of the weapon used to inflict injury.

Moreover, contrary to popular opinion, homicide is generally not a one-sided event. According to social science research, the typical homicide is the result of expressive confrontations in which both parties are not only known to each other (e.g. Deibert and Meithe, 2003; Maxon et al., 2000, Porkorny, 1965) but also active participants (Curtis, 1974; Hannon, 2004; Polk, 1993; 1997a; Sobol, 1995, 1997; Voss and Hepburn, 1968; Wikstrom, 1991; Wolfgang, 1958; Swisher and Latzman, 2008; Stretesky and Pogrebin, 2007; Athens, 2005; Matjasko et al., 2010). In this way, homicide victims contribute to the interaction that culminates in their deaths. In fact, in the case of mutual combat, it is usually difficult to distinguish between the "victim" and the "offender," except for the death, because both parties play an active role in the initiation and/or escalation of the violent interaction (Luckenbill, 1977).

Whatever the fact is, other researchers believe that a large number of killings are done by design and that the offender's specific intent to harm is the reason for the presence and use of a gun. Felson and Messner (1996), for example, insisted that "a substantial portion of homicide offenders really do intend to kill their victims and not merely to injure them" (p. 520). Furthermore, they suggested that "the presence of lethal intent increases the likelihood of a killing even though the association between intent and actual outcome is not perfect" (p. 523). Nielsen and colleagues, in addition to Brennan and Moore (2009), essentially make the same claim.

Meanwhile, explanations of escalated violence and fatal assault have mainly involved conceptual frameworks and casual analyses that make use of weapon instrumentality as the predicate of proposition. This hypothesis is understandable, given the lethality of guns and their availability in this country. Nonetheless, this position essentially considers the nature and effect of action—that is, gun use—at the expense of the purpose or intent of offender behavior. Yet, one's state of mind and ambition at the time of an event is potentially an influencing factor in lethal violence, especially if it is the reason for the involvement of a firearm.

To this extent, the plethora of research evidence suggests that an association between weapon instrumentality and severity of outcome in assault-related violence may be spurious. The relationship between the type of weapon used to inflict injury and the lethality of violent assault may actually be due to the co-variation between weapon choice and situation specific intent to do harm, with the offender's intent being the effective cause of incident outcome in violent conflict.

EMPIRICAL LITERATURE REVIEW OF WEAPON INSTRUMENTALITY

The empirical knowledge is clear and unanimous; guns are more strongly predictive of lethal outcome in assaultive violence than any other type of weapon (Doerner, 1983; Fingerhut, 1993; Hanke and Gundlach, 1995; Harris, Thomas, Fisher, and Hirsh, 2002; McDowall, 1991; Meithe and Regoeczi, 2004; Richardson, 2003; Shumaker and McKee, 2001; Weaver et al., 2004; Zimring, 1972, 1984, 1996). Before assuming, however, that this knowledge ultimately has policy implications for gun control in reducing lethal violence, it must be understood if the weapon instrumentality effect is distinct from other situational antecedents of violence or whether contextual risk factors, most importantly the offender's fatal intent (also known as the weapon facilitation effect), exert direct or indirect effects on lethal violence via weapon choice.

Efforts to assess and disentangle weapon choice and other contextual factors, including intent to do harm, as determinants of outcome from assaultive encounters have been few and limited. There are five previous investigations of lethality that access whether the weapon instrumentality effect is distinct from the offender's specific intent (and other contextual variables). Prior methodological strategies to investigate weapon and facilitation effects on lethal and non-lethal outcomes have entailed individual level criminal event analysis by way of three different data sources to determine the variables that are related to the lethality of assaultive violence. These sources are official record data, victim surveys, and offender interviews.

Owing to the traditional use of official crime data and victim self-reports, most previous investigations on this subject are limited in a critical respect: they do not include direct measures of the offender's situation-specific intentions to do harm. In the absence of the offender's voice or other effective ways to measure intent, which is a private event, researchers trying to disentangle weapon and facilitation effects have made inferences about intent based on offense and offender or victim characteristics. They have traditionally used these proxy variables to account and control for offenders' intentions in the escalation of violence and incident outcomes in assaultive encounters. Perhaps Toch (1980) said it best:

> We shall not treat, prevent, or predict violence until we have talked and truly listened to persons who are intimate with violence, who can tell us about the "how" and illuminate the "why". In the absence of this strategy , our science of violence seems fated to be strong on facts that are weakly buttressed by remote influences" (p.664).

Articles in this review are organized thematically. The goal is to discuss the topic from its emergence in the empirical literature to the most recent entry by means of conceptual presentation. The working methods used in this area of social science research are discussed, compared, and contrasted. The contributions and limitations of each investigation are also established. Ultimately, the analytic strategy for the intended evaluation is presented and supported.

Impact of Firearms on Attacks, Injuries, and Deaths

Kleck and McElrath (1991) made the first notable attempt to control for the offender's situation-specific intentions to do harm in hostile or threatening encounters. Their study assessed the impact of firearms on three types of outcomes, ranging from verbal threats to homicide, for conflictual encounters involving strangers. The sample, which was derived by merging assault victimization data from the National Crime Victim Surveys (NCVS) for 1979 through 1985 and criminal homicide cases from the 1982 Supplementary Homicide Reports (SHR), consisted of individual incidents of potential or actual violence. The authors attempted to answer three questions vis-à-vis weapon instrumentality effect in their evaluation of incident outcome in conflict situations: Does the possession of a firearm influence 1) whether a hostile situation escalates to an actual attack, 2) whether the attack results in injury, and 3) whether the injury results in death?

With respect to lethal intent, Kleck and McElrath (1991) hypothesized that offenders with more serious intentions to kill or with a stronger propensity toward violence choose more lethal weapons. For their research, propensity and intent were representative of offenders' "motivation", which was conceptualized as "how willing and able (apart from weaponry possession) aggressors were to attack and injure victims" (p. 681). To control for offenders' intent and propensity to do harm, the authors used a model that included measures for characteristics of the criminal event, in addition to the offenders' race, sex, and age. These measures were selected based on the assumptions that Black males between the ages of 12 and 29 and individuals who commit robberies, rapes, and burglaries are more intent on harming, inasmuch as they usually have more extensive violent crime histories and rates of violent offending.

Findings from the study suggested that the presence of a firearm in threatening and hostile situations among strangers reduced the probability of attack, while the presence of less lethal weapons increased the probability of whether a situation escalated to a physical assault. Moreover, in the event of an attack, guns reduced the chance of attack resulting in injury. However, if a wound was inflicted during the attack, results showed that guns were more likely to end in the death of the victim than assaults where no weapon or other weapons were used.

Further results indicated that victims injured in the course of a robbery were less likely to die, which appears to run counter to Kleck and McElrath's (1991) hypothesis that robbery incidents are highly predictive of lethal outcomes. Otherwise, the general pattern of findings for the three dependent variables—victim attack, victim injury, and victim death—held regardless of crime and offenders characteristics. These findings indicate that guns tend to inhibit the escalation of violence and death of the victim unless a gunshot wound is inflicted, which supports the weapon instrumentality thesis. Moreover, the findings suggest that prior intent to kill by the offender is generally not involved in violent interactions. Or as many students of homicide have suggested, most killings are the outcome of interpersonal violence that progressed beyond the degree of harm intended by the offender (Block, 1977; Block and Block, 1991; Brookman, 2003; Doerner, 1983; Felson and Messer, 1996; Felson and Steadman, 1983; Hardwick and Rowton-Lee, 1996; Harries, 1997; Katz, 1988; Luckenbill, 1977; Polk, 1993, 1998; Porkorny, 1965; Schmideberg, 1973; Weaver et al., 2004; Williams and Flewelling, 1988; Wilson, 1997; Wilson and Daly, 1985; Wolfgang, 1958; Zimring, 1972).

Kleck and McElrath's (1991) research was notable inasmuch as it was the first attempt to empirically disentangle weapon instrumentality and weapon facilitation effects in hostile and threatening encounters. In addition, they recognized that the likelihood of violence in general and lethality specifically depends on many different contextual and individual risk factors, including one's propensity for violence. The authors also acknowledged that the effects of weaponry and offender's intent on the escalation and outcome of violence are substantial when examined stage by stage.

Although their research was seminal, there are some significant exceptions to note. Overall, the study suffered from five important methodological limitations. In addition to response bias and underestimation of gun assaults involving injury to victim that is likely with the use of NCVS data (Weaver et al, 2004), their sources precluded a direct measure of offenders' specific intent. The absence of a more precise measure of lethal intention, of course, means that the investigators did not adequately settle whether the aggressor's premeditated plans to kill the victim are associated with weapon choice and/or incident outcome. Even Kleck and McElrath (1991) acknowledged that this was problematic inasmuch as "omitting direct measures of motivation tends to bias the gun coefficients in a positive direction making gun use seem to have more of a positive effect than it really does" (p. 688). Furthermore, they remarked that the effect of guns on the death outcome could be reduced or eliminated if motivation was properly measured and controlled for in future investigations.

Another significant shortcoming of Kleck and McElrath's (1991) research is that their analyses only included cases involving stranger violence. This criterion limited the external validity of the study inasmuch as stranger violence accounts for a smaller proportion of all interpersonal violence and is more likely to occur as a result of robbery than other types of assault (Fritzon, 2000; Miethe and Drass, 1999; Miethe and Regoeczi, 2004; Salfati, 1999, 2000; Salfati and Canter, 1999; Salfati and Haratsis, 2001). By excluding non-stranger assaults and homicides, not only did they eliminate the most common type of interpersonal violence (Deibert and Miethe, 2003; Felson and Steadman, 1983; Harries, 1997; Hewitt, 1988; Kuhn et al., 1999; Maxson et al., 2000; Miethe and Drass, 1999; Polk, 1994; Porkorny, 1965; Wells and Horney, 2002; Wolfgang, 1958) but they failed to heed the distinction between victim and offender relationships, which might be important for understanding weapon choice and the homicide process.

Tactical Decision-Making and Weapon Facilitation

In an exploration of lethal intent and weapon choice as determinants of death from violent assaults, Felson and Messner (1996) adopted Kleck and McElrath's (1991) procedure of merging NCVS data from 1987 through 1991 on assault victimization with SHR data from 1989 on criminal homicide. In their criminal event analysis, however, they included stranger and non-stranger violent encounters and only selected victimization incidents that resulted in injury, which they operationally defined as physical harm that required medical treatment. The main dependent variable for their study was incident outcome, which they dichotomized in four different ways: death versus any injury, death versus serious injury, serious non-lethal injury versus non-serious injury, and presence of a gun versus no gun present.

They also took a different approach from Kleck and McElrath (1991) in selecting a proxy variable for offender situation-specific intent to do harm and the statistical procedure they used to systematically examine its association with weapon choice on incident outcome. Whereas the authors in the previous study included offender and crime characteristics as proxy measures of intent, these investigators used only type of crime to examine the interaction between intent and weapon choice in affecting the likelihood of death resulting from violent encounters. The assumption driving their selection of the proxy variable was that offenders in "pure assault" incidents, which they defined as "assaultive incidents with injury that do not contain elements of other felonious activities" (p. 529), are more likely to value harm or to have lethal intent than offenders in robbery incidents. Nonetheless, they did not statistically control for the aggressor's situation-specific intentions to do harm as Kleck and McElrath did in their study; rather they accounted for intent by analyzing the type of crime and the odds ratio for the presence of firearms in encounters ending in the death of the victim. They did, however, statistically control for offenders' sex and race in the study to determine if these contextual antecedents exerted direct or indirect effects on lethal violence via weapon choice.

Felson and Messner (1996) assumed that other crime characteristics and victim attributes would affect the likelihood of lethal outcome in injurious attacks. In addition to weapon involved in the offense, they included the sex and race of the victim, victim-offender relationship, and the number of offenders involved in the violent conflict as independent variables in their study. Largely, they used rational choice as a theoretical underpinning to explain the reasons why offenders might decide to kill rather than simply injure their victims. They speculated that the desire to kill may reflect tactical concerns about third-party and target-imposed costs. Overall, they contended that offenders are more likely to make tactical decisions to kill victims who pose an immediate safety threat or are likely to retaliate in the future. Felson and Messner (1996) hypothesized that for tactical reasons offenders are more likely to kill male victims than female victims, and more likely to kill Black victims than White victims. They also hypothesized that multiple offenders in an incident would reduce the likelihood that a victim will be killed and that victims are more likely to be killed by non-strangers than by strangers following the logic of tactical concerns. Finally, they assumed that the use of a gun would increase the chance of the victim's death from a violent attack.

Owing to the dichotomous nature of all the variables of study, Felson and Messner (1996) used logistic regression procedures to analyze their data. The main hypotheses in their investigation were supported by the research findings. The authors found that offenders were almost four times more likely to kill the victim in a pure assault than in a robbery. As predicted, guns were also strongly related to fatal outcomes. Offenders who used a gun in conflict were over 40 times more likely to kill the victim than offenders who did not use a weapon at all, while offenders who used a knife were just four times more likely to kill the victim than offenders who did not use a weapon.

Felson and Messner (1996) designed their research on weapon choice and aggressor intentionality to evaluate two competing hypotheses around weapon instrumentality: the weapon facilitation hypothesis, which states that offenders who have a desire to kill their victims will use more lethal weapons making it easier to do so; and the compensation thesis, which postulates that offenders who are determined to kill their victims will do so regardless of the type of weapon they use by compensating with more force or targeting more vital areas on the body when less lethal weapons are available to them (see Wolfgang, 1958) .

With respect to offender's intent to do harm and the compensation-facilitation debate, since guns and knives were both more strongly related to lethal outcomes in pure assaults than in robbery, the research evidence supports the weapon facilitation argument over the compensation hypothesis. In other words, offenders who desire to kill their victims use more lethal weapons in assaultive violence. Insofar as weapon effects are concerned, their results support the weapon instrumentality thesis. That is to say, guns are more likely than other weapons to produce fatal injuries.

Other hypotheses that were borne out in the study include: offenders are more likely to kill the victim if the victim is male or Black or previously known to the offender or if the offender is alone. The study also indicated that guns were more likely to be used when confronting male victims or Black victims, which probably explains why assaultive encounters involving such victims are more likely to have lethal outcomes.

The offender's sex and race, however, had no significant effect on the likelihood of death resulting from a violent attack. This seems to suggest that Black men do not have a stronger propensity for harming their victims than other groups of offenders as Kleck and McElrath (1991) speculated and used as basis for selecting the proxy variable for aggressor's intention in their study.

Felson and Messner's (1996) research initiative improved on Kleck and McElrath's (1991) seminal work and advanced study in this area in several ways. Firstly, they included both stranger and non-stranger incidents in their evaluation of incident outcomes in assautive violence. This is important inasmuch as research consistently shows that the vast majority of homicides involve parties known to each other (Deibert and Miethe, 2003; Felson and Steadman, 1983; Harries, 1997; Hewitt, 1988; Kuhn et al., 1999; Maxson et al., 2000; Miethe and Drass, 1999; Polk, 1994; Porkorny, 1965; Wolfgang, 1958). Moreover, they only selected cases from the NCVS where assaultive incidents resulted in injury. This is particularly important in generating knowledge that would lend to a greater understanding of youthful lethality. Studying serious assaults alongside homicides potentially allows for a better understanding of the situational structures that differentiate outcomes for violent encounters. Considering minor and serious assaults together is a questionable methodology for determining whether homicides are fundamentally and qualitatively different from assaults. The violence dynamics between minor assault and homicide are essentially different in both process and outcome, so as not to make for a good comparative analysis in determining risk factors for lethality in assaultive encounters. Aggravated and injurious assaults, on the other hand, are potentially more comparable (Harries, 1997).

Felson and Messner (1996) were the first researchers in this area of study to empirically evidence that victim characteristics, specifically sex and race, play a significant role in determining the risk of death from hostile and violent encounters through weapon choice. However, the analysis was limited by missing data for these victim characteristics and should be interpreted with caution.

Of course, like Kleck and McElrath's (1991) research, this study had other limitations associated with the data. In addition to the response bias typically associated with gun assaults in the NCVS, the expected underreporting of assaults perpetrated by family members is potentially problematic for Felson and Messner's (1996) study. Stranger and non-stranger cases were included in their criminal event analysis; non-lethal incidents involving family members are likely to be underestimated relative to lethal incidents in the evaluation since underreporting is less problematic with homicides in the dataset from which they got their sample.

Moreover, as alluded to already, missing data for offender characteristics is a usual feature associated with SHR data in particular, and to some extent NCVS data. In Felson and Messner's (1996) investigation, in particular, missing data was a limitation in the analysis of victim-offender relationship. Owing to these limitations, any results involving offenders' race and sex or the victim-offender relationship must be interpreted with caution.

Finally, a major methodological limitation of this study was that intent was neither directly measured nor properly controlled in the study. Rather than resolving the weapon instrumentality-weapon facilitation debate per se, and ascertaining whether firearms have an independent effect on lethal outcomes in assaultive encounters, Felson and Messner (1996) essentially designed their research to evaluate the weapon facilitation hypothesis and the weapon compensation thesis. To that extent, the authors merely made inferences about intent based on characteristics of the violent encounter without statistically determining if the presence of situation-specific intent, as they operationalized it in their study, caused the relationship between weapon choice and incident outcome to change.

Predicting the Odds of Lethality

In a study by Weaver et al. (2004) results revealed that the type of weapon used in and the circumstances surrounding an assault exerted the strongest influence on lethal and non-lethal outcomes. These authors departed from the use of National Crime Victim Surveys and Supplemental Homicide Reports and drew event data for their evaluation from the National Incident-Based Reporting System (NIBRS), which is also organized and managed by an FBI program.

The sample for the study consisted of data from 1995 through 2000 on 238,419 aggravated assaults and 2, 583 homicides from law enforcement agencies in 18 states. Aggravated assault (non-lethal) and homicide (lethal) cases including a single victim and a single offender were indicators of incident outcome for violent encounters in this research initiative. Weaver and his group (2004) evaluated contextual variables that were significantly predictive of incident lethality in Kleck and McElrath's (1991) and Felson and Messner's (1996) studies, namely weapon involved, victim-offender relationship, location, and the sex, age, and race of both the victim and the offender. Additionally, they looked at the circumstance that inspired the assaultive encounter and whether it exerted direct or indirect effects on incident outcome through choice of weapon.

Weaver and his team (2004) accounted for offenders' specific lethal intentions to the same degree that Felson and Messner (1996) did, except they exclusively analyzed robbery cases in their evaluation. The logic behind this decision was that robbery offenders "rarely have an a priori intent to kill" (p. 362). The reason for gun possession among robbers, they maintained, is to gain compliance from their victims.

As indicated by the criminal lethality perspective, which was the theoretical underpinning of the investigation, it was expected that (a) the type of weapon involved in a threatening or hostile encounter should affect the odds of the event ending in the death of the victim, (b) the race, sex, and age of the victim and the offender should potentially influence the outcome of assault-related incidents, (c) where the conflict took place (private or public setting) should alter the lethality potential of violent encounters, and (d) the circumstance or type of conflict between the victim and the offender should potentially affect the lethality of an attack.

Logistic regression analysis was used to analyze the data and odds ratios were presented to compare incident outcomes as determined by various situational variables. In relation to weapon effect, as expected and in agreement with previous investigations of lethality, firearms increased the likelihood of an attack ending with the death of the victim. Specifically, in this study, the victim was nearly 12 times more likely to die if a gun was used in the incident. Also in keeping with Kleck and McElrath's (1991) and Felson and Messner's (1996) findings, the offenders' race had no significant effect on the likelihood of death resulting from a violent attack.

Different from the earlier studies, however, Weaver's (2004) evaluation did not find that Black victims were more likely to die in assault-related incidents than White victims. Furthermore, the greater lethality of incidents involving family members compared to those incidents involving acquaintances or strangers as revealed in their analysis was unexpected as well as surprising. The theory of relational or social distance as it distinguishes victim-offender association by incident outcome, suggest that acquaintances are generally more susceptible than family members to being killed by their offender in assaultive encounters (Deibert and Miethe, 2003; Felson and Steadman, 1983; Harries, 1997; Hewitt, 1988; Kuhn et al., 1999; Maxson et al.,

2000; Miethe and Drass, 1999; Polk, 1994; Porkorny, 1965; Wells and Horney, 2002; Wolfgang, 1958). This finding may be explained by the sampling methodology used in the study.

Firstly, intersexual assault cases and assault-related incidents occurring during the course of a domestic quarrel were included in the analysis. Research indicates that lethal assault is typically intrasexual, consisting of male-to-male violence (Adler and Polk, 1997, Bailey, 2000; Cook and Laub, 2002; Daly and Wilson, 1988, 2001; Fox and Zawitz, 2004; Krienert, 2003; Mear et al., 1998; Polk, 1993, 1994, 1998, 1997b; Wilson and Daly, 1985). Moreover, knowledge suggests that conflicts between men and women are distinguishable from intrasexual conflicts (Daly and Wilson, 1988, Wilson and Daly, 1985; Philip and Maume, 2007), just as violence between intimate partners is distinct in social context from activities with other victim-offender associations (Daly and Wilson, 1988, Wilson and Daly, 1985). Still, this finding might be explained by the use of data that primarily included criminal events involving adult offenders. According to the literature on juvenile homicide, friends and acquaintances have continually been the modal category for lethal violence, while those involving family members have declined over time and stranger homicides have become more common over the last two decades (Blumstein, 1995a; Carter, 1998; Cornell et al., 1987b; Ewing, 1990; Gonzalez, 2001; Miethe and Regoeczi, 2004). Therefore, it is probable that the correlation between victim-offender relationship and weapon choice would have been altered if juvenile offenses were the focus of the study or properly related in size to the adult counterpart.

Results also showed that assault-related incidents occurring in private locations, particularly the home, were significantly more likely than violent encounters that took place in public settings to result in fatal outcomes. This finding can likewise be explained by the sampling methodology used in the study and expected to be altered when looking at juvenile lethality.

Finally, with respect to unraveling weapon and facilitation effects, the results revealed that robbery incidents involving a gun were positively related to fatality; specifically, they were almost 16 times more likely to end with the death of the victim than assault. Again, these findings suggest that the effect of a firearm is distinct from the offenders' specific intent to do harm in violent encounters.

In addition to the aforementioned methodological limitations, including the absence of a direct measure of offenders' intent and failure to properly control for this variable as addressed in relation to the prior studies, the representativeness of the sample in this investigation was restricted by the voluntary nature of data collection procedures for the NIBRS. At the time of the study, only a portion of law enforcement agencies in 18 states participated in the program. Nevertheless, using the NIBRS data set allowed the authors access to more detailed information on assaultive violence, including more valid cases of offender and victim characteristics and held less potential for underreporting of non-stranger assaults than traditional sources. Further, their work advanced research in this area and understanding of lethality by illuminating other event characteristics that may determine lethality through the type of weapon involved irrespective of the aggressor's premeditated lethal intent (e.g. circumstance surrounding the conflict).

Another contribution Weaver and his team (2004) made to the investigation of lethality was the use of detailed categories to characterize the association between the victim and the offender in regard to direct and indirect effects on lethal violence. While Kleck and McElrath (1991) only analyzed stranger assaults and Felson and Messner (1996) used the abbreviated classification system of stranger versus non-stranger to examine relationships in their study, which potentially masked important variations in the relationship between victim-offender association and homicide, the typology for this study included the categories of family, acquaintance, stranger, and unknown. This level of distinction between relationships is important for understanding the homicide process (Decker, 1993; Lundsgaarde, 1977; Miethe and Regoeczi, 2004; Polk and Ranson, 1989; Silverman and Kennedy, 1993).

Disentangling Instrumentality and Lethal Intent

Wells and Horney's (2002) study is the only investigation to use offenders' self-reports as a direct measure of intent to do serious harm, which researchers consider to be a better methodology for determining and predicting specific intent (Kleck and McElrath, 1991; Toch, 1980; Brennan and Moore, 2009; Nielsen et al., 2005). Their research consisted of more than 700 interviews with male offenders who were convicted of a felony and sentenced to at least one year in a

Midwestern correctional facility from November 1997 through December 1998.

Although the study did not specifically examine situational influences on lethality, it assessed the effects of weapons and offenders' situation-specific intent on the escalation of violence. Each participant was asked to recall and give a detailed account of multiple incidents of violence and "avoided violence" that they had been involved in over a three-year period. For each event that was recounted, interviewers inquired about weapons involved in the encounter and the respondent's specific intent to do serious harm (i.e., injure the victim) in that situation. Another set of variables, victims' gun possession and offenders' substance use at the time of the incident, were used as situation-level control variables in the analysis. In addition, their study was the first to use a within-person design to control for offenders' propensity for violence.

Hierarchical linear modeling was used to analyze more than 2,000 hostile incidents described by offenders. Their hypothesis that the effects of weapon possession on the likelihood of an attack occurring will depend on the offender's intent to seriously harm the victim was not confirmed by the data. Overall, their findings were similar to what Kleck and McElrath's (1991) study suggested. The results showed that offenders' intent to seriously injure the victim was significantly related to the likelihood that an attack will occur. All the same, the probability of attack by the offender is lowered when the victim has a gun. Relative to attacks with other weapons or no weaponry, firearms decreased the odds that the victim will be injured; nevertheless, guns increased the likelihood of serious injury sixty-fold if the victim was wounded.[26] Moreover, the probability of the offender attacking or injuring the victim did not significantly change when the measure of specific intent was included in the model. Finally, the study also identified a significant positive relationship between substance use by the offender at the time of the incident and the likelihood that he would physically attack the victim. These findings also support the weapon instrumentality thesis and suggest that the effects of the weapon used in an assault on incident outcome do not depend on the offender's intent to seriously harm the victim.

A major contribution of Wells and Horney's (2002) initiative was the direct measure of offenders' situation-specific intent do harm. Their within-person analysis, which allowed them to more precisely control for offenders' propensity for violence, also advanced the study of weapon and facilitation effects. Furthermore, they introduced the variable of offenders' substance use at the time of the event to their equation model.

General knowledge tells us that substance use surrounding conflict increases the likelihood of escalated violence among males in general and juveniles males in particular (Graham et al., 1998; Rossow, Pape, Wichstrom, 1999; Wiley and Weisner, 1995; Graham et al., 2001; Huang et al., 2001; Lennings et al., 2003; Lennings and Pritchard, 1999; Salts et al., 1995). In fact, the comorbidity of substance use and violent offending among adolescents is well documented (Busch, Zagar, and Hunghes, 1990; Cornell et al., 1987b; Elliot, Huizingua, and Menard, 1989; Ewing, 1990; Hardwick and Rowton-Lee, 1996; Heide, 1999; Johnston, O'Mally, and Bachman, 1993; Lennings, Copeland, and Howard, 2003; Lewis, et al. 1988; Office of National Drug Policy [ONDP], 2000; Rojek, 1999). Ordinarily, drugs and alcohol act in the brain on mechanisms responsible for regulating the functions of mood, thoughts, and motivation. Insofar as this is true, the psycho-pharmacological effects[27] of these substances can cause poor judgment, mood disturbances, and impaired reality testing, which may influence crime and violence in young people. Young males are more susceptible than their female counterparts to intoxication effects, which tend to trigger hyper masculine aggression, especially where other response alternatives are unavailable.[28]

A study by the Australian Institute of Criminology, entitled *Alcohol, drugs, and crime: A study of juveniles in detention* (Prichard and Payne, 2005) indicated that almost three-fourths (70%) of teenagers use drugs and/or alcohol immediately preceding a violent crime. In another Australian study that also made use of young violent offenders in detention, one-third of the sample reported that the use of alcohol or other drugs had made them violent at some prior time (Lennings et al., 2003). Similarly, Cornell and his partners (1987b) found that almost three-fourths (73%) of adolescent homicide offenders in their sample were under the influence of recreational drugs and/or alcohol at the time of their murderous misdeeds. Findings by Carcach (1997), Carter (1998), Dolan and Smith (2001), and Polk (1993) approach the same point of view. Meanwhile, other scholars posit that the causal relationship between substance use and violence is stronger when both the victim and the offender have been using (Wieczorek et al., 1990; Wolfgang, 1958). Certainly, Wells and Horney's (2002) data support the current state of knowledge.

However, their investigation was limited by their measure of incident seriousness. The outcome variable in this research was characterized by attack versus no attack. Only by comparing and contrasting cases that result in different degrees of attack do we potentially develop a fuller understanding of interpersonal violence in general and lethality in particular. The findings were also restrained by the cross-sectional nature of the assessment, which limited external generalizability.

Although information about the physical setting of the event, the circumstances attending the conflict, the presence of a social audience, and the victim-offender relationship was obtained for each of the nearly 2,000 incidents that were recounted in the analysis, another significant limitation of the study is that the authors neglected to control for these potentially confounding influences on incident outcome. Nor did they assess whether these contextual variables are related to intent and/or weapon effects, even though it appears that they had the opportunity to.

While the findings of Wells and Horney's (2002) study are consistent with previous and subsequent research, conclusions about weapon effects, intent, and severity of outcome should be interpreted with caution. The sample used in their evaluation possibly included incidents involving both inter- and intrasexual conflicts, as well as domestic quarrels. The research clearly indicates that assaultive violence typically involves male-to-male activity (Bailey, 2000; Cook and Laub, 2002; Daly and Wilson, 1988, 2001; Fox and Zawitz, 2004; Krientert, 2003; Polk, 1993; Athens, 2005; Yonas et al. 2007; Wilkinson et al., 2009), and that confrontations between men and women and intimate partners are distinguished from these interactions (e.g., Daly and Wilson, 1988).

Disentangling Instrumentality and Lethal Intent: A Replication Study

In their efforts to disentangle weapon instrumentality and lethal intent, Phillip and Maume (2007) also turned away from conventional data and research sources for criminal event analysis, and used a matched pair design to examine the relationship among weapon instrumentality, intent, and incident outcomes. Data for their evaluation was drawn from 100 face-to-face interviews with male offenders convicted of aggravated assault or homicide that were the consequence of an argument or other dispute with another male. In its nature, however, their study did not observe weapon instrumentality and intent as determinants of lethality. Rather, the focus was to assess the effect of guns and offenders' intention to do harm on disputes ending in serious physical conflict (i.e., assault or homicide) and those that ended without physical conflict. For the evaluation, an alternative research design based on matched pairs of conflicts, where respondents described the violent conflict that led to their incarceration in addition to similar non-violent conflicts from the same time period, was used to control for both offenders' situation-specific intentions to do harm and their violent tendencies. Kleck and McElrath (1991) originally emphasized the importance of analyzing individual potential for violence; Phillip and Maume (2007) applied this idea to their evaluation. However, their work differed from the earlier study in the conceptualization and operationalization of this variable. Moreover, they adapted the within-person research design as a way of controlling for offenders' propensity for violence from Wells and Horney's (2002) study.

There were three primary independent variables in Phillip and Maume's (2007) investigation of escalated violence: offenders' violent tendencies, presence of a gun, and use of a gun, which was a proxy variable to control for the offender's level of anger—an additional way of accounting for situational intent to do harm. Measures for the presence and use of a gun came from qualitative data about the violent conflict for each matched sample. The categories for presence of a gun included: no gun present, presence of a gun coincidental, and presence of a gun is the result of intent to harm. The use of a gun, however, was measured by respondents self-reported level of anger during the conflict on a scale from 0 to 10. The justification for this method of operationalization was based on the assumption that the angriest aggressors are most likely to be intent on harming their victim. In addition, Phillip and Maume (2007) controlled for six other situational confounders in their model, including victim-offender relationship, respondent alcohol use, respondent drug use, and presence of an audience.

Logistic regression analysis was used to tabulate odds ratios for lethality. Once more, results showed that firearms increased the likelihood of a dispute resulting in violence. In their study, the odds of a conflict escalating to violence were 9.5 times greater if a gun was involved. Overall, the impact of guns on escalated conflict held when potential individual and situational confounders, including offenders' specific intentions to do harm were controlled and accounted for in the analysis. The findings are in general agreement with prior investigations in this area and it appears that the relationship between guns and violence is not spurious.

In spite of the consensus in findings, however, Phillip and Maume's (2007) study is restricted by the absence of a direct measure of offenders' specific intent, its self-report methodology, the use of a local cross-sectional sample and a relatively small sample size, among other limitations. These considerations notwithstanding, their project had some important redeeming features. Above all, the research purview addressed the most common type of injurious and lethal violence: male-to-male dispute-related assaults (Anderson, 1997; Harries, 1997; Daly and Wilson, 1988; Daly and Wilson, 2001; Felson and Steadman, 1983; Felson and Tedeschi, 1995; Luckenbill, 1977; Meithe and Regoeczi, 2004; Polk, 1993, 1994; 1997b; Wilkinson and Fagan, 1996; Wilson and Daly, 1985; Wolfgang, 1958; Alder and Polk, 1997; Bailey, 2000; Cook and Laub, 2002; Fox and Zawitz, 2004; Krienert, 2003; Mear et al, 1998; Messerchmidts, 1993, 1997, 2000; Oliver, 2001; Bernard, 1990; Daly and Wilson, 1988; Fox and Zawitz, 2004; Kuhn et al., 1999; Uniform Crime Report, 2004; Wilkinson et al., 2009).

Furthermore, they introduced social audience effects to their equation model. The impact of guns on the escalation of violence remained when this social context was controlled and accounted for. However, prior research tells us that the presence of a social audience increases the likelihood of escalated violence among males in general and juvenile males in particular (Decker, 1995; Deibert and Miethe, 2003; Felson, 1982; Felson and Steadman, 1983; Oliver, 2001).

In summary, even though the research in this review employs various quantitative strategies, the findings consistently support the weapon instrumentality thesis. Moreover, knowledge indicates that weapon effects are distinct from other situational antecedents of violence, including offenders' specific intentions to do harm. Nevertheless, the evidence on weapon and facilitation effects is restrained by methodological problems. No assessment to date has focused exclusively on violent encounters involving juvenile male offenders; this alone typifies a gap in the knowledge. Owing to this and other limitations of research on the relationship between weapon choice and intentionality in assaultive violence, the proposed criminal event analysis will include self-reports for adolescent males who have been adjudicated for homicide or aggravated assault in New York state. The goal of the investigation is to ascertain the relationship between offenders' situation-specific intent to do harm, weapon choice, and severity of outcome in violent conflicts involving juvenile male perpetrators. Moreover, this analysis will endeavor to determine whether other well-known situational antecedents exert direct or indirect effects on lethal violence via offenders' intent and/or weapon choice.

CHAPTER 5:
The Research Strategy

SECONDARY ANALYSIS: DESIGN AND RATIONALE

The data for the study is based on a re-examination of quantitative information relating to the prior experiences of young males who were adjudicated for the crime of homicide or aggravated assault, and the characteristics of their violent crimes. To that extent, this investigation describes the lifestyle of violent adolescent male offenders as it is influenced by culture and learning. In the end, however, the purpose of this thesis was to determine the role of firearms and offender intentionality on the outcome of assaultive violence involving juvenile male perpetrators.

Secondary analysis is a common and acceptable mode of inquiry in quantitative research (Rubin and Babbie, 2008, Yegidis and Weinbach, 2002). Moreover, it is suited to the purpose of this investigation, and inside the bounds of practicality. In addition to these data being accessible,[29] there is a goodness of fit between the purpose of the proposed inquiry and the nature and quality of the original data (Sales, Lichtenwalter, and Fevola, 2006). As well, examination of existing knowledge obviates the enormous expense of time and money that would be required to implement a research project of this magnitude (Sales, Lichtenwalter, and Fevola, 2006). Likewise, secondary data research also allows the investigator to eschew various bureaucratic obstacles; permits wider use of data from an inaccessible subject population; and avoids burden and/or risk to human subjects, while maximizing the use of existent information (Yegidis and Weinbach, 2002; Sales, Lichtenwalter, and Fevola, 2006).

The form of secondary review that was used for this study is the additional subset analysis, where part of the dataset from the original research is employed to address the distinct interests and questions of the present inquiry (Hinds et al., 1997). Adequately assessing the contextual effects of lethal violence requires data with certain features. Firstly, a dataset that contains a range of proximal variables, especially the offender's situation-specific intent to do harm, is absolutely essential for the intended criminal event analysis. For that reason, official record data and victimization reports are inadequate sources (Phillip and Maume, 2007; Wells and Horney, 2002); offender self-report data, on the other hand, is more likely to satisfy this requirement. Secondly, given that aggravated assault is believed to resemble homicide (Brookman, 2003; Cook and Laub, 1998, 2002), having a dataset that includes offense information for both aggravated assault and homicide events is advantageous.

Moreover, inasmuch as none of the previous investigations into weapon instrumentality and facilitation effects on the outcome of violent events has focused exclusively on juvenile perpetrated violence, which generally differs in important ways from adult violence (Cook and Laub, 1998, 2002; McCurley and Synder, 2004), there is a significant gap in knowledge about the role of weapons and offenders' specific intent to do harm on lethal outcomes involving adolescent offenders.

Data from the Learning About Violence and Drug among Adolescents (LAVIDA) project (Crimmins, Brownstein, Spunt, Ryder, and Warley, 1998) satisfy all three conditions. In fact, LAVIDA contains an inclusive survey of background and immediate situational factors for comparable samples of violent juvenile offenders. Practicality aside, LAVIDA is appealing and suited to the generation of new knowledge and hypotheses of criminal lethality in general and juvenile homicide in particular. For one, these data provide an opportunity for analyzing aggravated assault and homicide offenses, which will facilitate a richer understanding of violent encounters and lethal behavior involving adolescents. Moreover, these data consist of interviews with young males who have been identified as violent and homicidal by the Juvenile Justice System in New York State. This type of self-report data is the best way to learn directly about criminal homicide among teenage boys.[30] Finally, given that the dataset reflects assaultive violence from the most recent and most severe period of juvenile lethality in the nation's history, the results of the study can potentially give evidence that will help to address current and future trends in juvenile violence.

THE ORIGINAL STUDY: LEARNING ABOUT DRUGS AND VIOLENCE AMONG ADOLESCENTS

Learning About Drugs and Violence Among Adolescents (LAVIDA), the original study from which data for the current investigation was drawn, was funded by the National Institute on Drug Abuse (grant no. R01 DA08676), and the data were generated under the auspices of the Institute on Trauma and Violence at National Development and Research Institutes, Inc. (NDRI) in New York City. Drs. Susan Crimmins (Principal Investigator) and Judith Ryder (Project Director) maintained direction and oversight of the project. Formal consent was given by the Principal Investigator of the study to use these data for this analysis.[31]

LAVIDA was a retrospective, correlational study designed to assess the role of drug use and trafficking in youth violence. Self-reports were obtained from male and female adolescents who were adjudicated for one of four violent offenses, namely aggravated assault, sexual assault, robbery, or homicide, and remanded to the care and custody of the New York State Office of Children and Family Services (OCFS)[32] between September 1995 and May 1996. The eligible population for the LAVIDA study originally consisted of 1,291 youths between the ages of 10 and 21. Given limited resources and the impracticality of attempting to interview the entire population, two sampling methods were employed. First, because female, sexual assault, and homicide offenders were inadequately represented, the sample was stratified by sex and offense. A disproportionate stratified sample called for the inclusion of all such offenders in the population. Next, a random sample technique was employed to select male, aggravated assault, and robbery offenders from the population. These sampling criteria generated a pool of 931 prospective research subjects (see Figure 2, LAVIDA Sampling Plan and Outcomes). From that sample, 441 youths were contacted for interviews. Of the 490 youths who were not contacted, 376 had been released from the OCFS system before they could be interviewed; 75 were transferred from OCFS to the New York State Department of Corrections due to changes in New York State's correctional policy beginning in 1996;[33] 33 youths were never approached because of administrative deadlines for completing field work; three youths had escaped; two were eliminated from the sampling frame because they had participated in a similar pilot study;

and one youth was deemed too unstable by OCFS staff to be interviewed.[34]

Figure 2. LAVIDA Sampling Plan and Outcomes

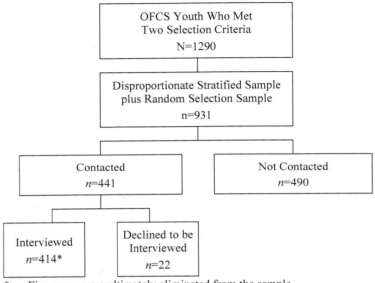

*   Five cases were ultimately eliminated from the sample.

A total of 419 of the 441 offenders agreed to be interviewed, yielding a response rate of 95%.[35] Eventually five completed interviews were eliminated from the sample: one youth had completed a pilot for a similar NDRI study, and the other four cases had large amounts of missing data. The final LAVIDA sample comprised 414 respondents,[36] aged 12 to 20 years old, with a median age of 16. Almost 90% (*n=363*) were male.

Nearly 60% (*n=240*) self-identified as Black (i.e. African American, Caribbean-American, Haitian) and over 20% (*n=87*) identified as Latino (i.e. Puerto Rican, Dominican, Mexican). About three-fourths of the youths lived in the New York City area prior to OCFS custody. The distribution by type of offense was 145 (35%) robbery offenders, 115 (28%) aggravated assault offenders, 83 (20%) homicide offenders, and 71 (17%) sexual assault offenders.

The original study involved semi-structured interviews, containing both open- and close-ended questions. The interview schedule was designed to generate detailed information about each respondent's life prior to incarceration (e.g. home environment, peer relations, exposure to trauma and violence, and prior involvement in illegal activities), as well as the instant offense for which they were currently confined.

The questionnaire was pilot tested with 40 youths from OCFS facilities and a teen drop-in center in New York City with a group of adolescents who resembled the population of interest (Bradburn et al., 2004). Any wording of instructions, questions, or probes that sounded stilted, awkward, or was misunderstood in the pilot test, as determined by debriefings with respondents and interviewers, was revised as needed. When pilot testing was completed, the final draft of the questionnaire schedule was generated.

Since respondents were wards of the State, consent was first obtained from OCFS and the Division of Criminal Justice Services to interview potential subjects on a voluntary basis. At the outset, each OCFS facility was contacted for a presentation, wherein the purpose of the research was explained, and staff assistance was requested in calling potential respondents out and escorting them to private rooms in OFCS facilities to meet with trained research staff for a single in-depth interview.

At the beginning of each session, youths were given a brief description of the research, informed that their participation was voluntary (i.e. they could refuse to participate or to answer any questions, and they could stop the interview at any time without any negative consequences), and assured that the information collected during the interview would be anonymous and held in the strictest confidence (Federal Certificate of Confidentiality, No. DA-95-94). The sensitive nature of the questionnaire and the potential for painful recall was also explained to prospective respondents, and they were advised that counseling services would be available by the project should they become distressed as a result of their participation in the interview.

Respondents who agreed to participate were required to sign a consent form indicating their understanding of the study and willingness to take part in the research. Respondents were assigned identification numbers to protect their personal identities. Audio tapes,[37] completed interview schedules, and consent forms were stored in locked file cabinets at NDRI headquarters to maintain confidentiality. Interviews with respondents lasted on average about an hour and one-half. At the conclusion of the interview, respondents received a certificate of participation which was placed in their institutional file. Interviews were transcribed and coded. Senior staff performed quality control checks on randomly selected interview schedules to check coding and transcription quality for verbatim responses. These checks were also conducted to identify areas where staff required more training or where a code was not working.

Self-report interviews with adolescents are generally valid and reliable (Williams et al., 1998). Nevertheless, several measures were taken to counteract possible response bias. To begin with, deliberate deception due to fear of detection was eliminated as respondents had already been convicted of their crimes. Consequently, the research was independent of eventual judicial disposition, and juveniles were not at-risk of self-incrimination. In addition, researchers were clear and unambiguous about their status as outsiders and lack of authority in the Juvenile Justice System. Deliberate distortion also was minimized by the assurance of privacy, anonymity, and confidentiality. Moreover, interviewers were trained to identify inconsistencies and to gauge the truthfulness of respondents' accounts. At the end of each interview, they noted their perceptions of the subjects' responses, and any questions as to an interview's validity were discussed in staff meetings. On the whole, respondents described experiences and behaviors that are generally considered socially undesirable and admitted to their crimes. Even if there was some boasting, deliberate deception does not appear to be a concern in this study, inasmuch as what the youth described resembles existent knowledge in the areas of juvenile homicide and violence, as well as information provided in official record data.

Furthermore, steps were taken in the original investigation to significantly minimize response bias due to memory distortion. For instance, questions were bounded by short reporting periods (Bradburn, Sudman, and Wansink, 2004; Incardi, Horowitz, and Pottieger, 1993),[38] by reference to family, community life, and peer activities (McCraken, 1988), or by use of ordinal level rating scales. With respect to the criminal event, however, memory bias is not likely to have been a significant problem on account of the relative recency and saliency of the event.

Measures were also taken to ensure standardization of interviews. More specifically, the reliability and internal validity of the LAVIDA data were protected by the following protocol:

- Training staff in interviewing, engagement, and probing skills to build rapport and educe sufficient information.

- Providing didactic instruction to staff in the areas of child maltreatment, trauma, substance use and abuse, gang membership, and interpersonal violence as a means of minimizing bias and sensitizing staff to issues that juvenile participants may have faced.

- Having staff memorize the interview schedule and engage in role play to promote consistency in asking questions/probes and to reduce the likelihood of asking leading questions (Fowler and Manglone, 1990).

- Using simple, clear, non-judgmental, and gender neutral language in the questionnaire schedule that could be understood by adolescents and that avoided influencing their responses.

- Training staff to record verbatim responses and to code data.

- Having data coded and transcribed after interviews were completed and precluding staff from transcribing or coding interviews they conducted.

- Randomly selecting interviews for quality control checks to identify training needs, code revisions, and other quality issue concerns.

- Holding weekly debriefings to prevent secondary trauma and burnout among frontline staff (Renezetti and Lee, 1993).

JUVENILE LETHALITY: THE PRESENT INVESTIGATION

Sample Distribution

The present study involves a two group comparison of homicide (n=76) and aggravated assault (n=65) offenses using data collected in the LAVIDA project. All of the respondents (n=141) in this subset analysis consist of assaultive encounters involving juvenile male offenders and male victims. Male offenders are the focus of study because males are overwhelmingly responsible for assaultive violence worldwide. Insofar as this is true, much can be learned about lethal violence by studying male samples. Furthermore, cases involving male victims are chosen for this evaluation because research indicates that assaultive violence is typically intrasexual, consisting of male-to-male violence (Alder and

Polk, 1997; Bailey, 2000; Cook and Laub, 2002; Daly and Wilson, 1988, 2001; Fox and Zawitz, 2004; Krienert, 2003; Mear et al., 1998; Polk, 1993, 1994, 1998; Wilson and Daly, 1985). Moreover, knowledge suggests that conflicts between males and females are distinguishable from intrasexual violence (Daly and Wilson, 1988; Philip and Maume, 2007).

The sub-group sample range in age from 14- to 20-years-old, with a median age of 17 at the time of the interview.[39] The largest ethnicity represented in this subset is Black (i.e. African American, Caribbean American, Haitian), representing 87 of the 141 cases or 62% of the sample. Hispanic male juveniles represent the second largest proportion of the sample; 33 juveniles or 23% of the whole sample self-identified as Puerto Rican, Dominican, Mexican, or Cuban. Bi-racial or multiracial youth comprised 6% (n=8) of the sample. The remaining cases consist of juvenile males who self-identified as Caucasian (5%) or as "other" (4%). Homicide offenses in this subset analysis were more likely than the aggravated assault group to involve offenders who self-identified as Black($X^2 _{(df=2)}$ = 7.914; p = .019). This finding is consistent with the current state of knowledge concerning juvenile homicide.

Research Questions, Hypotheses and Study Variables

This research is founded on the supposition that homicides committed by adolescent males are generally aggravated assaults with fatal outcomes. With that basic understanding, this project aims to answer the following questions: Are outcomes in assaultive encounters involving juvenile male perpetrators similar in nature or differentiated by specific circumstances surrounding the event? More specifically, is the weapon instrumentality effect distinct from other situational antecedents of violence in determining death from assault? Do certain risk factors, most importantly, offenders' specific intent, exert direct or indirect influence on lethal violence via weapon choice? In the case of lethal intent, is the desire to kill one's victim related to the instrumental goal of establishing or maintaining honor/face for juvenile male offenders?

With respect to honor contests and assaultive violence in general, this research is also designed to answer two specific questions. First, are violent encounters involving juvenile male perpetrators characterized by offender and victim attributes that reflect the concept of male honor? Second, are assaultive encounters involving juvenile male perpetrators influenced by normative values, experiences, and lifestyles that reflect the approval or tolerance of violence?

Foremost, it was hypothesized that the type of weapon involved in the assaultive encounters would have an independent influence on potential lethality. Particularly, it was expected that the presence of a firearm would increase the likelihood of an assault ending in the death of the victim. Additionally, it was assumed that the offender's lethal intent would increase the likelihood of the presence of a gun, as well as fatality in assaultive encounters.

The specific motive surrounding the offense was also expected to exert an influence on the potential for lethal outcome. In accordance with the literature, it was hypothesized that homicide events would be more likely than aggravated assault events to have occurred during the course of a robbery. However, since the current state of knowledge suggests that male-to-male violence is commonly associated with honor contests, it was not expected that outcomes would be distinguished by offenders' perception of victim-precipitation, irrespective of the motive for offending. It was also predicted that assaultive violence involving drug trafficking and third parities would positively influence the potential for fatal outcome. In addition to firearms, these situational risks were assumed to influence offenders' intent to kill by intensifying conflict and raising identity stakes for young males.

Moreover, since the current state of knowledge suggests that violent crime disproportionately occurs among members of the underclass, it was expected that both aggravated assault and homicide offenses in this sample would be characterized by offender and victim attributes that reflect male honor violence. Finally, it was assumed that these encounters would be preceded by normative values, experiences, and lifestyles that reflect the approval or tolerance of violence.

Measures[40]

All measures for this investigation are taken from semi-structured interviews with violent juvenile male offenders. Participants were asked to complete one-on-one interviews that examined their lived experiences, including the instant offense, prior to incarceration. The primary concepts for this study are weapon instrumentality, offenders' specific intent to do harm, and severity of outcome. Third party effects and drug trafficking at the time of the offense are also included in the analysis to properly gauge the effects of potentially confounding variables on incident outcome in assaultive encounters involving juvenile male perpetrators.

Criterion variables

The criterion variable for this study, severity of outcome, refers to whether a violent encounter eventuates in injury or death of the victim. To operationalize severity of outcome, a subset of adjudicated homicide and aggravated assault offenses were compared. Inasmuch as these two violent crimes are believed to resemble one another (Block and Block, 1991; Brookman, 2003; Cook and Laub, 1998, 2002; Felson and Messner, 1996; Giacopassi et al., 1992; Harries, 1997; Porkorny, 1965; Zimring, 1972, 1997), using this operation to measure the outcome variable is well grounded. Severity was coded as a dichotomous variable. Cases adjudicated as homicide (i.e. assault that ended with the death of the victim) was assigned a value of one (1) and those adjudicated as aggravated assault (i.e. assault that did not end with the death of the victim) was assigned a value of zero (0).

Explanatory variable

A great deal of knowledge concerning the circumstances of violent encounters was obtained by asking participants *"What happened"* to bring them to OCFS custody. Interviewers were instructed to probe for specific situational factors that were not elicited by this question. Open-ended responses were analyzed and coded into offender and victim characteristics and offense attributes that provided the physical and social context for the interpersonal violence that transpired. Coding schemes in the original investigation were derived from the narratives. Nominal definitions and coding schemes for the antecedent variables of interest in the current study are presented below.

Weapon instrumentality

This variable ascribes causal importance for lethality to the type of weapon used in violent encounters. For the purpose of this investigation, weapon instrumentality refers to the type of instrument employed in the encounter for which the youth was adjudicated and remanded to the care and custody of OCFS. This weapon may have been used by the youth, his victim, or someone else who was present at the time of the offense. It may have been employed in attack, in defense, or for another tactical purpose, such as intimidation or to gain compliance. If subjects did not volunteer this information, they were asked *"What weapons were involved [in the offense]?"* The response pattern for this variable was as follows: "None", "Gun", "Knife", "Fire", "Razor", "Other cutting tools", "Bat", "Screwdriver", "Blunt instrument", "Fists", "Bottles", and "Pillow". To transform these data into a classification of offense type by weapon involved, response alternatives were collapsed into three categories: no weapon (0), gun (1), and other weapon (2).

Offender's specific intent

In both criminal justice and social science the assessment of intentionality is customarily based on objective measures, such as inferences from conditions and facts surrounding the event or the reasonable person's standard of foreseeability. This test of intention refers to the offender's basic or general intent to do harm. An offense of specific intent, however, is predicated on the offender's conscious plan to achieve a particular harm relative to the resultant criminal act. Ipso facto, specific intent constitutes the mental component of criminal behavior; therefore, intent can only be inferred from a subjective test of what is in the offender's mind at the time of or prior to the offense.

Hence, for this investigation, intent is defined as the purpose underlying the youth's actions at the time of the encounter for which he was adjudicated and remanded to the care and custody of OCFS, as it relates to the outcome of the event. That is, whether the offender set out to cause the harm that was ultimately suffered by his victim. The outcome of the event refers to either aggravated assault or homicide.

The word or concept of intent was not precisely utilized in the original study. Notwithstanding this consideration, the present research effectively takes an original indicator in a new conceptual direction (Sales, Lichtenwalter, and Fevola, 2006). The identified variable for this analysis elicits the sequence of major events for these assaultive encounters. Up to three events were accounted for in the initial investigation; only the first code, however, was used in the current analysis as it is considered to demonstrate the offender's expressed ambition in the commission of the instant offense. Ultimately, this validation test constitutes the act of violence with regard to the offender's purpose to accomplish a particular type of harm.

Specifically, in the original study, after participants reported on their violent encounters, narratives were analyzed and quantified for up to three major events in the course of action, beginning with the initial goal of their behavior. For instance, a youth recounted that during a robbery attempt the victim failed to comply with his demands; he shot the victim and the victim died. This account should have been coded to reflect robbery, dispute, and homicide as the sequence of events that followed.

The response pattern for this variable was "Dispute", "Robbery", Property Damage", "Threatened with a Weapon", "Sexual Assault", Physical Assault, and "Homicide". Using the first code in the series, the sequence of events were transformed into a dichotomous variable to contrast lethal intent (1) with spontaneous reactivity and violence originating out of other crimes (0)—i.e. no intent to kill.

Offender's perception of victim-precipitation

Offender's perception of victim-precipitation is defined as whether or not the youth believed his victim's actions were morally or legally responsible for the encounter that ended in his injury or death. This variable was evaluated by responses to the following query: *"Did the victim do anything to make the event happen?"* If respondents did not understand the question, interviewers were instructed to say *"For example, did the victim hit you, threaten you, or insult you?"* Response options for this variable were yes (1) or no (0).

Motive

Motive refers to the underlying cause of the encounter for which the youth was adjudicated and remanded to the care and custody of OCFS. One item in the battery was used to measure the youth's motive for his violent action: *"Why did it happen?"* Up to three responses were coded for this item; only the first coded response was used in the analysis. Respondents reported a variety of reasons for engaging in the violent disputes that eventuated in their current incarceration. The full range of responses for this variable is listed in Appendix A. These responses were recoded into four categories: confrontational dispute, conflict resolution dispute, revenge, and robbery. Recoding decisions were guided by the current state of knowledge on modus operandi for male perpetrated assault in general and male-on-male violence in particular. A detailed description of the recoding scheme for this variable can be found in Appendix B.

Systemic drug-relatedness

Systemic drug-relatedness refers to whether the encounter for which the youth was adjudicated and remanded to the care and custody of OCFS involved the illegal distribution of drugs. Involvement by distribution refers to the offender, his victim, or someone else who was present at the time of the event participating in any activity connected to the illegal trade or supply of drugs, including buying, selling, or being a lookout. Systemic drug-relatedness was measured by responses to three indicators: (a) *At the time of the offense, were you involved in drug trafficking, including buying or selling drugs or being a lookout?;* (b) *At the time of the offense, was the victim involved in drug trafficking, including buying or selling drugs or being a lookout?;* and (c) *At the time of the offense, was anyone else who was present involved in drug trafficking, including buying or selling drugs or being a lookout?* Response options for each item included yes (1) or no (0). A positive response to any of the questions indicated systemic drug-relatedness.

Presence of a social audience

The social audience effect is connoted by others being involved as co-offenders or spectators in the encounter for which the youth was adjudicated and remanded to the care and custody of OCFS. Presence of a social audience was observed by youths' responses to the following query: *"Besides you and the victim, how many other people were involved?"* Respondents reported 0 to 70 other people being present at the time of the encounter. To transform these data, information was recoded so that a response of zero maintained that score, while all other values were changed to a score of one—indicating the presence of a social audience.

METHODOLOGICAL LIMITATIONS AND ANTICIPATED CONTRIBUTIONS

This investigation was conducted with the assumption that juveniles in the sample who were convicted in a court of law for homicide are, in fact, guilty of that crime. In itself, this may restrict the conclusions that may be drawn from the examination. Findings of this study should be viewed with caution for several other reasons as well. In particular, the following limitations of the study are important to note.

First, sample data for the investigation was based on a re-examination of quantitative information relating to crime characteristics of young males who were adjudicated for the crime of aggravated assault or homicide and remanded to the care and custody of the New York State Office of Children and Family Services between September 1995 and May 1996. These data allowed for a test of the relationship between weapon instrumentality, offenders' specific intent to do harm, and severity of outcome for a sample drawn from the most recent epidemic of juvenile violence in United States history. While there is no evidence to suggest that the structure or process of homicide in general or among juveniles in particular have changed in any significant way since this time, it is possible that contextual effects in hostile interactions are different for contemporary criminal events. Therefore, the findings of the analysis should be interpreted with caution.

Although there is little empirical evidence to suggest that juvenile homicide in New York differs from that in other large cities, these findings pertain to a single place and time. Insofar as this is true, the external validity of the data is attenuated. In addition, the cross-sectional nature of the data precludes claims about causality.[41] Thus, the research can identify variables that are related to juvenile homicide, but can not conclusively establish which, if any, factors directly cause lethal violence. Furthermore, the relatively small sample size could limit generalizability of the findings, as well as weaken the statistical power of the data.

The sample of offenders used in the study is drawn from a population of institutionalized youths.[42] This sample is biased insofar as there are other youths who have killed and assaulted but avoided detection, apprehension, or conviction[43]. Particularly for aggravated assault offenders, the pool of prospective subjects gets smaller from arrest to incarceration (Wolfgang, 1958). To say nothing of the biases in the court system that distorts offender samples (Feld, 1999; Teplin et al., 2005). Racial and ethnic minorities are more likely to be arrested for a violent crime, more likely to be convicted when arrested, and more likely to be incarcerated when convicted. Ipso facto, minorities are likely to be disproportionately represented in offender samples (NIDA, 2003a; Piquero and Brame, 2008; Piquero and Sealock, 2010). Incarcerated samples may differ from non-institutionalized samples in other ways as well (Swisher and Latzman, 2008; Matjasko et al., 2010). In fact, all social pathologies may be overstated with institutionalized offender samples.

While self-report data are generally reliable and valid (Elliot, Huizinga, and Menard, 1989; Gruber et al., 1996; Hawkins, 1992; Williams et al., 1999), the findings of this study rest on the veracity of respondents' self-reports. Detailed information provided by juveniles was not corroborated by other sources. Moreover, while both victim and perpetrator variables play a critical role in generating, escalating, and determining the outcome of violent events, victims' voices and background perspectives are conspicuously absent from the analysis. Moreover, background measures for juvenile perpetrators in this study are not expressly indicative of the code of the street. Any implications or conclusions about male honor contest violence reached from this study will have to be tempered by these facts.

The operationalization of other variables in this analysis, including offenders' specific intent to do harm, is also problematic. In many cases, indicators were measured by participants' responses to a single item from the original question battery. In addition, the accuracy of coding for the intent variable was unable to be verified because transcribed instruments and audio tapes from the initial investigation were destroyed in the 911 attack on the World Trade Center in New York City.

Finally, the scope of the data does not permit an evaluation of all the potentially confounding situational, individual, and environmental risk factors for incident outcome in male-to-male interpersonal violence. Of course, one can only speculate as to how these methodological limitations may have affected the findings; this is a potential topic for future research. In fact, the conclusions as well as the other limitations of this study bring forth fruitful avenues for further inquires that might be used to address the problem of youth violence in general and juvenile homicide in particular. The most important avenue is obviously qualitative study of contextual effects in male-to-male violent interactions involving juvenile offers. The matter of specific intent to do harm and the weapon instrumentality effect-offender lethality debate requires special attention on the basis of the current research.

Nevertheless, this research represents the most comprehensive criminal event analysis of lethal and non-lethal outcomes in juvenile perpetrated assaultive violence to date. Despite the limitations, the anticipated benefits of this study for social work practice and social welfare are manifold. To begin with, the findings of this research have potential implications for social welfare policy, as well as the development and delivery of risk-focused prevention. This investigation also builds on past research concerning weapon and facilitation effects, and make general contributions to knowledge in the areas of criminal lethality and juvenile homicide. Moreover, this study contributes to knowledge and education in many professional fields, including social work, criminology, sociology, public health, and psychology. Specifically, this analysis has special significance for forensic social work research, recommending areas for future investigations where social work and social welfare can and should influence the research agenda on interpersonal violence.

Violent Encounters Involving Juvenile Male Offenders

DATA ANALYSIS STRATEGY

The technique for generating counts of predictors by outcomes, as well as computing statistics and corresponding p-values to examine the null hypotheses of this study, met all assumptions for nonparametric inferential testing, namely the chi-squared analysis (see Abu-Bader, 2006; Weinbach and Grinnell, 2001). To begin with, the sample was randomly selected. By that fact, the sample is presumed to be representative of the population from which it was drawn, and the chi-squared statistic for the sample can be used to estimate the population's parameters. Second, the size of the sample exceeds the minimum number of cases required to form assorted two-dimensional contingency tables. Moreover, the criterion and all effect variables are at nominal levels of measurement; that is, the joint distributions under investigation are frequencies not scores.

Measures of the strength of the relationships between predictor and criterion variables are determined by the phi or Cramer's V coefficients (r), which was squared to convey the amount of variance in the severity of incident outcome that is accounted for by each predictor variable (r^2). These statistics are only assessed when the chi-squared test reveals significant results. Non-directional (i.e. two-tailed) research hypotheses are offered for all situations. The alpha (a) criteria for rejecting the null hypothesis in each case is set at the standard .05. Therefore, H_o is only rejected if $p \leq .05$.

OFFENSE PROFILE: OFFENDER AND VICTIM CHARACTERISTICS

This section contains a descriptive analysis of offense profile through presentation of offender and victim characteristics. There were 141 cases in the research study; 76 homicide offenses and 65 aggravated assault offenses. All cases included male juvenile offenders and one or more male victims. Numerical data in this portion is organized by frequency and chi-squared analyses. The objective of this summary review is to verify the principal features of male honor contests. In specific, these attributes include offenders' race/ethnicity, number of victims involved, victims' sex,[44] victims' race/ethnicity, and victims' age. Overall, this component of the analysis is an attempt to answer the following research question: Are assaultive encounters involving juvenile male perpetrators characterized by offender and victim attributes that reflect the concept of male honor?

Offenders' Race/Ethnicity

The data in Table 1 show that the largest portion of offenses involved perpetrators who self-identified as Black (62%). Juvenile males who self-identified as Hispanic (23%) represent the second largest portion of race/ethnicity for offenders. The remaining portion of offenses encompassed perpetrators who self-identified as either bi- or multiracial (6%), White (5%), or "other" (4%). When analyzed by offense type, it was revealed that the percent of violent encounters involving Black offenders was equivalent within offense categories (62%). Meanwhile, aggravated assault offenders were two to six times more likely than homicide offenders to self-identify as Hispanic (15% vs. 30%), bi- or multiracial (8% vs. 4%), White (8% vs. 3%) and "other" (6% vs. 1%). Altogether, though, 92% of the homicide offenders and 77% of the aggravated assault offenders were Black and Hispanic.

To ascertain if differences were statistically significant, all 141 cases were included in a 2 x 3 contingency table that examined offense type by offenders' race/ethnicity.[45] Since the p-value is less than the accepted value of .05 ($X^2_{(df=2)} = 7.914$; $p = .019$), it is concluded that there is a significant difference between the homicide and non-homicide group with respect to offenders' race/ethnicity.

Table 1. Offender and Victim Characteristics

	Homicide (n=76)	Aggravated Assault (n=65)	All Offenses (N=141)
Offenders' Race/Ethnicity			
Black	62%	62%	62%
Hispanic	30%	15%	23%
Bi/Multiracial	4%	8%	6%
White	3%	8%	5%
Other	1%	6%	4%
Number of Victims			
One victim	89%	92%	91%
More than 1 victim	11%	8%	9%
Victims' Sex			
Male	93%	85%	89%
Female	7%	15%	11%
Victims' Race/Ethnicity			
Black	57%	46%	53%
Hispanic	21%	19%	20%
Bi/Multiracial	3%	5%	4%
White	19%	29%	24%
Victims' Age			
Juvenile	34%	59%	46%
20-29	37%	11%	25%
30-older	29%	30%	29%

*   percentages may not equal 100 percent due to rounding

Still, the Cramer's V co-efficient suggest that the relationship between offense type and offenders' race/ethnicity is weak to moderate (r = .238), with offenders' race/ethnicity explaining about 6% of the variance in incident outcome (see Table 2).

Table 2. Chi-Square Correlations Between Victim-Offender Characteristics and Severity of Incident Outcome[a]

	n	$X^2_{(df)}$	*p*	*r*
Offenders' Race/Ethnicity[c]	141	7.914 $_{(2)}$	.019[b]	.238[e]
Number of Victims Involved	140	.366 $_{(1)}$	.545	.051
Victims' Sex	157	2.191 $_{(1)}$	.139	.118
Victims' Race/Ethnicity	127	2.273 $_{(3)}$	.518	.134[e]
Victims' Age	116	11.871 $_{(2)}$	.003[b]	.320[e]

[a] Severity of incident outcome: 0 = *aggravated assault*, 1 = *homicide*.

[b] Meets the alpha criteria of $p \leq .05$ for rejecting the null hypothesis.

[c] For the original classification, 6 cells had expected counts less than 5; the categories of White, bi/racial, and "other" were collapsed in the chi-squared analysis to address this problem .

[e] Carmer's V co-efficient used because table was larger than 2x2.

Number of Victims Involved

The number of victims involved in the violent encounter was operationalized by youths' responses to the following query: "How many victims were involved". Respondents, reported one to eight victims. To transform these data, information was recoded so that a response of one maintained that value, while all other responses were changed to a value of two—indicating that more than one victim was involved in the assaultive encounter. The vast majority of violent encounters involving juvenile male perpetrators (91%) had only one victim. Of the 76 homicide offenses, 67 or 89% included one victim; for aggravated assaults one victim was reported in 92% of the cases. Although homicides were slightly more likely to include multiple victims, the difference was not statistically significant when the *p*-value was examined.

Victims' Sex

To determine whether assaultive encounters involving juvenile male perpetrators are characterized by offender and victim attributes that reflect the concept of male honor, differentiating cases by sex of the victim is essential. For this reason, all 157 valid cases[46] in the database were included in this evaluation. Combined, the vast majority of offenses (89%) involved male victims. Just 17 of the 157 violent encounters or 11% of all the offenses had female victims. Moreover, homicides were less likely (7%) than aggravated assaults (15%) to include female victims, but a little more likely (93%) than aggravated assaults (85%) to include male victims. Nevertheless, a chi-squared test did not demonstrate significant differences between the offense groups with respect to the sex of the victim.

Victims' Race/Ethnicity

Offender reports were used to evaluate race/ethnicity for victims of assaultive violence. According to this information, more than one-half (53%) of the victims were Black. In the remaining cases, one-quarter (24%) of the victims were White, one-fifth or 20% were Hispanic, and only 4% of the victims were reportedly bi- or multiracial. When offenders' race/ethnicity was examined by outcome status, the most notable revelation were the within offense differences for Black and White offenders. As Table 1 shows, there was ample disparity between the homicide and aggravated assault groups with respect to these racial classifications. White victims were more likely to be involved in confrontations that resulted in serious bodily injury (29%) than they were to be involved in confrontations that eventuated in death (19%). For Black victims, however, the circumstances were altogether different. They were more likely to be victims of homicide (57%) than they were to be victims of aggravated assault (46%).

To determine if the difference between homicide and aggravated assaults regarding victims' race/ethnicity was statistically different, the chi-squared statistic was used. A 2 x 4 contingency tale was generated for this analysis. Of the 141 cases in the sample, 14 were eliminated due to missing data for the race/ethnicity variable. Results do not show a significant difference between the homicide and the non-homicide group with respect to the race/ethnicity of the victim.

Victims' Age

Offender reports were also used to asses the age of victims in this sample. According to these reports, victims ranged in age from 12 to 52, with a median age of 19 years. The pattern of responses for the age variable were collapsed into the following typology: "juvenile," "20-29 years old," and "30 years of age or older." Combined, almost one-half of the victims (46%) were juvenile males. Of the remaining adult victims, 25% were reportedly 20 to 29 years old and 29% were 30 years of age or older. When the distribution was analyzed by offense, the data showed that the percent of homicide offenses that involved other juveniles (34%) was much lower than the percent of aggravated assault cases that involved other juveniles (59%). Moreover, the percent of adolescent homicides that involved victims who were in their 20s (37%) were more than three times higher than the percent of juvenile perpetrated aggravated assault cases that involved victims in this age cohort (11%). However, as Table 1 reveals, the percent of cases involving victims who were 30 years of age or older was equivalent within offense categories.

To determine whether these differences were significant or occurred by chance or sampling error, the chi-squared test was used. A total of 116 cases were included in a 2 x 3 contingency table that inspected offense type by victims' age; 25 cases were eliminated from the analysis because of missing data for the age variable. Results of the chi-squared test indicate that for victims' age there is a significant difference between homicides and aggravated assaults perpetrated by adolescent males ($X^2_{(df=2)}$ = 11.871; p = .003). The Cramer's V coefficient suggests that the relationship between offense type and age of the victim is moderate (r = .320), with victims' age explaining 10% of the variance in severity of outcome for assaultive encounters involving juvenile male offenders.

Background Information for Offenders

Using the same procedures and summary framework as the previous analysis, quantitative background information for juvenile male perpetrators of homicide and aggravated assault was explored. The intention was twofold. First, the design was to further inquire into characteristic elements of honor contests involving adolescent males. Second, the intent was to test the hypothesis that juvenile violence is influenced by street culture and lifestyles that are conducive to assaultive violence. Variables in this subdivision include: neighborhood violence, neighborhood drug trafficking, availability of guns in neighborhood, association with violent peers, gun ownership, gun use, gun carrying, and drug dealing. Altogether, these analyses endeavor to answer the following research question: Are assaultive encounters involving juvenile male perpetrators influenced by normative values, experiences, and lifestyles that reflect the approval or tolerance of violence?

Neighborhood Context

Background questions for neighborhood context were operationalized by offenders' "yes" or "no" responses to the following questions: *"Would you describe your neighborhood as being violent?"; "Was there drug dealing in your area?"*; and *"Were guns easily available in your neighborhood?"* As evidenced by the findings of a descriptive analysis, this cohort of violent juvenile male offenders resided in neighborhoods characterized by violence, drug trafficking, and the availability of guns. Moreover, there were no statistically significant differences between homicide and aggravated assault offenders as to area of residence.

Peer Group Influence

Association with violent peers was measured by offenders' affiliation with a group of friends prior to OCFS custody who engaged in violent behavior. In the larger study, peer delinquency was determined by five items from the questionnaire battery. The first component of the measure tapped into general adolescent peer affiliation; youths were asked whether or not they had a group of friends that they spent time with prior to OCFS custody. Response categories for this item were "yes" and "no". Respondents who indicated that they belonged to a group of friends were then asked several follow-up questions about their involvement with the group and the group's collective activities.

For the present analysis, peer group influence was observed by three questions in the series: *"Did the group ever do violent things together?"*; *"Did the group ever sell drugs?"*; and *"Did the group ever use weapons?"* Each item had two response categories: "yes" and "no". A positive response to any of the questions meant that the youth affiliated with a group of violent peers. Almost all of the offenders in this study (92%) reportedly associated with peer groups that engaged in violence and other anti-social behavior. Furthermore, the percent of offenders who affiliated with violent peers was almost identical when analyzed by offense type (see Table 3). Since the *p*-value for this bivariate distribution is greater than the accepted value of .05 (see Table 4), it is concluded that there is no significant difference between homicides and aggravated assaults concerning violent peer group influence.

Gun Ownership, Carrying, and Use

For this analysis, gun ownership was determined by "yes"/ "no" responses to: *"Did you ever have your own gun?"* Nearly three-fourths (72%) of the youth said they had possession of a gun as their property some time before OCFS custody. As the data in Table 3 show, homicide offenders were slightly more likely (78%) than aggravated assault offenders (65%) to have owned a gun. However, there was no significant difference between juveniles who committed homicide and juveniles who did not in regards to gun ownership.

Table 3. Background Information for Offenders

	Homicide (n=76)	Aggravated Assault (n=65)	All Offenses (N=141)
Neighborhood Violence			
No	20%	31%	25%
Yes	80%	69%	75%
Neighborhood Drug Trafficking			
No	5%	5%	5%
Yes	95%	95%	95%
Guns Available in Neighborhood			
No	19%	25%	22%
Yes	81%	75%	78%
Associate with Violent Peers			
No	7%	9%	8%
Yes	93%	91%	92%
Own a Gun			
No	22%	35%	28%
Yes	78%	65%	72%
Carry a Gun			
No	0%	2%	1%
Yes	100%	98%	99%
Use a Gun			
No	10%	25%	17%
Yes	90%	75%	83%
Involved in Drug Dealing			
No	41%	29%	36%
Yes	59%	71%	64%

*   Percentages may not equal 100 percent due to rounding.

Table 4. Chi-Square Correlations Between Background Variables and Severity of Incident Outcome[a]

	n	$X^2_{(df)}$	*p*	*r*
Neighborhood Violence	141	$2.285_{(1)}$	.131	.127
Neighborhood Drug Trafficking	137	$.029_{(1)}$	.865	-.015
Gun Availability in Neighborhood	138	$.746_{(1)}$	.388	.074
Association with Violent Peers	97[c]	$.217_{(1)}$	.641	.047
Gun Ownership	139	$.3.247_{(1)}$	.072	.153
Gun Carrying	117	$1.400_{(1)}$	.237	.109
Gun Use	138	$5.590_{(1)}$	.018[b]	.201
Involvement in Drug Trafficking	140	$2.221_{(1)}$	.136	-.126

[a]   Severity of incident outcome: 0 = *aggravated assault*, 1 = *homicide*.
[b]   Meets the alpha criteria of $p \leq .05$ for rejecting the null hypothesis.
[c]   Association with violent peers was derived from a gateway question; there were a total of 97 cases for this variable.

Gun carrying, on the other hand, referred to having a firearm at one's disposal or holding a firearm on one's person in public prior to OCFS custody. This construct was measured by the question: *"When would you have a gun on you?"* Respondents reported a multitude of reasons for having a gun on their person. Any response other than "I did not carry a gun" signified gun carrying. Nearly all of the offenders (99%) carried firearms. When examined by offense type, of course, the percentage of homicide offenders (100%) who reportedly carried a firearm was nearly equivalent to the percentage of aggravated assault offenders (98%) who carried a gun.

Finally, gun use connoted that youth employed firearms for any reasons, but especially to threaten or shoot at someone prior to OCFS custody. For the analysis, gun use was observed by "yes"/"no" responses to: *"Did you ever use a gun?* Altogether, 83% of the 141 offenders said they had used a gun before OCFS custody. Among the 76 homicide offenders, 90% had used a gun at some point and time before custody, whereas 75% of the aggravated assault offenders had ever used a gun. To determine if these differences were significant, the chi-squared test was used. The analysis included 138 cases; three cases were eliminated due to missing data. When gun use was cross tabulated with offense type, results indicated that there is a statistically significant difference between the two groups of violent juvenile offenders as far as gun use is concerned ($X^2_{(df=1)}$ = 5.590; p = .018). The correlation coefficient shows that there is a low to moderate association between the two variables (r = .201). In fact, the coefficient of determination, the phi coefficient in this case, suggests that gun use accounts for 4% of the variance in offense type.

Drug Dealing

The distribution of drugs refers to the ancillary activities that are involved in the illicit supply and trade of black market drugs. These activities include transporting, guarding, steering, and selling. Involvement in drug trafficking was assessed by youths' "yes" or "no" responses to the query, *"Have you ever been involved in drug dealing; for example, selling, acting as a lookout, transporting, or guarding?"* Sixty-four percent of the juveniles said that they had been involved in drug dealing. When examined by offense type, it was revealed that the homicidal group was less likely (59%) than the assault group (71%) to have been involved in illegal drug trade at some time prior to the instant event. Nevertheless, there was no significant difference in drug trafficking between homicidal and nonhomicidal juveniles in this sample.

SITUATIONAL RISK FACTORS FOR SEVERITY OF INCIDENT OUTCOME

In this segment, descriptive (i.e. frequencies) and inferential (i.e. chi-square) statistics for situational risk factors in the production of lethal violence are explored. The purpose of this criminal event analysis is to determine how incident characteristics—namely, offenders' specific intent to do harm, type of weapon involved, systemic drug-relatedness, and social audience effects—are associated with fatal outcomes for this cohort. Fundamentally this is a test of the fatal assault thesis; ipso facto, this part of the investigation is designed to answer the following research question: Are lethal outcomes in assaultive encounters involving juvenile male perpetrators related in nature or differentiated by specific circumstances surrounding the event?

Weapon Instrumentality

Firearms were the most popular means of violent attack. Forty-six percent of the assaultive encounters involved a gun; 44% involved other weapons, namely knives, razors, screwdrivers, bottles, bats, some other cutting tool or blunt instrument, fists, or fire. Only 11% of the violent attacks occurred without a weapon. When the distribution was analyzed by offense, the data showed that the percent of homicide offenses that did not involve a weapon (1%) was much lower than the percent of aggravated assaults that did not involve a weapon (22%). As Table 5 also reveals, the percent of homicides that involved a firearm (68%) was much higher than the percent of aggravated assaults that involved a firearm (20%). Meanwhile, the percent of homicide cases involving a weapon other than gun (31%) was much lower than it was for aggravated assaults (58%).

To determine if these differences were significant, the chi-squared test was used. The analysis included 138 cases; three cases were eliminated due to missing data. For this classification a 2 x 3 contingency table was generated. When the type of weapon involved was cross tabulated with the severity of incident outcome, results indicate that the observed relationship between the type of weapon involved and the severity of incident outcome did not occur by chance or sampling error ($X^2_{(df=2)} = 35.726$; $p = .000$). As the correlation coefficient in Table 6 shows, there is a moderate to strong association between the two variables ($r = .509$). In fact, the coefficient of determination, the Cramer's V coefficient in this case, suggests that the type of weapon involved in assaultive encounters involving juvenile male perpetrators solely accounts for 26% of the variance in severity of incident outcome.

Offenders' Specific Intent to do Harm

Overall, nearly two-thirds of offenders reported that they did not set out to kill their victims (62%). Intentionality was remarkable, however, when compared by offense. The vast majority of homicides originated with lethal intent (71%), while none of the aggravated assaults reportedly proceed with intent to kill the victim. A contingency table that examined 140 valid cases of offense by offenders' specific intent was generated to examine significance for this bivariate distribution. The results of the chi-squared test indicates that there is a statistically significant association between specific intent to do harm and incident outcome in assaultive encounters involving juvenile male perpetrators ($X^2_{(df=1)}$ = 73.916; p = .000). The phi coefficient reveals that the relationship between the two variables is strong (r = .727), with lethal intent explaining 53% of the variance in severity of outcome in assaultive encounters involving juvenile male perpetrators.

Offenders' Perception of Victim-Precipitation

The vast majority of youth in the sample believed their victims were responsible for what happened (76%). When analyzed by offense, findings indicate that assault offenders were slightly more likely (80%) than their homicidal counterparts (72%) to attribute the violence to their victims. However, the difference between the two groups of offenders is not statistically significant at the standard confidence level of $p \leq .05$.

Motive

In keeping with the current state of knowledge, violent offenses in this sample were generally dispute-related (86%). From this larger category, 38% were classified as confrontational disputes, 31% were classified as conflict resolution disputes, and 17% were classified as having revenge as a motive. Just 14% of the offenses were robbery-related; nevertheless, when compared by offense, homicides (19%) were more than twice as likely as aggravated assaults (9%) to have robbery as a motive. Still, the null hypothesis can not be rejected since results do not show a statistically significant difference between the two groups with respect to motive.

Systemic Drug-Relatedness

Overall, violent encounters did not involve illegal trade (89%). Homicide events, however, were about three times (16%) as likely as aggravated assaults (5%) to have the offender, the victim, or some one else who was present involved in illegal drug trade at the time of the offense. The chi-squared analysis for this bivariate distribution included all 141 cases. Results indicate that the observed differences seen in this analysis are not likely to have occurred by chance or sampling error. That is to say, there is statistically significant relationship between involvement in illegal drug trade at the time of a violent encounter and the severity of outcome for assaults involving juvenile male offenders ($X^2_{(df=1)}$ = 4.602; p = .032). The phi coefficient reveals that the relationship between the two variables is not as powerful as it is for weapon type and offenders' specific intent to do harm ($r = .181$); nevertheless, involvement in the illegal drug trade at the time of the event accounts for about 3% of the variance in severity of outcome in assaultive encounters involving juvenile male perpetrators.

Presence of a Social Audience

As Table 5 shows, spectators were present in the vast majority of these encounters (74%). By contrast, homicides were more likely (81%) than aggravated assaults (66%) to have an audience present. To assess whether the difference distinguishes the two offenses, a cross tabulation was performed on 128 valid cases; 11 cases were eliminated from the sample due to missing data for the predictor variable. Results of the analysis revealed that homicides are statistically more likely than aggravated assaults to have an audience present ($X^2_{(df=1)} = 4.197$; $p = .041$). The phi coefficient shows that the association between event outcome and the presence of a social audience is also not as strong ($r=.181$) as it is for the bivariate associations for weapon choice and specific intent to do harm (see Table 6). The presence of a social audience accounts for just 3% of the variance in severity of incident outcome, leaving 97% of the variance unaccounted for. Nevertheless, the level of significance observed in the joint distribution of this pair of variates meets the criteria for rejecting the null hypothesis.

Disentangling Weapon Instrumentality and Offenders' Specific Intent

As stated in chapters one, two, and three, the principal endeavor of this research was to disentangle weapon instrumentality and offenders' intentionality in determining death from assault. To that extent, this investigation attempted to answer the question: Are lethal outcomes in assaultive encounters involving juvenile male perpetrators a primary function of type of weapon involved (i.e. firearms) or the primary function of offenders' specific intent to do lethal harm? Consequently, this section was supposed to involve a multivariate chi-square analysis to inspect weapon and facilitation effects on lethal outcomes, controlling for the influence of each respective predictor variable (i.e. type of weapon involved and offenders' specific intent).

Table 5. Situational Risk Factors for Severity of Incident Outcome

	Homicide (n=76)	Aggravated Assault (n=65)	All Offenses (N=141)
Type of Weapon Involved			
None	1%	22%	11%
Firearm	68%	20%	46%
Other Weapon	31%	58%	44%
Offenders' Specific Intent			
No Intent to Kill	29%	100%	62%
Intent to Kill	71%	0%	38%
Victim-Precipitated			
No	28%	20%	24%
Yes	72%	80%	76%
Motive			
Confrontation	39%	37%	38%
Conflict Resolution	26%	37%	31%
Revenge	16%	18%	17%
Robbery	19%	9%	14%
Systemic Drug-Relatedness			
No	84%	95%	89%
Yes	16%	5%	11%
Social Audience			
No	19%	35%	26%
Yes	81%	66%	74%

*   Percentages may not equal 100 percent due to rounding.

Table 6. Chi-Square Correlations Between Situational Risk Factors and Severity of Incident Outcome[a]

	n	$X^2_{(df)}$	p	r
Offenders' Specific Intent[c]	140	73.916 $_{(1)}$	.000 [b]	.727
Type of Weapon Involved	138	35.726 $_{(1)}$	.000 [b]	.509
Systemic Drug-Relatedness	141	4.602 $_{(1)}$	.032 [b]	181
Presence of a Social Audience	128	4.197 $_{(2)}$	.041 [b]	.181 [d]
Motive	119	2.716 $_{(1)}$	.099	-.151
Offenders' Perception of Victim-Precipitation	127	.989 $_{(1)}$	.320	-.088

[a]   Severity of incident outcome: $0 = $ *aggravated assault*, $1 = $ *homicide*.

[b]   Meets the alpha criteria of $p \leq .05$ for rejecting the null hypothesis.

[c]   There was one cells in this analysis with a count of less than 5.

[d]   Cramer's V co-efficient used because table was larger than 2x2.

However, there was no indication of lethal intent for any of the aggravated assault cases in this sample. As a result, the contingency tables produced for this analysis contained cells with no frequencies. Because cells could not possibly be collapsed and there was no alternate test that could be performed in this case, this investigation lacked the necessary statistical means to disentangle the association between specific intent, weapon instrumentality, and severity of incident outcome.

Nevertheless, bivariate analysis for offenders' specific intent and incident outcome had the recommended percentage of cells with expected frequencies of at least five cases. Therefore, according to the overall analysis, the preponderance of the weapon instrumentality effect is called into question. Although, the type of weapon predicted whether the offense ended in the death of the victim or not, offenders' specific intent to do harm accounted for a larger portion of the variance in severity of incident outcome in juvenile perpetrated violence (see Table 6).

SITUATIONAL RISK FACTORS FOR LETHAL INTENT

This phase of the investigation gives attention to the theory of tactical concerns and coercive power in determining death from assault. On the authority of this explanation, the aim is to explore conditional dynamics in the immediate event that potentially account for lethal intent among juvenile male perpetrators. In this analysis, offenders' specific intent to do harm is treated as the criterion variable; type of weapon involved, systemic drug-relatedness, and the presence of a social audience are the antecedent study variables. This test attempts to address the following research question: Are lethal outcomes in assaultive encounters involving male perpetrators a function of offenders' willful choice to kill their victims as it relates to situational contingencies that reflect the instrumental goals of establishing or maintaining honor?

Type of Weapon Involved

The data in Table 7 shows that among the 138 valid cases for this analysis, 63 violent encounters or 46% of the cases involved a firearm, and 75 encounters or 55% of the sample offenses did not involve a gun. As can be seen within the intent matrix, however, intent to kill was more likely decided where a gun was involved (64%) than it was where a gun was not involved (35%). In fact, in the chi-square analysis, firearms were found to be significantly correlated with the offender's decision to kill his victim(s) ($X^2_{(df=2)} = 13.449$; $p = .001$). The correlation coefficient indicates that there is a weak to moderate association between the two variables ($r = .312$), with firearms explaining nearly 10% of the variance in the offender's decision to kill his victim(s) or not (see Table 8).

Offenders' Perception of Victim-Precipitation

To analyze offenders' intent by perception of victim-precipitation, a 2 x 2 contingency table was generated. Of the 141 cases in the sample, 14 were eliminated from the analysis due to missing data. In summary, the data shows that in situations where there was no intent to kill, offenders were more likely to justify their violent behavior by attributing blame to the victim. Moreover, the results of the chi-squared test indicates that this finding is statistically significant ($X^2_{(df=1)} = 5.593$; $p < .018$). The phi coefficient reveals that the relationship between the two variables is weak to moderate ($r = -.210$), with perception of victim-precipitation explaining less than 5% of the variance in offenders' intent to do harm.

Table 7. Situational Risk Factors for Lethal Intent

	Lethal Intent (n=53)	No Lethal Intent (n=87)	All Offenses (N=140)[a]
Firearm Involved			
No	37%	65%	55%
Yes	64%	35%	46%
Victim-Precipitated			
No	36%	18%	24%
Yes	64%	83%	76%
Motive			
Confrontation	36%	38%	37%
Conflict Resolution	36%	29%	31%
Revenge	18%	17%	17%
Robbery	10%	17%	14%
Systemic Drug-Relatedness			
No	83%	93%	89%
Yes	17%	7%	11%
Social Audience			
No	14%	33%	26%
Yes	86%	67%	74%

* Percentages may not equal 100 percent due to rounding.
[a] One case was eliminated from the sample because of missing data.

Table 8. Chi-Square Correlations Between Situational Risk Factors and Lethal Intent[a]

	n	$X^2_{(df)}$	*p*	*r*
Type of Weapon Involved	138	$13.449_{(2)}$	$.001^{b}$	$.312^{c}$
Offenders' Perception of Victim-Precipitation	127	5.5	$.018^{b}$	-.210
Presence of a Social Audience	128	$93_{(1)}$ $5.483_{(1)}$	$.019^{b}$	.207
Systemic Drug-Relatedness	140	$3.501_{(2)}$	.061	$.158^{c}$
Motive	118	$.814_{(1)}$	.367	.083

[a]   Lethal intent: 0 = no lethal intent, 1 = lethal intent.

[b]   Meets the alpha criteria of $p \leq .05$ for rejecting the null hypothesis.

[c]   Cramer's V co-efficient used because table was larger than 2x2.

Motive

The preponderance of violent attacks was motivated by some form of dispute. When motive was cross tabulated with offenders' intent to do harm, a small difference was observed between situations where lethal intent was decided and those where it was not vis-à-vis robbery as a motive. Specifically, robbery was more likely to be the motive in situations that did not evidence lethal intent than it was in situations where there was a desire to kill the victim.

For the chi-squared analysis, a 2 x 2 contingency table was generated. Of the 141 cases in the sample, 23 were eliminated from the analysis due to missing data. Ultimately, 118 cases were examined. Results do not show that this difference is statistically significant; therefore, do not reject the null hypothesis.

Systemic Drug-Relatedness

Overall, drug trade at the time of the violent encounter appears to be of less importance than other risk factors. In most situations (89%), the offender, the victim(s), or someone else who was present at the time of the event was reportedly participating in the distribution of narcotics. Nonetheless, when intent and drug-relatedness were cross tabulated, it was revealed that offenders were more than two times as likely to have the intention to kill their victims where drug trafficking was involved (17%) than they were where it was not (7%).

Again, the chi-squared statistic was used to determine if the relationship between the decision to kill and drug-relatedness was significant ($X^2_{(df=1)} = 3.501$; $p = .061$). The probability value is greater than the accepted value of .05. Since the null hypothesis fails to be rejected at the .05 level, it is concluded that the observed difference is likely to have occurred by chance or sampling error. That is to say, there is no significant difference between the drug-relatedness of violent encounters and offenders' specific intent to do harm. Nevertheless, this finding is suggestive.

Presence of a Social Audience

As expected under the rubric of male honor contest violence, spectators were present in three-fourths (74%) of these confrontations. Moreover, the presence of a social audience was possibly more of a tactical concern in situations where lethal intent was expressed (86%) than it was in situations where it was not (63%). The chi-squared test indicates that although third parties were on hand the majority of the time for both groups, the difference between the lethal and non-lethal cohorts approached significance ($X^2_{(df=1)} = 5.483$; $p = .019$). The correlation between the presence of spectators and the decision to kill, however, is somewhat weak ($r = .207$). The social audience effect accounts for just 4% of the variance in the decision to kill, leaving 96% of the difference to be explained by other factors.

CHAPTER 7:
Developing Youth Violence Prevention and Intervention Strategies

DISCUSSION OF FINDINGS

While the empirical literature is clear and unambiguous about guns being more strongly predictive of lethal outcome in assaultive violence than any other type of weapon (Doerner, 1993; Hanke and Gundlach, 1995; Harris, Thomas, Fisher, and Hirsh, 2002; Meithe and Regoeczi, 2004; Weaver et al., 2004; Zimring, 1972; 1984; 1996), many social scientists and theorists argue that the relationship between firearms and fatal violence is spurious (Kleck and McElrath, 1991; Zimring, 1972; Philip and Maume, 2007; Wilkinson et al., 2009; Spano and Bolland, 2010; Nielsen et al., 2005). Spuriousness is explained by offenders' specific intent to do lethal harm being the reason for the presence of firearms in the first place. This discourse on criminal intent and offender lethality relates to supply- and demand-side theories and strategies in the reduction of gun violence and homicide among juveniles. In the political debate surrounding gun control and sentencing policies, these very ideas are used to support suppression and punishment strategies. Nevertheless, this is an important research problem for social science that deals with theory and practice of social administration. Even if death is a consequence of weapon technology, ascertaining with what objective youth possess, carry, and use firearms, in addition to what promotes destructive intentions among juveniles can facilitate an informed approach to public welfare.

Victim-Offender and Background Characteristics

The findings of this study support a more complex explanation of juvenile lethality than has been proposed in discussions of gun control and sentencing policies. As was anticipated, adolescent violence is characterized by offender and victim attributes that reflect the concept of male honor. By design, all cases in this investigation included both male offenders and victims; nevertheless, the largest portion (89%) of the sampling frame contained male-to-male violent offenses. The maleness of homicide and serious assault is well documented in the literature (e.g. Bailey, 2000; Block and Block, 1991; Cook and Laub, 2002; Daly and Wilson, 1988; Krienert, 2003; McCurley and Synder, 2004, Polk, 1998; Fox and Zawitz, 2004; Wolfgang, 1958; Yonas et al., 2005; Piquero and Sealock, 2010), as is the intrasexual nature of assault and the preponderance of male-to-male violence. Moreover, it is important to note that sex differences in violent offending transcend age, social class, and race/ethnicity; this phenomenon has been maintained globally and historically.

Other victim-offender demographic findings furnish support that compulsory masculinity may be a critical risk factor in adolescent violence in general and homicide in particular. Honor contest participants are characteristically young and occupy the lowest socioeconomic position in society (Polk, 1997a; 1999; Oliver, 2001; Stewart et al., 2008; Brezina et al., 2004; Swisher and Latzman, 2008; Anderson and Meier, 2004; Stretesky and Pogrebin, 2007). These data suggest that young male offenders belonged to the American underclass. Overwhelmingly, these perpetrators resided in disorganized communities, as evidenced by violence, drug trade, and the availability of guns in their neighborhoods (see Table 3). Ostensibly, their actions were preceded by a process of enculturation owing to continuous firsthand contact with area and peer violence, drug trafficking, and experiences with guns. Inasmuch as community dangerousness and drug trafficking have been identified as important determinants of homicide (Prothrow-Stith, 1991; Kubrin and Weitzer, 2003; Oliver, 2001; Chaiken, 2000; Lizotte and Sheppard, 2001; Allen and Lo, 2010), it appears that environmental (i.e. structural and cultural) factors may have an impact on juvenile violence.

Results also showed that nearly three-fourths of the victims were younger than age 30. A significant finding was that homicides (37%) were more than three times as likely as aggravated assaults (11%) to involve male victims who were in their twenties. Contrarily, aggravated assault offenses (59%) were almost twice as likely as homicides (34%) to involve victims who were between the ages of 12 and 19. These findings are consistent with the state of knowledge on victim age trends in juvenile homicide. For example, a macro-level study completed by Cook and Laub (1998, 2002) attempted to determine age trends in violent crime victimization for criminal homicides, robberies, and aggravated assaults involving juveniles. Data for the study were drawn from four national-level sources: the Uniform Crime Reports, the National Crime Victim Survey, the Supplemental Homicide Reports, and the National Center for Health Statistics. Results showed that three-fourths of killers age thirteen to seventeen were younger than their victims by five or more years (see also Brookman, 2003; Decker, 1993; Kuhn et al., 1999). Research by Brewer and associates (1998) examined homicides in Houston from 1990-1994 and amplified differences in age of victim for juvenile homicide by contrasting it with adult homicide trends. Per their findings, juvenile killers were, on average, ten years younger than their victims, whereas adult murderers were usually three years older or younger than the people they killed. While these findings suggest that the majority of victims of adolescent homicide are adults, other research shows that juveniles typically kill older juveniles (Blumstein and Cork, 1996; Duxbury, 1980; McCurley and Synder, 2004).

Whatever the case, the risk of death is greater for older victims because they are more likely to encounter armed juveniles. As compared to younger or same age adversaries, adolescents are apt to use firearms against older opponents because they have greater physical size or better fighting skills in most cases (Wolfgang, 1958; Miethe and Regoeczi, 2004). Defense of self alone, however, is not the heart of the matter. In many inner city homicides involving juveniles and older murder victims, presumably what is at issue is performance expectations and gunplay as an impression management strategy. Oliver (2001) hinted at this in his ethnographic research into the violent social world of Black males: "In addition to resorting to violence to defend themselves against physical assault, some respondents believed that it matters how a man performs in a violent confrontation because his performance has implications for reputation" (p. 129). Stretesky and Pogrebin (2007), as well as other scholars in the field, drew this same conclusion. Consequently, juveniles may brandish or use guns in confrontations with older adversaries to protect both their physical and their social selves, as well as aggrandize their reputation and status.

Findings pertaining to offender and victim race/ethnicity were also important in relation to male honor contest violence. The majority of all offenders (62%) as well as victims (53%) in the sample were Black. Moreover, the largest portion of homicide offenses involved Black victims (57%) and Black offenders (62%). In fact, homicide offenses were significantly more likely to involve Black offenders than any other race/ethnic group. The ratio of Black offenders to Black victims is logical and in accordance with other empirical information. The vast majority of assaultive violence involve victims and offenders of the same race/ethnicity (Block and Block, 1991; Decker, 1993; Martinez, 1997). Furthermore, analysis of homicide trends in the United States indicates a preponderance of Black-on-Black cases among intra-racial homicides (Miethe and Regoeczi, 2004, Kuhn et al., 1999; Decker, 1993). The disproportionate rate of Black-on-Black violence has been attributed to residential segregation. Blacks are more spatially segregated and disproportionately confined to socially and economically deprived communities, irrespective of socioeconomic status, than any other racial/ethnic group (Massey, 2005; Shihadeh and Maume, 1997; Ousey, 1999; Hawkins, 1990; Stewart et al., 2008; Wilkinson et al., 2009; Piquero and Sealock, 2010; Allen and Lo, 2010). This means that Black males are exposed to higher rates of violence, other environmental hazards, and masculine role strain. In this sense, violence and disputatiousness among young Black males are promoted through both a psychology of danger and perceptions of tenuous masculinity.

While there were a few statistical differences between homicides and aggravated assaults involving juvenile male perpetrators, altogether the two offenses were more alike than different as regards predisposing, structural-cultural risk factors. This indicates that background characteristics, such as neighborhood context and antisocial peer group affiliation, as well as gun ownership, carrying, and use are preconditions of aggressive crimes. Therefore, the implication of the first hypothesis was borne out by observation. The supposition that homicide and aggravated assault offenses would differ by the situational variables in this study was also substantiated. Consistent with the criminal event perspective, results demonstrate the importance of immediate contextual factors in determining potential lethality of violent encounters. By that fact, homicides and aggravated assaults are differentiated by specific circumstances surrounding the event. In general, offenders' intent, the type of weapon involved, offender's perception of victim-precipitation, systemic drug-relatedness, and the presence of third parties influenced intent to kill, as well as lethal and nonlethal outcomes in assaultive encounters.

Offenders' Perception of Victim-Precipitation

While the vast majority (76%) of youth believed their victims did something to cause the violence, offenders' perception of victim-precipitation did not affect severity of incident outcome in this sample. Ironically, though, when cases were compared by offenders' intentionality, results show that in situations where there was no desire to kill, offenders were more likely to justify their violent behavior by attributing blame to the victim than they were in circumstances that arose with lethal intent. This finding was unexpected; however, one way to interpret it is through the disquisition on capital punishment and recidivism rates for convicted murders as compared to other violent offenders (Alvarez and Bachman, 2007). The argument here is simply that people who kill generally express a great deal of remorse about their behavior, particularly compared to those who commit other types of violent crime. On one hand, it might be socially and psychologically more problematic for one to justify his premeditated actions to kill. On the other hand, this might be explained by the fact that psychotherapeutic treatment of homicide offenders differ from that of most other aggressive offenders when it comes to confronting denial of responsibility for the crime and fostering grief and remorse[47] (Cornell, 1998). The youth in this study had been in the care and custody of the juvenile justice system for a period of time before they were interviewed for the original investigation. Inasmuch as counseling intervention is a typical component imposed on juvenile cases (Lipsey, Wilson, and Cothern, 2000), it is likely that these youth had been exposed to psychotherapeutic treatment. Still, the difference in perception of victim-precipitation for those offenders who intended to kill and those who did not may have been genuine; perhaps moral anguish arose in youth who had a premeditated desire to kill their victim from recognition of the immutable permanency of their actions.

Motive

The greatest portion of violent encounters (86%) was motivated by some form of dispute. Less than 15% of the cases involved robbery as a motive; however, when compared by offense, homicides (19%) were twice as likely as aggravated assaults (9%) to originate from larceny. At the same time that lethal intent is perceivably not a factor in most robberies (Block and Zimring, 1973; Decker, 1993, 1996; Meithe and Drass, 1999; Miethe and Regoeczi, 2004; Kleck and McElrath, 1991), the interrelationship between aggravated robbery and homicide has been well established in the literature (Wolfgang, 1958; McDowall, 1991; Polk, 1994; Zimring, 1984; Kubrin and Hertig, 2003), particularly with respect to juveniles (Cook and Laub, 1998; Gonzalez, 2001). Notwithstanding the preceding information, the difference between homicides and aggravated assaults in this study did not prove to be significant at the standard criteria of $p \leq .05$.

Systemic Drug-Relatedness

Generally, violent encounters did not involve illegal drug trade (89%). Homicides (16%), however, were three times more likely than aggravated assaults (5%) to have offenders, victims, or someone else who was present at the time of the confrontation involved in buying or selling drugs. This finding is consistent with other studies that have found drug trafficking to be associated with juvenile homicide (McLaughlin, Daniel, Joost, 1999; Fagan and Wilkinson, Van Horn, 1992; Boyum and Klienman, 2003; Nielsen et al., 2005; Yonas et al., 2007, Allen and Lo, 2010). Violence is a common part of the drug-distribution system. This might be explained by the nature of the business or by personal propensity for violence among those who engage in illegal drug trade. Another plausible explanation may be derived from impression management theory and notions of male honor and character. Given the enhanced status that is bestowed upon dealers in disorganized neighborhoods, they are suitable targets for violence by other males who wish to advance their position in the street. In these settings, drug dealers are also motivated offenders for the reason that they are likely to be sensitive and responsive to maintaining their personal advantages in the community by use of violence.

In any case, the relationship between drug-relatedness and severity of incident outcome is ultimately understood by the close connection between firearms and drug trafficking. Involvement in drug trade increases exposure to guns; moreover, the presence of firearms increases the potential for gun violence. Studies suggest that the presence of firearms in hostile encounters involving males, particularly juvenile males, elicits aggressive behavior and increases the probability of gun assault (Bailey, 2000; Blumstein and Cork, 1996; Kubrin and Hertig, 2003; Wilson, 1997; Cook and Laub, 2002; Fagan and Wilkinson, 1998; Goldstein, 1991; Black and Hausman, 2008; Wilkinson et al., 2009; Spano and Bolland, 2010; Nielsen et al., 2005). Ipso facto, drug trafficking may have an indirect effect on severity of incident outcome through the type of weapon involved.

Further analysis was done to look at the relationship between drug-relatedness and specific intent to do harm. It was hypothesized that drug-trafficking would increase the intensity of conflict and the magnitude of threat to manhood, thereby determining the offender's lethal intent. Where drug-trafficking was observed, intent to kill was more likely (17%) than not (7%) to be the outcome. Nevertheless, the difference in intent was not statistically significant at the standard $p \leq$ .05.

Presence of a Social Audience

Another significant result concerning situational risk factors was the preponderancy of the social audience among homicide cases. Spectators were present in the vast majority of all offenses (74%); nevertheless, homicides (81%) were statistically more likely than aggravated assaults (66%) to have people, besides the victim and the offender, present at the time of the encounter. This information seems agreeable with existing knowledge about social audience effects on hostile encounters and severity of incident outcome (Decker, 1995; Deibert and Miethe, 2003; Felson, 1982; Felson and Steadman, 1983; Oliver, 2001; Wilkinson et al., 2009; Swisher and Latzman, 2008; Anderson and Meier, 2004; Ronel, 2010). It also supports Goffman's theory of charter (i.e. honor) and impression management. For males in particular, the presence of third parities is often germane to the development and escalation of social conflict. There are at least two plausible explanations for this: a) disputes involving adolescent boys, as compared to those involving girls, are more likely to have the support and participation of onlookers (Steadman, 1982; Decker, 1995; Felson, Ribner, and Siegel, 1994; Tedeschi and Felson, 1994); b) the presence of spectators raise the identity costs of backing down for young males, particularly for those who have limited options for doing gender (Daly and Wilson, 1988; 2001; Polk, 1997a, 1999; Oliver, 2001; Krienert, 2003; Deibert and Miethe, 2003; Athens, 2005; Stretesky and Pogrebin, 2007; Yonas et al., 2007; Rich and Grey, 2005; Wilkinson et al., 2009; Brennan and Moore, 2009; Ronel, 2010).

In keeping with the theory of compulsory masculinity and tactical concerns, it was also expected that the presence of a social audience would determine offenders' intent to kill. Bivariate analysis revealed that where spectators were present, lethal intent was statistically more likely (86%) than not (67%) to be at issue.

Weapon Instrumentality

Ultimately this investigation attempted to ascertain whether homicide involving juvenile perpetrators is commonly the result of chance or the intention to kill, and to decipher the role of firearms in assaultive violence among adolescents. The vast majority of offenses in this subset analysis involved some kind of weapon (90%); however, homicides (99%) were statistically more likely than aggravated assaults (78%) to involve a weapon. Relevant to the issue of weapon instrumentality in particular, homicides (68%) were also statistically more likely than aggravated assaults (20%) to involve a firearm. This finding is in conformity with the knowledge that guns are the primary method of killing in the United States (Weaver et al., 2004; Harries, 1997; Kleck and McElrath, 1991; Meithe and Regoeczi, 2004; Wells and Horney, 2002; Zimring, 1968; 1972; 1984; 1996; Nielsen et al., 2005; Spano and Bolland, 2010; Wilkinson et al., 2009).

Further analysis was done to examine the relationship between type of weapon involved and specific intent to do harm. Corresponding to the notion that guns contribute to the escalation and lethality of violence, this investigation was a test of the weapon facilitation thesis, as well as the conjecture that firearms intensify conflict and the magnitude of threat to manhood for young males, thereby determining lethal intent. Results support both contentions; firearms appear to condition the effects of offender intentionality. Where firearms were involved, intent to kill was statistically more likely (64%) than not (35%) to be decided.

This particular finding has implications for research, practice, and policy. In criminal justice, forensic social work, and social science, the assessment of intentionality is customarily based on objective measures, such as inferences from conditions and facts surrounding the event or the reasonable person's standard of foreseeability. This test of intention is referred to as basic or general intent to do harm. As regards the presence or type of weapon involved in a criminal event, however, this protocol may not sufficiently ascertain specific intent to do harm or the propensity for lethal violence among juveniles. Even more troubling is that in the policy arena youthful lethality has been inferred from statistics on gun possession, carrying, and use among adolescents and utilized to reason the existence of the juvenile super predator. This certainly explains the emphasis on stricter sentencing policies above all else in addressing the problem of adolescent homicide. Yet, in this investigation about one-third of the offenses that involved a firearm did not evidence offenders' specific intent to kill.

Offenders' Specific Intent to do Harm

With respect to intentionality, the vast majority of confrontations did not evidence premeditation (62%). When offenders had lethal intent, however, violent interactions were significantly more likely (71%) than not (29%) to end in the death of the victim. These findings give the impression that, overall, homicides involving juveniles in this sample were not fatal assaults; that is to say, violence that progressed beyond what was intended by the offender. In the present observation, homicides were essentially the result of offenders' specific intent to do lethal harm.

In keeping with the concept of the juvenile super predator, to some, these data might suggest that violent adolescent offenders are natural born killers. That is to say, there is (or was) a breed of juvenile perpetrators who are ruthless sociopaths with no moral consciousness. Perhaps these youth are brought into life this way; or, maybe, they are created this way as a result of violent values that are widespread among certain ethnocultural reference groups. However, the findings of the present study support a more complex explanation of juvenile lethality than is proposed by the myth of the adolescent super predator or discussions of gun control and juvenile sentencing policies.

Youthful violence in this investigation was characterized by attributes and circumstances that reflect the concepts of compulsory masculinity and male honor contest violence. Overwhelmingly, the sample contained male-to-male dispute-related violent offenses that centered on character, respect, and/or honor. The vast majority of both victims and offenders were young, Black and Hispanic adolescents. Results indicate that these offenders resided in disorganized communities and were exposed to normative values, experiences, and lifestyles that reflect the approval and/or tolerance of violence. Again, 75% of the youth described their neighborhood as violent, 95% reported rampant drug trafficking in their community, and 78% of the violent offenders in this study said guns were readily available in their area of residence. Therefore, an alternative possibility is that external social factors cause gun violence and murderous intent among youth. Perchance structural deficiencies rather than individual or cultural pathology is the root cause of the problem. The findings of this study, which was undertaken on a set of assumptions and concepts that reflect the person-in-environment perspective, are consistent with a host of knowledge derived from observations of risk factors associated with adolescent violence. Meanwhile there is little theoretical or empirical support within the literature for the notion of the juvenile super predator.

The essence of the theory of hyper masculinity and male honor contest violence is contained explicitly and implicitly in the discourse on cultural intersectionality, social disorganization theory, and the subculture of violence thesis as it is related to disputatiousness and assaultive violence among young, poor, ethnic minority males. This assertion is even supported in criminology. Merton's theory of strain is one of the most popular criminological theories, and it has been instrumental in explicating the concentration of crime by age, sex, race and socioeconomic class. With respects to the masculine nature of violence and strain theory, according to Merton (1968), in American society, the masculine role intrinsically carries elements of strain. Money, power, success, and bravado constitute the social construction of manhood; yet, opportunities to fulfill prototypes and idealized examples of masculinity are largely ascribed on the basis of particularistic group membership. Race x class x sex stratification and blocked opportunities to do gender result in a compensatory process where toughness and the acquisition of money and material goods by any means necessary are admired and even obligatory.

As posited by social disorganization theory (Sutherland, 1924), structural inequalities create neighborhoods plagued by economic and social deprivation. In the adaptation process that arises as a consequence of social exclusion and the by-product of oppression, specific behavioral and interactional patterns develop among inhabitants of socially disorganized communities. Violence in these environments are promoted through conditions and codes that encourage it, and, moreover, through the absence of mechanisms to discourage such behavior. Children are socialized into delinquent subcultures by adults and delinquent peer groups in the neighborhood, which are often unsupervised due to the high prevalence of single-parent households (Sampson, 1987a) and the lack of structured activities (Lee and Ousey, 2005; Oliver, 2001) in these communities. The dearth of positive male role models and father figures in disorganized neighborhoods, to influence and guide adolescent males in the right direction, can have a big impact on gender identity and role behavior in young boys (Stretesky and Pogrebin, 2007; Parker and Reckdenwald, 2008; Allen and Lo, 2010). Rites of passage for teenage males in poor communities relate closely to the enculturation of "ghetto specific manhood roles", namely the tough guy, the hustler, and the player (Oliver, 2001).

Many theorists and social scientists have maintained that neighborhood characteristics are culpably involved in the epidemic of violence among young, lower-class males (Prothrow-Stith, 1991; Brooks et al, 1993; Sampson, Morenoff, and Gannon-Rowley, 2002; Kubrin and Weitzer; Oliver, 2001; Fagan and Wilkinson, 1998; Harries, 1997; Faser, 1996; Pebley and Sastry, 2003, Lee and Ousey, 2005; Sampson, 1987a, 1997; Stewart et al., 2008; Yonas et al., 2007; Matjasko et al., 2010; Swisher and Latzman, 2008; Duke et al., 2009; Rich and Grey, 2005; Parker and Reckdenwald, 2008; Brennan and Moore, 2009; Ronel, 2010; Allen and Lo, 2010). It has also been established that neighborhood effects vary by race and ethnicity, largely as a result of class and racial segregation in this country. There is overwhelming evidence to support the claim that Blacks are more likely than Whites—even poor Whites—and other ethnic minority groups to live in extremely impoverished areas (Massey, 2004, 2005; Kubrin and Hertig, 2003; Ousey, 1999; Messner and Tardiff, 1986; Miethe and Regoeczi, 2004; Shihadeh and Maume, 1997; Massey and Fischer, 1999; Stewart et al., 2008; Taylor et al., 2010; Piquero and Brame, 2008; Felson et al., 2007). In fact, Massey (2004) discovered that nearly one-half (48%) of all metropolitan Blacks, irrespective of income level, live under conditions of hypersegregation in disorganized communities. By that very fact, Black males are exposed to far higher rates of social disorder, violence, and role strain than any other social group.

This furnishes support for the subculture of violence theory as it relates to marginalized males in disorganized communities. Violence is learned behavior. Youth who are exposed to violence in their families and communities are at greater risk of becoming violent themselves (Kracke, 2001; Hawkins, 2000; Spano et al., 2010; Matjasko et al., 2010; Brennan and Moore, 2009; Ronel, 2010; Piquero and Sealock, 2010). For disadvantaged males, in particular, assaultive behavior is not only promoted through the strain of witnessing and experiencing violence, it is advanced through social learning as it relates to risky patterns of behavior such delinquency and crime, with special emphasis on participation in drug trafficking and gun ownership as a way of doing gender. Furthermore, violent encounters between similarly situated males in disorganized communities occur readily because respect is paramount; these youth are more apt than those who have other outlets to shore up their personal worth and self-image to respond aggressively to the most trivial of slights. For them, violence serves a tactical purpose for survival, as well as aggrandizing their masculine reputation and status.

Children and adolescents in truly disadvantaged surroundings are often exposed to violence in their homes and communities (Heide, 1999; Lorion and Saltzman, 1993; Martinez and Richters, 1993; Matjasko et al., 2010; Spano et al., 2010; Brennan and Moore, 2009). From an early age, they customarily witness and experience injury, suffering, and death. Chronic and repeated exposure to violence promotes the formation of attitudes that are favorable to violence, as well as the internalization of "scripts" that use violence as an appropriate method of problem-solving (Fagan and Wilkinson, 1998; Salfati and Haratsis, 2001; Tedeschi and Felson, 1994; Swisher and Latzman, 2008; Brennan and Moore, 2009). The adolescent offenders in this study were exposed to rampant violence in their communities and their peer groups; three-quarters (75%) of the youth reported that their neighborhood was violent and 92% stated that they associated with peers who engaged in violent activities.

Proximity to subcultures of violence and delinquency increases one's chance of engaging in deviant and illegal activities, because children and adolescents are disposed to forming friendships with and mimicking those whom they encounter often. Moreover, exposure to antisocial models provides opportunities for learning and engaging in antisocial behavior (Mears et al, 1998; Duxbury, 1980; Heimer, 1997; Yonas et al., 2007; Matjasko et al., 2010; Stretesky and Pogrebin, 2007; Parker and Reckdenwald, 2008).

However, violence also begets trauma, which produces the violence-trauma-violence cycle. The relationship between exposure to violence and subsequent violent behavior is consistent in many studies that rely on self-report data (Baron and Hartnagel, 1998; Cao, Adams, and Jensen, 1997; Fagan and Wilkinson, 1998), with the exception of a study by Lennings, Copeland and Howard (2003), which found no relationship between exposure to violence and self-reported violent behavior. Bias arising from sample selection, however, could explain the findings of their investigation. Lennings and associates evaluated 95 adolescent detainees. Since these participants were awaiting pretrial release, arraignment, or disposition, their responses to the query about committing violent offenses might not have been in agreement with fact or reality.

One's pattern of living can also increase the likelihood of exposure to violence. These lifestyle factors include involvement in delinquency, association with deviant peers, participation in drug trafficking, acquisition and use of guns, and disputatiousness (Baron and Hartnagel, 1998; Ingram, 1993; Luckenbill and Doyle, 1989; Nofziger and Kurtz, 2005; Sampson and Lauritsen, 1990; Tepline, McCelland, Abram, and Mileusnic, 2005; Williams et al., 1998; Matjasko et al., 2010; Wilkinson et al., 2010; Brennan and Moore, 2009; Yonas et al., 2005; Yonas et al., 2007; Stretesky and Pogrebin, 2007; Nielsen et at., 2005; Spano and Bolland, 2010; Allen and Lo, 2010). The vast majority of youthful offenders in the present investigation was involved in drug dealing (64%), associated with violent peer (92%); and owned (92%), carried (99%), or used (83%) guns. Ostensibly, deviant lifestyles make juveniles more susceptible to victimization and witnessing violence, which in turn increases their probability of violent offending (Nofziger and Kurtz, 2005; Spano et al., 2010; Brennan and Moore, 2009; Parker and Reckdenwald, 2008; Piquero and Sealock, 2010). Whatever the case, it comes as no surprise that young murderers are likely to have a history of victimization and exposure to violence (Busch et al., 1990; Heide, 1999).

The life circumstances of disadvantaged and marginalized young males often foster hopelessness, fatalism, and a belief that one's existence is meaningless and futile. Some scholars suggest that disadvantaged youth may express suicidal intent by way of high risk violent behavior (Joe and Kaplan, 2001; Poussaint and Alexander, 2000). Still, others have postulated that masculine violence is related to a general foreshortened life expectancy among disadvantaged youth.

The relationship between exposure to violence, feelings of hopelessness, and risky behavior among youthful males has been established by several studies. For example, ethnographic research of gun violence among youth, identified adolescents with foreshortened life expectancy as more likely to carry guns (Fagan and Wilkinson, 1998). Research by Durant and his colleagues (1994) examined the relationship between self-reported exposure to violence and use of violence by Black adolescents living in disadvantaged communities. Results showed that the use of violence is positively associated with hopelessness and has an inverse relationship with expectancy of being alive at age 18. Similarly, a preliminary investigation (N=76) of data from the original study (*Learning About Violence and Drugs among* Adolescents) suggested that short time horizons among violent juvenile offenders correlated with exposure to trauma and violence and participation in illegal activities, including drug trafficking (Schmidt, Ryder, Crimmins, Spunt, and Brownstein, 1996) . Hopelessness as a result of social and economic oppression and a determinant of violent behavior was discussed more recently by Stewart et al.(2008), Brezina et al. (2004) and Duke et al. (2009).

Daly and Wilson, (2001) hypothesized that risk-prone behavior among males, especially criminal violence and homicide, is an outcome of steep future discounting. The thought of having nothing to gain, means having nothing to lose. On the matter of discounting the future, Sorrell (1977) put it well:

> If….[a youngster's] current life is miserable and gives little hope of anything better in the future, he is susceptible to the most fleeting of impulses and seldom stops to exercise judgment. Every opportunity for illegal activity is met with 'Why not?....What do I have to lose?' (p. 318).

Perchance, these identifiable social problems and patterns of behavior account for some of the disparities in juvenile victimization and offending by socioeconomic status, race/ethnicity, sex, and neighborhood of residence. If these youth are disputatious, if they see violence as their only means of conflict resolution or as a rite of passage, if they are unconcerned with the destruction of human life or the personal consequences of their actions; if they are undeterred by legal sanctions, perchance this signifies general hopelessness and/or a foreshortened sense of future (Anderson, 1994; Bell and Jenkins, 1991; Fagan and Wilkinson, 1998; Lorizon and Saltzman, 1993; Stewart et al., 2008; Brezina et al., 2004; Duke et al., 2009)

All things considered, violence and lethality among adolescents may largely be explained by the trauma of institutional oppression and the intersection between race, class, and sex stratification in this country. Theoretically, if we change these structures we eliminate situations that cause great distress and destruction, thereby abating gun violence and homicide among youth.

Disentangling Weapon Instrumentality and Offenders' Specific Intent

The question remains: Does offenders' specific intent to do harm influence death from assault by means of the type of weapon involved or does it exert direct effects on incident outcome? The first part of the question alludes to the weapon facilitation thesis, which postulates that people with fatal intent will use more lethal weaponry (i.e. firearms) in assaultive encounters. In effect, the facilitation thesis corresponds to the weapon instrumentality effect hypothesis and the notion that guns contribute to lethal violence. The latter part of the question references the weapon compensation hypothesis. Proponents of this theory admit that people who intend to kill their victims will use more lethal weapons, namely firearms, to accomplish the task. However, they maintain that when firearms are not available, offenders who intend to kill their victims will do so irrespective of the type of weapon involved; they will use more force and/or target more vital areas on the body— whatever it takes to achieve their destructive goal. Ipso facto, death from assault is primarily a function of offenders' lethality.

To answer the question, weapon effects needed to be inspected, controlling for the influence of offenders' specific intent. In the dataset used for this investigation, however, there was no indication of lethal intent for any of the aggravated assault offenses. Under the circumstances, the investigation lacked the necessary statistical means to disentangle the association between specific intent, weapon instrumentality, and severity of incident outcome. This is unfortunate inasmuch as that information is essential to developing appropriate prevention strategies.

Case in point: If homicide is primarily a function of the type of weapon involved, decreasing the overall level of conflict and violence among youth is expedient. Along with surveillance and other suppression strategies, school-based violence intervention programs designed to develop social competency and problem-solving skills in children and adolescents could be sufficiently valuable (Payne and Button, 2009; Matjasko et al., 2010; Wilkinson et al., 2009; Duke et al., 2009). One such option is Responding In Peaceful and Positive Ways (RIPP). Endorsed by the Department of Education and the Substance Abuse and Mental Health Services Administration, RIPP is an evidenced-based program that includes a variety of lessons and activities designed to promote critical thinking and conflict resolution skills, as well as physical and mental well-being among youth. RIPP's curriculum-based prevention-intervention model also offers peer mediation and adult mentorship. With-in school evaluations of RIPP show that students who participate have a greater knowledge of effective problem-solving skills, fewer fight-related injuries, fewer disciplinary violations for violent offenses, increased use of peer mediation programs, lower approval of violent behavior, and more peer support for non-violent behavior. In response to weapon instrumentality effects, RIPP's curriculum could be adapted to educate youth about the dangers and consequences of owing, carrying, and using weapons, especially firearms.

A different approach to designing and delivering violence prevention curricula in local schools is offering structured, supervised, and prosocial recreational activities in the community. The Settlement House Movement showed that building centers where children and youth in disadvantaged communities can gather for social and cultural activities is beneficial. Rooted in the tradition of that social movement, the Boys and Girls Clubs of America strives to offer socially and economically troubled youth prosocial opportunities for participation through the presence and involvement of caring, supportive adults. The Boys and Girls Clubs offer a series of programs aimed at positive peer group activities and "helping young people to realize their full potential as productive, responsible, and caring citizens." These programs include sports and special events, as well as personal and social development programs that promote self-esteem and cultural pride.

A third approach to reducing levels of youth violence is mass media campaigns. In addition to public service announcements, posters, television, magazine, and radio spots featuring musicians, actors, and other celebrities who appeal to juveniles can be used to increase awareness and change attitudes about violence. When used in conjunction with service activities, media campaigns have demonstrated effectiveness in changing individual behavior and attitudes associated with youth violence (Whitaker, Baker, and Arias, 2008; Allen and Lo, 2010). In fact, for any of these strategies to be successful in reducing or preventing youth violence they must be used in conjunction with strategies that seek to change policy and social structures within disadvantaged communities (Gottfredson and Bauer, 2008; Stewart et al., 2008; Yonas et al., 2007; Brennan and Moore, 2009; Swisher and Latzman, 2008; Duke et al., 2009; Spano and Bolland, 2010; Piquero and Brame, 2008; Allen and Lo, 2010).

If juvenile homicide is mainly a function of offender lethality, a different set of prevention-intervention approaches is advisable. First and foremost, there is a need for more qualitative research to understand what causes young males to wish or desire to kill another human being. With that information, the goal should be to prevent rather than to wait and intervene through corrections and rehabilitation for youth who kill. Based on the assumption that juvenile violence is a product of social disorganization and social learning, several primary and secondary strategies are indicated.

Approaches that avert or decrease favorable attitudes toward violence and increase optimism for the future among youth, as well as adults in disenfranchised neighborhoods are indispensable. Strengthen families and communities have traditionally been supported by the social work profession since it is understood that these structures are related to healthy development and positive social outcomes for youth. Because children and adolescents are more frequently exposed to grown-ups in their immediate environment, adult family members and community residents are largely responsible for their socialization. Therefore, it is not enough to work with children through schools, community centers, and media campaigns. Juveniles require consistent anti-violence messages and they need to be nurtured in safe and supportive environments.

Social interventions that enhance the climate of depressed and crime-ridden neighborhoods have strong potential for prevention. To this effect, community-based initiatives should provide a host of neighborhood resources, namely counseling and therapeutic services, drug and alcohol treatment, social centers, community organizations, and cultural institutes. In addition, university partnerships and adult training and apprenticeship programs should be offered. For the purpose of dealing directly with at-risk youth, street gang intervention programs would also be advantageous in many cities. The main objective, however, should be to champion the cause of social and economic justice and equal access to education, career advancement, and monetary remuneration for society's most vulnerable citizens. To a large extent the social work profession has deserted this mission.

PRACTICE IMPLICATIONS OF THE STUDY

This investigation did not conclusively decipher gun and offender lethality effects for homicides involving juvenile male perpetrators; nevertheless, several implications can be drawn from this observation. Results confirm the masculine, intrasexual nature of violence among juveniles. These data also indicate that assaultive violence involving juvenile male perpetrators characteristically include individuals who occupy the lowest socioeconomic position in society—that is, the truly disadvantaged. These youth reside in economically and socially deprived communities that play a central role in the transmission of values, attitudes, and behaviors that are favorable toward violence. Ipso facto, violence and lethality among adolescents is dramatically dependent upon the community in which youth are nurtured.

Nevertheless, these structural and cultural variables are ultimately better at explaining aggressive behavior than they are at interpreting outcome from serious assault. While structural and cultural factors predispose youth to assaultive behavior, with respect to lethal violence, all homicides are not planned and all planned homicides do not eventuate in death. Since 1958, theorists and social science have postulated that homicide is a dynamic situation that can be modified in form or character according to various actions and events immediate to the social situation. Therefore, it is posited that situational contingencies are more likely than distal predisposing factors to ultimately determine the production of homicide; this study confirms that supposition.

Notwithstanding, in the present investigation, homicides and aggravated assaults involving juvenile male offenders were more alike than different with respect to situational risk indicators as well. All things considered, any of the offenders in the assault group could have committed a homicide if the right situation and opportunity had presented itself. For instance, whether or not others were present; whether or not someone was buying or selling drugs at the time; whether or not the victim was wounded, and how and where on the body he was wounded. Clearly, the nature of homicide is dynamic and complex, and the availability and use of firearms is only one part of the problem.

This knowledge implies that the best plan for reducing the incidence and prevalence of homicide is utilizing strategies that decrease the overall level of conflict and violence among youth. School-based delivery is one entry point for providing services to juveniles and their families; in addition, community-based programming is a way of engaging youth who are not in school. Furthermore, policies and practices that reduce neighborhood social and economic decline, and provide meaningful opportunities for advancement and alternatives to crime and violence have more long-term potential than suppression strategies. Suppression tactics such as aggressive law enforcement and prosecution aimed at recovering illegal guns and securing long prison sentences for dangerous youth are tertiary in nature. These interventions are used where problems already exist. Ostensibly, they are not meant to prevent young people from killing by taking steps to eliminate or minimize contributory factors before violence occurs. Moreover, there is no evidence which demonstrates the long-term effectiveness of gun control or stricter sentencing policies on juvenile violence. This is not surprising since these activities do not address root causes. Notwithstanding these considerations, gun laws and social control of juvenile offenders through a system of imprisonment and rehabilitation are the guiding principles of social policy.

Regrettably, any practice or public discourse in social work and social welfare concerning juvenile homicide and violence is at this level. Forensic social work almost exclusively focuses on youth who are already involved with courts or other correctional services (i.e. probation, parole, penal institutions, and child welfare). The field has partnered with the criminal and juvenile justice systems and social workers in this area of practice have largely gone from being agents of social change to being agents of social control. In this capacity the objective of practice is to change the individual, not the structural arrangements of society that impact behavior.

Without addressing root causes, that is to say the structural-cultural link to adolescent violence, the potential for generational continuance of antisocial values and behaviors is great. For every gun taken off of the street, the demand for another is exponential in inner city neighborhoods. For every drug dealer, killer, or other criminal confined to prison, there are at least a dozen other disadvantaged boys who are ready, willing, and able to engage in violence and other illicit activities. Therefore, the motivation for violence, as well as the demand for gun possession and use must be addressed if juvenile homicide is to be successfully abated.

To that extent, social work should take the helm. In an effort to prevent juvenile violence, the field should develop a system of solutions that revolve around strengths-based, community-oriented practice and professional development. This model includes five core elements:

Professional Advocacy: Apply social justice principles more consistently and more vigorously to structural problems. A basic function of social work is to speak up for social and economic justice and to safeguard human rights. The National Association of Social Workers alone has almost 200,000 members nation-wide. The profession has a tremendous amount of power that could be utilized for organizing overt reactions to oppressive sentencing, family, and economic policies, as well as advocating for family and neighborhood resources, better quality education for disadvantaged youth, and adequate funding for social service programs.

Community Mobilization: Employ a range of social organization techniques to empower local residence to come together and organize around common goals regarding safety and neighborhood crime, the availability of alcohol and drugs, the availability of guns, community attachment and stability issues, physical disorder, and troubled youth. Besides more traditional community organizing initiatives, prepare residence to stand along side social work in public demonstration. This not only has the potential to bring about policy change, it also increases self-efficacy and decrease a sense of helplessness among disenfranchised citizens.

Social Interventions: Design, implement, and monitor comprehensive services for children, teens, and families established on the positive youth development framework. Since juvenile males in socially and economically oppressed communities are at high risk for violent and lethal offending, *intervene early.* Target youth and families who are not involved in the system. Provide a comprehensive menu of services to counteract the various factors that make children vulnerable to violence. Realistically, all of the necessary services can not be provided successfully in one agency setting (Jenkins and Welsh, 2003), so develop inter-agency collaborations within social work and linkages with other organizations in the community.

Intent to treat is not enough; intensive outreach is required inasmuch as help-seeking behavior is influenced by personal and cultural factors, as well as by experiences the truly disadvantaged has had with "helping" professionals and society (Hepworth, Rooney, Rooney, Storm-Gottfried, and Larsen, 2006). To effectively recruit and engage these clients in services, social work will need to provide a corrective experience. This has implications for culturally competent practice.

In regard to compulsory masculinity in particular, community-based risk reduction efforts should include Rites of Passage programming for boys and adolescent males. Supporting Adolescents with Guidance and Employment (SAGE) is one model specifically developed for African American youth. In addition to group and one-on-one mentoring, SAGE includes a cultural heritage curriculum, summer jobs training and placement, and entrepreneurial experience. Program evaluations demonstrate that SAGE can increase self-esteem, educational aspirations, and prosocial beliefs regarding violence, as well as reduce the likelihood of violence-related and other health-risk behaviors among African American males.

Professional Recruitment and Development: Recruit more African American and Latino males into the social work profession. Many African American and Latino boys are in need of positive male role models. As mentors and service providers, these helping professionals can provide purposeful demonstrations of positive masculinity for disadvantaged boys. To engage the interest of African American and Latino males in professional social work practice (i.e. MSW), recruitment should take place at the high school as well as the undergraduate level. For maximum impact, summer jobs programs, scholarships, and university-agency partnerships should be created. These approaches provide opportunity and incentive for young males to expand their educational and career options.

In other areas of social work education, engage up-and-coming professionals in more sociological rather pathological discussions of distress and disorder. Incorporate models and theories of psychotherapy and social work practice into that framework. Moreover, ensure that students are exposed to this sort of discourse, in addition to culturally competent practice, in the practicum component of education. Also model and encourage social action in the field and in the classroom by providing opportunities and incentives for students and practitioners to participate in policy change efforts.

Finally, give more regard to evidence-based practice in social work education. The profession espouses the idea that the interventive process should be supported by empirical research findings; therefore, research methods should be incorporated into every part of the curriculum. Moreover, effective social welfare practice requires critical examination of the wide range of solutions used to address complex problems; research knowledge is the means to that end. Also, the profession should endeavor to set the research agenda for juvenile homicide and other social problems. For all these reasons, social workers need to be genuine consumers and producers knowledge.

Administrative Leadership: In the tertiary capacity social work has limited authority over treatment planning. To more effectively correct or alleviate the problem of youth violence, the profession must be at the core of leadership developing and implementing the plan of action and evaluating programmatic outcomes. Not only does this require training and education, but political savvy as well. The field needs to build a mass base of support among individuals, families, communities, organizational stakeholders, politicians, and the media for the purpose of delivering risk-focused prevention programming that best meets the needs of society's most vulnerable citizens. This may sound unreasonably idealistic; nonetheless, it is within the range of possibility. For example, in January 2009, Barak Obama took the oath of office as the first African American President of the United States. Many variables factored into this historical occasion, but, without a doubt, through social organization techniques social work played a major role in this phenomenal event.

The information in this report might prove to be a useful corrective for those who have or want to champion the task of preventing murderous behavior among adolescents. Hopefully, the prevention and intervention recommendations described herein will persuade policy makers and the fields of social work and social welfare to invest more resources in primary prevention of juvenile homicide.

CONCLUSION

This study was intended to be a building point for more extensive investigation of juvenile lethality. Given that public policy continues to be fashioned on gun control and the retribution approach, and that these strategies have not been shown to be successful in reducing juvenile homicide it behooves social work researchers to assess this problem in a more inclusive manner. Such efforts should be driven by theoretical conceptualizations (e.g. compulsory masculinity) that seek to not only identify the etiology of juvenile homicide, but also attempt to predict and prevent its manifestation. The overall goal should be to develop an understanding of the roots of youthful violence—juvenile homicide in particular, since it is the ultimate form of violence.

Research on the question of why adolescents kill must continue if there is an opportunity to stop one child from taking the life of another human being. Moreover, the social work profession must lend its voice and knowledge to the discourse on juvenile violence. To that extent, national policy and the administrative response to it might entail a new dimension of risk-focused prevention that can better serve at-risk youth, families, and communities, as well as better protect society from murderous teens.

Endnotes

1. In regard to homicide offending, as determined by Supplementary Homicide Reports for the years 1976—2005 combined, female perpetrators accounted for just 11% of all homicide offenders (Fox and Zawitz, 2007).

2. Zimring and Hawkins (1999) are among the few scholars who refute the drug market-lethal violence nexus set forth by Blumstein. They rebutted his theory on the basis of few homicides being outwardly related to the drug trade. What they failed to consider in their argument, however, is that in official records data, drug-related homicide is strictly measured by murders that occur during the commission of a narcotics felony, such as drug trafficking. All other ways in which a system of drug distribution and use can be related to homicide is neglected. For that reason, crime and arrest data do not offer proof of the true incidence of drug-related homicide. Moreover, it did not appear that these authors understood Blumstein's explanation of the gun diffusion process and its connection to the growth of crack-cocaine markets, and, ultimately, lethal violence.

3. Freud published the first study on adolescent homicide (Nelson, 2000).

4. Sutherland preferred this wording over the term socially disorganized communities.

5. For more detailed information on social disorganization, social learning, and the subculture of violence theories see work by Cohen (1955), Wolfgang and Ferricuti (1967), Miller (1958), and Sutherland and Cressey (1974).

6. Because race is poorly operationalized in race-based studies of homicide, it is not known for certain that this information specifically applies to African Americans as opposed to (or in combination with) other "Black" or "non-White" ethnic groups. Nevertheless, these categories generally allude to African Americans.

7. However, according to findings by Brewer and colleagues (1998), Cheatwood and Block (1990) and Goetting (1989), juveniles are more likely than adults to be involved in interracial homicide.

151

8. Chaiken's (2000) research evidence is inconsistent with this supposition; however, the limitations of her study and/or the reporting of her methodology, as described earlier, might explain her paradoxical findings.

9. See Zimring (1998) for a description of the three gun markets and a discussion on the challenges of regulating handguns for youths.

10. The Index of Gun Density was composed of the proportion of Detroit robberies committed with a gun and the proportion of Detroit suicides committed with a gun.

11. Like most other disaggregate studies that examine race, there is no indication of which ethnic groups comprise the race dichotomy.

12. These authors also used data from the Rochester Youth Development Study (RYDS). RYDS was funded by the Office of Juvenile Justice and Delinquency Prevention and part of their Program of Research on the Causes and Correlates of Delinquency, which comprised three coordinated research studies: the Denver Youth Survey, the Pittsburg Youth Study, and the Rochester Youth Development Study. The project began in 1987, when participants were in the seventh and eight grades, and terminated in 1997 after twelve regularly scheduled waves of interviews with youths and their primary caregivers. Data on juvenile subjects were also collected from agency reports (i.e. school, police, courts, and social service).

13. See Zimring, 1972, 1996, 1998; Kleck and McElrath, 1991; Kleck, 1991; Wells and Horney, 2002; Felson and Messner, 1996; Weaver, Wittekind, Corzine, Corzine, Peete, and Jarvis, 2004; Decker, 1995; Yonas et al., 2005 for more information on the role of third parties in violent encounters.

14. Research indicates that third parties are more likely to instigate or participate in conflict than to mediate it (Felson, 1982; Felson and Steadman, 1983)

15. Felson et al. (1984) found that mediation appeared to have no effect on whether or not someone was killed in the encounter. One explanation for this finding is that spectators tend to do nothing until the interaction between the victim and the offender is so far escalated any attempt to bring about a peaceful settlement is futile.

16. Refer to earlier discussion on the preponderance of Black-on-Black crime.

17. See Felson and Messner (1996), Zimring (1996), and Wolfgang (1958) for further discussion on weapon facilitation and compensation effects.

18. Although Wolfgang's typology of motive was not the first to appear in the homicide literature, it was seminal in the creation and development of theories and classification systems for masculine violence.

19. Generally, these categories correspond with the instrumental/expressive dichotomy of motive.

20. In the criminological literature, the phrase "similarly situated males" is used in two distinct ways. It either means "in the same place at the same time", which is how Luckenbill (1977) used the expression, or "from the same position in life", which is this author's preferred phraseology.

21. In the literature, homicides emerging from immediate escalating disputes are generally referred to as confrontational, altercation, social conflict, or male honor/character contest homicide.

22. In the literature, homicides resulting from long-standing disputes are generally referred to as conflict resolution, revenge, or retaliation homicide, as well as righteous slaughter.

23. Pallone and Hennesy (1993) referred to this phenomenon as "tinder box criminal violence".

24. There are only a few exceptions to this empirical rule in the literature (see Dolan and Smith, 2001; Porkorny, 1965; Wolfgang, 1958)

25. Some researchers have found that knives are just as lethal or possibly more lethal in some situations.

26. Wells and Horney (2002) did not qualify the difference in weapon effects for "injury" versus "serious injury" by means of wounding. In the absence of adequate clarification of these constructs, Kleck and McElrath's (1991) conceptualization seems logical here.

27. Psychopharmacological effects are similar in character for intoxication, withdrawal, and craving.

28. Rohensow and Bacharowski (1984) admonished that acute intoxication effects and violence as a corollary, are in large part contingent on the method and amount of ingestion, the situation, type of provocation, and sex of the antagonist, as well as available response alternatives.

29. As a Research Associate on the LAVIDA project, the Principal Investigator of the present study was intimately involved in the research process; consequently, she has first-hand knowledge of the context in which the original data were collected and processed.

30. Self-report studies of general population samples are not suitable for investigations of juvenile homicide because few seriously violent offenders are in the community, or they are otherwise elusive (Farrington, 1998; Williams et al., 1998).

31. Identifiers for research subjects were never given to the current investigator.

32. Formerly known as the Division for Youth (DFY).

33. The policy change required violent juvenile offenders who were 18 years and older to be transferred to the adult corrections system.

34. This was the only remaining female homicide offender in the sampling frame.

35. High response rates are common in prison-based research (Krienert, 2003).

36. Information on the representativeness of the sample is available from Crimmins et al. (1998).

37. With the respondents' permission, interviews were tape recorded.

38. As an example, respondents were asked how many times they experienced a particular traumatic event or engaged in a delinquent activity in the last year before coming to OCFS.

39. At the time of the interview nearly 21% of the respondents were 18 years of age or older.

40. Measures for the inferential component of this study are included in this section. Indicators used in the descriptive analysis are presented with those findings.

41. In truth, this is inevitable in homicide research because prospective studies of this phenomenon are really not feasible or practical.

42. Again, this is inevitable in homicide research as general population samples are not likely to meet the demand or requirement for seriously violent youth.

43. There are six types of cases that do not make it to incarceration: 1) homicides and assaults that are not reported or detected; 2) homicides and assaults where no suspect has been identified by police; 3) homicides and assaults where a suspect is identified by police but not brought to trial (e.g. there was no grand jury indictment or the assault/homicide was classified as excusable/justified); 4) homicides and assaults where a suspect is identified by police but has escaped arrest; 5) homicides and assaults where a suspect is identified by police, brought to trial but acquitted; and, 6) in the case of homicide, where the police and/or coroner has ruled the case not to be a homicide when it actually was.

44. Respondents could report demographic facts on as many as three victims. However, statistical data for all victim characteristics were generated by use of information for the first victim mentioned only. This procedure was intended to circumvent the complexities of data transformation, which was considered unnecessary since the current analysis is designed to be a summary review and over 90% of the cases involved just one victim.

45. Since more than 20% of the cells had expected frequencies of less than 5, the categories of White, bi-racial/multiracial, and "other" were collapsed for the chi-squared analysis.

46. There were a total of 160 homicide and aggravated assault cases in the LAVIDA dataset; three cases were eliminated from the present analysis due to missing data for the victims' sex variable.

47. The only exception to this is treatment of sex offenders.

Response Pattern for Motive Variable

Subjects reported a variety of reasons for engaging in the violent disputes that eventuated in their current incarceration. The full range and number of responses for this variable is:

"To get money/goods" (1)
"To get money for drugs" (2)
"To get drugs" (3)
"Revenge/anger/retaliation" (4)
"Jealousy" (5)
"Self-defense" (6)
"Defense of others" (7)
"Victim 'dissed' subject/other" (8)
"Victim resisted crime" (9)
"Argument with victim" (10)
"Seek excitement/instigate" (11)
"Subject/perp under influence of alcohol or drugs" (12)
"Scare tactic" (13)
"Psychiatric condition" (15)
"To erase debt" (16)
"Problems with victim" (21)
"No reason/just happened" (22)
"Self-enhancement" (23)
"Victim under the influence of alcohol or drugs" (25)
"Victim robbed subject/other" (28)
"Subjects responsibility/ character" (31)
"Victim assaulted subject/other" (35)
"Accident" (36)

"Victim threatened subject" (26)
"Result of drug war" (27)
"Victim robbed subject/other" (28)
"Subject wanted to send message" (29)
"Didn't happen" (30)
"Victims responsibility" (38)
"Third party responsible" (39)
"Hate crime" (40)
"Aftermath of previous victimization" (41)
"Co-perp wanted money/goods" (43)

Recoding Scheme for Motive Variable

Recoding decisions were guided by the current state of knowledge on modus operandi for male perpetrated assault in general and male-on-male violence in particular.

Robbery: Offender said or indicated that the violence occurred as he and/or a co-perpetrator was trying to get money, goods/property, or money for drugs from someone else's possession. Codes = 1, 2, 43.

Character Contest[1]: Offender mentioned or alluded to enhancing or protecting self or reputation as the focal concern. Codes = 6, 7, 8, 23, 12, 25, 11, 22, 5.

Conflict Resolution[2]: Offender stated or suggested that the violence was an attempt to resolve an immediate dispute or an on-going conflict between him and the victim. Codes = 10, 21, 31, 35, 39.

Revenge[3]*:* Offender claimed that the instant offense was a counterattack against the victim for a previous wrong he initiated. Codes = 4, 28, 35.

[1] For an description of character contest violence see Brookman, 2003; Deibert and Miethe, 2003; Kubrin and Hertig, 2003; Miethe and Regoeczi, 2004; O'Brien, Stockard, and Issacson, 1999; Polk, 1993, 1994, 1999.

[2] For a discussion on conflict resolution violence see Block and Block, 1991; Brookman, 2003; Fagan and Wilkinson, 1998; Miethe and Regoeczi, 2004; Oliver, 2001; Polk, 1994, 1997.

[3] For an explanation of revenge assault see Brookman, 2003; Katz, 1988; Kubrin and Hertig, 2003.

Bibliography

Abu-Bader, S.H. (2006). Using statistical methods in social work practice: A complete SPSS guide. Chicago, IL: Lyceum Books.

Adler, C. and Polk, K. (1997). *The killing of children in Victoria, 1985-1995: A report to the Criminology Research Counsel 32/93-94*, Criminology Department, the University of Melbourne, Victoria.

Akers, R.L. (1994), *Criminological Theories: Introduction and evaluation.* Los Angeles, CA: Roxbury Publishing.

Allen, A.N. and Lo, C.C. (2010). Drugs, guns, and disadvantaged youths: Co-occurring behavior and the code of the street. *Crime and Delinquency,* 1-22. doi: 10.1177/0011128709359652

Alvarez, A. and Bachman, R. (2007). *Violence: The enduring problem.* Thousand Oaks, CA: Sage Publications.

Anderson, E. (1994, May). The code of the street. *Atlantic Monthly.*

Anderson, E. (1997). Violence and the inner-city street code. In J. McCord (Ed.), *Violence and children in the inner city* (pp. 1-30). New York: Cambridge University Press.

Anderson, E. (1998). The social ecology of youth violence. *Crime and Justice, 24,* 64-103.

Anderson, L.A and Meier, R.F. (2004). Interactions and the criminal event perspective. *Journal of Contemporary Criminal Justice, 20* (4), 416-440.

Applegate, B.K. and Davis, R.K. (2006). Public views on sentencing juvenile murders. *Youth Violence and Juvenile Justice, 4* (1), 55-74.

Athens, L. (2005). Violent encounters: Violent engagements, skirmishes, and tiffs. *Journal of Contemporary Ethnography, 34* (6), 631-678.

Athens, L. (1985). Character contests and violent criminal conduct: A critique. *The Sociological Quarterly, 26* (3), 419-431.

Austin, R.L. (1980). Adolescent subculture of violence. *The Sociological Quarterly, 21*, 545-561.

Avakame, E.F. (1997). Urban homicide: A multilevel analysis across Chicago's census tracts. *Homicide Studies, 1* (4), 338-358.

Bailey, S. (2000). Juvenile homicide. *Criminal Behaviour and Mental Health, 10*, 149-154.

Ball-Rokeach, S.J. (1973). Values and violence: A test of the subculture of violence thesis. *American Sociological Review 38* (6), 736-749.

Baron, S.W. and Hartnagel, T.F. (1998). Street youth and criminal violence. *Journal of*

Research in Crime and Delinquency, 35 (2), 166-192.

Baron, S.W., Kennedy, L.W., and Forde, D.R. (2001). Male street youths' conflict: The role of background subcultural and situational factors. Justice Quarterly, 18 (4), 759-789.

Bell, C.C. and Jenkins, E.J. (1991). Traumatic stress and children. *Journal of Health Care for the Poor and Underserved, 2*, 172-185.

Bender, L. (1959). Children and adolescents who have killed. *American Journal of Psychiatry, 116*, 510-513.

Benekos, P.J. and Merlo, A.V. (2008). Juvenile justice: The legacy of punitive policy. *Youth Violence and Juvenile Justice, 6* (1), 28-46.

Bennett, W.J., DiIulio, J.J., and Walters, J. (1996). *Body count: Moral Poverty and how to win America's war against crime and drugs.* New York: Simon and Schuster.

Bernard, T.J. (1990). Angry aggression among the "truly disadvantaged". *Criminology, 28* (1), 73-95.

Bjerregaard, B. and Lizotte, A.J. (1995). Gun ownership and gang membership. *Journal of Criminal Law and Criminology, 86* (1), 37-59.

Black, S. and Hausman, A. (2008). Adolescents' views of guns in a high-violence community. *Journal of Adolescent Research, 23* (5), 592-610.

Blau, J.R. and Blau, P.M. (1982). The cost of inequality: Metropolitan structure and violent crime. *American Sociological Review, 47*, 114-129.

Block, R. (1977). *Violent crime*. Lexington, MA: D.C. Heath.

Block, R. (1981). Victim-offender dynamics in violent crime. *Journal of Criminal Law, 72,* 743-761.

Block, C. R. and Block R. (1991). Beginning with Wolfgang: An agenda for homicide research. *Journal of Crime and Justice, 14* (2), 30-70.

Block, C.R. and Block, R. (1993). *Street gang crime in Chicago*. Research in Brief.

Washington, D.C.: U.S. Department of Justice, Office of Justice Program, National Institute of Justice.

Block, R. and Zimring, F. (1973). Homicide in Chicago, 1965-1970. *Journal of Research in Crime and Delinquency, 10,* 1-12.

Blumstein, A. (1995a, August). Violence by young people: Why the deadly nexus. *National Institute of Justice Journal*, 2-9.

Blumstein, A. (1995b). Youth violence, guns, and the illicit-drug industry. *Journal of Criminal Law and Criminology, 86* (1), 10-36.

Blumstein, A. and Cork, D. (1996). Linking gun availability to youth gun violence. *Law and Contemporary Problems, 59* (1), 5-24.

Blumstein, A. and Rosenfeld, R. (1999). Trends in rates of violence in the U.S.A. S*tudies on Crime and Crime Prevention, 8,* 139-146.

Boyum, D. and Kleiman, M.A.R. (2003). Breaking the drug-crime link. *Public Interest, 152,* 19-38.

Bradburn, N., Sudman, S., and Wansink, B. (2004). *Asking questions: The definitive guide to questionnaire design for marketing research, political polls, and social and health questionnaires*. San Francisco, CA: John Wiley and Son, Inc.

Braga, A.A. and Pierce, G.L. (2005). Disrupting illegal firearms markets in Boston: The effects of Operation Ceasefire on the supply of new handguns to criminals. *Criminology and Public Policy, 4* (4), 717-748.

Brennan, I.R. and Moore, S.C. (2009). Weapons and violence: A review of theory and research. *Aggression and Violent Behavior, 14,* 215-225.

Brearley, H.C. (1929). Homicide in South Carolina: A regional study. *Social Forces, 8,* 218-221.

Brewer, V.E., Damphousse, K.R., and Adkinson, C.D. (1998). The role of juveniles in urban homicide: The case of Houston, 1990-1994. *Homicide Studies, 2* (3), 321-339.

Brezina, T., Agnew, R., Cullen, F.T., and Wright, J.P. (2004). The code of the street: A quantitative assessment of Elijah Anderson's subculture of violence thesis and its contribution to youth violence research. *Youth Violence and Juvenile Justice, 2* (4), 303-328.

Brookman, F. (2003). Confrontational and revenge homicides among men in England and Wales. *The Australian and New Zealand Journal of Criminology, 36* (1), 34-59.

Brooks-Gunn, J., Duncan, G.J., Kiebanov, P.K., and Sealand, N. (1993). Do neighborhoods influence child and adolescent development? *American Journal of Sociology, 99* (2), 353-395.

Burgess, R.L. and Akers, R.L. (1966). A differential association-reinforcement theory of criminal behavior. *Social Problems, 14,* 128-147.

Busch, K.G., Zagar, R., Hughes, J.R., Arbit, J., and Bussell, R.E. (1990). Adolescents who kill. *Journal of Clinical Psychology, 46* (4), 472-485.

Butts, J. and Travis, J. (2002, March). *The rise and fall of American youth violence: 1980 to 2000.* Washington, DC: Urban Institute Justice Policy Center.

Calhoun, D., Dodge, A.C., Journel, C.S., and Zahnd, E. (2005). The supply and demand for guns to juveniles: Oakland gun tracing project. *Journal of Urban Health, 82* (4), 552-559.

Canada, G. (1996). *Fist, stick, knife, gun.* Boston, MA: Beacon Press.

Cao, L., Adams, A. and Jensen, V.J. (1997). A test of the Black subculture of violence thesis: A research note. *Criminology, 35* (2), 367-379.

Carcach, C. (1997). *Youth victims and offenders of homicide.* Paper presented at the Australian Institute of Criminology Conference, Adelaide, Australia.

Carter, H.J. (1998). Comparative study of characteristics associated with male, juvenile homicidal and nonhomicidal populations. *Dissertation Abstracts International* (UMI No. 9840069).

Chaiken, M.R. (2000, March). *Violent neighborhoods, violent kids.* Washington, DC: U.S. Department of Justice, Office of Juvenile Justice and Delinquency Prevention.

Channing Bete Company, Inc. (2004). Risk and protective factors. South Deerfield, MA.

Cohen, A.K. (1955). *Delinquent boys: The culture of the gang.* Glencoe, IL: Free Press.

Cook, P.J. (1985). Is robbery becoming more violent? An analysis of robbery murder trends since 1968. *Journal of Criminal Law and Criminology, 76.*

Cook, P.J. (1991). The technology of personal violence. In M. Tonry (Ed.), *Crime and justice: A review of research*, Volume 14. Chicago, IL: Chicago University Press.

Cook, P.J. and Laub, J.H. (1998). The unprecedented epidemic in youth violence. *Crime and Justice, 24*, 27-64.

Cook, P.J. and Laub, J.H. (2002). After the epidemic: Recent trends in youth violence in the United States. *Crime and Justice, 28*, 1-20.

Cook, P.J. and Ludig, J. (1997). *Guns in America: Results of a comprehensive national survey on firearm ownership and use.* Summary report. Washington, DC: Police Foundation.

Cork, D. (1999). Examining space-time interaction in city-level homicide data: Crack markets and the diffusion of guns among youth. *Journal of Quantitative Criminology, 15* (4), 379-406.

Cornell, D.G. (1993). Juvenile homicide: A growing national problem. *Behavioral Sciences and the Law, 11*, 389-396.

Cornell, D.G. (1998). Child and adolescent homicide. In V.B. Van Hasselt and M. Hersen (Eds.), *Handbook of psychological approaches with violent offenders: Contemporary strategies and issues* (pp. 131-152). New York: Springer.

Cornell, D.G., Benedek, E.P., and Benedek, B.A. (1987a). Juvenile homicide: Prior adjustment and a proposed typology. *American Journal of Orthopsychiatry, 57* (3), 383-393.

Cornell, D.G., Benedek, E.P., and Benedek, B.A. (1987b). Characteristics of adolescents charged with homicide: Review of 72 cases. *Behavioral Science and the Law, 5* (1), 11-23.

Crespi, T.D. and Rigazio-DiGilio, S.A. (1996). Adolescent homicide and family pathology: Implications for research and treatment with adolescents. *Adolescence, 31*, 353-367.

Crimmins, S.M., Brownstein, H.H., Spunt, B.J., Ryder, J.A., and Warley, R.M. (1998). *Learning about violence and drugs among adolescents (LAVIDA).* Final report to the National Institute on

Drug Abuse. Grant No. R01 DA08679. Washington, D.C.: National Institute of Health.

Curtis, L.A. (1974). Victim-precipitation and violent crime. *Social Problem, 21,* 594-605.

Daly, M. and Wilson, M. (1988). *Homicide.* New York: Aldine de Gruyter Publishers.

Daly, M. and Wilson, M. (2001). Risk-taking, intrasexual competition, and homicide. *Nebraska Symposium on Motivation, 47*, 1-36.

Darby, P.J., Wesley, W.D., Kashani, J.H., Hartke, K.L., and Reid, J.C. (1998). Analysis of 112 juveniles who committed homicide: Characteristics and a closer look at family abuse. *Journal of Family Violence, 13* (4), 365-375.

De Porte, J.V. and Parkhurst, E. (1935). Homicide in New York State: A statistical study of the victims and criminal in 37 counties in 1921-1930. *Human Biology, 7*, 47-73.

Decker, S.H. (1993). Exploring victim-offender relationships in homicide: The role of individual and event characteristics. *Justice Quarterly, 10* (4), 585-612.

Decker, S.H. (1995). Reconstructing homicide events: The role of witnesses in fatal encounters. *Journal of Criminal Justice, 23* (5), 439-450.

Decker, S.H. (1996). Deviant homicide: A new look at the role of motives and victim-offender relationships. *Journal of Research in Crime and Delinquency, 33* (4), 427-449.

Decker, S.H., Bynum, T.S., and Weisel, D.L. (1998). A tale of two cities: Gangs as organized crime groups. *Justice Quarterly, 15*, 395-423.

Decker, S.H. and Curry, G.D. (2000). Addressing key features of gang membership: Measuring the involvement of young gang members. *Journal of Criminal Justice, 28*, 473-482.

Decker, S.H., Pennel, S., and Caldwell, A. (1997). *Illegal firearms: Access and use by arrestees.* Washington, DC: U.S. Department of Justice, Office of Justice Programs, National Institute of Justice.

Decker, S.H. and Van Winkle, B. (1996). *Life in the gang: Family, friends, and violence.* New York: NY: Cambridge University Press.

Deibert, G.R. and Miethe, T.D. (2003). Character contests and dispute-related offenses. *Deviant Behavior: An Interdisciplinary Journal,* *24,* 245-267.

Denno, D.W. (1990). *Biology and violence: From birth to adulthood.* Cambridge: Cambridge University Press.

Denton, N.A. and Massey, D.S. (1988). Residential segregation of Blacks, Hispanics, and Asians by socioeconomic status and generation. *Social Science Quarterly, 69,* 797-817.

Doerner, W.G. (1983). Why does Johnny Reb die when shot? The impact of medical resources upon lethality. *Sociological Inquiry, 53* (1), 1-15.

Doerner, W.G. (1988). The impact of medical resources on criminally induced lethality: A further examination. *Criminology, 26* (1), 171-179.

Dolan, M. and Smith, C. (2001). Juvenile homicide offenders: 10 years experience of an adolescent forensic psychiatry service. *The Journal of Forensic Psychiatry, 12* (2), 313-329.

Duke, N.N., Borowsky, I.W., Pettingell, S.L., and McMorris, B.J. (2009). Examining youth hopelessness as an independent risk correlate for adolescent delinquency and violence. *Maternal Child Health Journal.* doi: 10.1007/s10995-009-0550-6

Durant, R.H, Cadenhead, C., Pendergrast, R.A., Slavens, G., and Linder, C.W. (1994). Factors associated with the use of violence among urban Black adolescents. *American Journal of Public Health, 84* (4), 612-617.

Duxbury, E.D. (1980). Violence by youth; violence against youth. *American Behavioral Scientist, 23* (5), 667-680.

Egley, A. (2000, November). *Highlights of the 1999 National Youth Gang Survey.* Washington, DC: U.S. Department of Justice, Office of Juvenile Justice and Delinquency Prevention.

Elliott, D.S., Huizinga, D. and Menard, S. (1989). *Multiple problem youth: Delinquency, substance use and mental health problems.* New York: Springer-Verlag.

Empy, L.T. and Stafford, T. (1991). *American delinquency: Its meaning and construction* (3rd ed.). Belmont, CA: Wadsworth Publishing.

Ensminger, M.E., Anthony, J.C. and McCord, J. (1997). The inner city and drug use: Initial findings from an epidemiological study. *Drug and Alcohol Dependence, 48* (3), 175-184.

Ewing, C. (1990). *When children kill: The dynamics of juvenile homicide.* Lexington, MA.:D.C. Health Company.

Fagan, J., Piper, E. and Moore, M. (1986). Violent delinquents and urban youths. *Criminology, 24* (3), 436-471.

Fagan, J. and Wilkinson, D.L. (1998). Guns, youth violence, and social identity in inner cities. *Crime and Justice, 24,* 105-188.

Fagan, J., Zimring, F.E., and Kim, J. (1998). Declining homicide in New York City: A tale of two trends. *Journal of Criminal Law and Criminology, 88* (4), 1277-1306.

Farrington, D.P. (1995). The development of offending and antisocial behavior from childhood: Key findings from the Cambridge study in delinquent development. *Journal of Child Psychology and Psychiatry, 36,* 929-964.

Farrington, D.P. (1997). Early prediction of violent and nonviolent youthful offending. *European Journal on Criminal Policy and Research, 5,* 52-66.

Farrington, D.P. (1998). Predictors, causes, and correlates of male youth violence. In M. Moore and M. Tonry (Eds.), *Crime and justice: An annual review of research,* (Vol. 21, pp. 421-475). Chicago, IL: University of Chicago Press.

Feld, B.C. (1999). *Bad kids.* New York: Oxford University Press.

Felson, R.B. (1982). Impression management and the escalation of aggression and violence. *Social Psychology Quarterly, 45* (4), 245-254.

Felson, R.B., Baccaglini, W.F., and Ribner, S.A. (1985). Accounting for criminal violence: A comparison of official and offender versions of the crime. *Sociological and Social Research, 70,* 93-95.

Felson, R.B., Deane, G., and Armstrong, D.P. (2008). Do theories of crime or violence explain race differences in delinquency? *Social Science Research,* 37, 624-641.

Felson, R.B. and Messner, S.F. (1996). To kill or not to kill? Lethal outcomes in injurious attacks. *Criminology, 34* (4), 519-545.

Felson, R.B., Ribner, S.A., and Siegel, M.S. (1984). Age and the effect of third parties during criminal violence. *Sociology and Social Research, 68 (4), 452-462.*

Felson, R. B. and Steadman, H. J. (1983). Situational factors in disputes leading to criminal violence. *Criminology, 21* (1), 59-74.

Felson, R.B. and Tedeschi, J.T. (1995). A social interactionist approach to violence: Cross-cultural application. In B. Ruback and N.A. Weiner (Eds.), *Interpersonal violent behavior*. New York: Springer.

Fingerhut, L.A. (1993). *Firearm mortality among children, youth, and young adults 1 -34 years of age: Trends and current status, United States 1985-1990*. Hyattsvile: National Center for Health Statistics.

Foster, J., Barkus, E., and Yavorsky, C. (2006). *Understanding and using advanced statistics*. Thousand Oaks, CA: Sage Publications.

Fowler, F. and Mangione, T. (1990). *Standardized survey interviewing: Minimizing interviewer- related error*. Newbury Park, CA: Sage Publication.

Fox, J.A. and Zawitz, M.W. (2007, July). *Homicide trends in the United States.* Washington, DC: U.S. Department of Justice, Bureau of Justice Statistics.

Fox, J.A. and Zawitz, M.W. (2004, November). *Homicide trends in the United States: 2002 update*. Washington, DC: U.S. Department of Justice, Bureau of Justice Statistics.

Frankel, E. (1939). One thousand murderers. *Journal of Criminal Law and Criminology, 29*, 672-688.

Fraser, M.W. (1996). Aggressive behavior in childhood and early adolescence: An ecological-developmental perspective on youth violence. *Social Work, 41* (4), 347-361.

Freedman, D. and Hemenway, D. (2000). Precursors of lethal violence: A death row sample. *Social Science and Medicine, 50,* 1757-1770.

Fritzon, K. (2000). The contribution of psychological research to arson investigation. In D.V. Canter and L.J. Alison (Eds), *Profiling property crimes: Offender profiling services* (Vol 4, pp. 147-184). Thousand Oak, CA: Sage Publication.

Giacopassi, D.J., Sparger, J.R. and Stein, P.M. (1992). The effects of emergency medical care on the homicide rate: Some additional evidence. *Journal of Criminal Justice, 20*, 249-259.

Giddens, A. (1972). *Emile Durkheim: Selected writings*. London: Cambridge University Press.

Gil, D.G. (1996). Preventing violence in a structurally violent society: Mission impossible. *American Journal of Orthopsychiatry, 66* (1), 77-84.

Goetting, A. (1989). Patterns of homicide among children. *Criminal Justice and Behavior, 16* (1), 63-80.

Goffman, E. (1967). *Interaction ritual: Essays in face-to-face behavior.* Chicago: Aldine Publishing.

Goffman, E. (1983). The interaction order. *American Sociological Review, 48,* 1-17.

Golden, M. and Almo, C. (2004). *Reducing gun violence: An overview of New York City's strategies.* Vera Institute of Justice.

Goldstein, A.P. (1991). *Delinquent gangs: A psychological perspective.* Chicago, IL: Research Press.

Gonzalez, J.R. (2001). Analyses of physical abuse, sexual abuse, and weapon accessibility among juvenile murderers. *Dissertation Abstracts International.* (UMI No. 3043000).

Gottfredson, D.C., McNeil, R.J. and Gottfredson, G.D. (1991). Social area influences on delinquency: A multilevel analysis. *Journal of Research in Crime and Delinquency, 28* (2), 197-226.

Graham, K., Leonard, K.E., Room, R., Wild, T.C., Pihl, R.O., Bois, C., et al. (1998). Current directions in research on understanding and preventing intoxicated aggression. *Addiction, 93,* 659-676.

Graham, K. and West, P. (2001). Alcohol and crime: examining the link. In N. Heather, T.J. Peters, and T. Stockwell (Eds.), *International handbook of alcohol dependence and problems* (pp. 439-470). San Francisco, CA: John Wiley and Sons.

Gruber, E., DiClemente, R.J., Anderson, M.M., and Lodico, M. (1996). Early drinking onset and its association with alcohol use and problem behavior in late adolescence. *Preventive Medicine, 25,* 293-300.

Hagan, J. and Foster, H. (2001). Youth violence and the end of adolescence. *American Sociological Review, 66,* 874-899.

Hanke P.J. and Gundlach, J.H. (1995). Damned on arrival: A preliminary study of the relationship between homicide, emergency medical care, and race. *Journal of Criminal Justice, 23* (4), 313-323.

Hannon, L. (2004). Race victim-precipitated homicide and the subculture of violence thesis. *The Social Science Journal, 41*, 115-121.

Harer, M.D. and Steffensmeier, D.L. (1992). The differing effects of economic inequality on Black and White rates of violence. *Social Forces, 70*, 1035-1054.

Hardwick, P.J. and Rowton-Lee, M.A. (1996). Adolescent homicide: towards assessment of risk. *Journal of Adolescence, 19*, 263-276.

Harries, K.D. (1997). *Serious violence: Patterns of homicide and assault in America* (2nd ed.). Springfield: Charles C. Thomas Publisher.

Harris, A.R., Thomas, S.H., Fisher, G.A., and Hirsch, D.J. (2002). Murder and medicine: The lethality of criminal assault 1960-1999. *Homicide Studies, 6* (2), 128-166.

Hawkins, D.F. (1983). Black and White homicide differentials: Alternative to an inadequate theory. *Criminal Justice and Behavior, 10* (4), 407-440.

Hawkins, D.F. (1985). Black homicide: The adequacy of existing research for devising prevention strategies. *Crime and Delinquency, 31* (1), 83-103.

Hawkins, J.D., Catalano, R.F., and Miller, J.Y. (1992). Risk and protective factors for alcohol and other drug problems in adolescence and early adulthood: Implications of substance use prevention. *Psychological Bulletin, 112*, 64-105.

Hawkins, J.D., Herrenkohl, T.I., Farrington, D.P., Brewer, D., Catalano, R.F., Harachi, T.W., et al. (1998). A review of predictors of youth violence. In R. Loeber and D.P. Farrington (Eds.), *Serious and violent juvenile offenders: Risk factors and successful interventions.* Thousand Oaks, CA: Sage Publication.

Hawkins, J.D., Herrenkohl, T.I., Farrington, D.P., Brewer, D., Catalano, R.F., Harachi, T.W., et al. (2000). *Predictors of youth violence.* Washington, DC: U.S. Department of Justice, Office of Juvenile Justice and Delinquency Prevention.

Heimer, K. (1997). Socioeconomic status, subcultural definitions, and violent delinquency. *Social Forces, 75* (3), 799-833.

Henry, B., Avshalom, C., Moffitt, T., and Silva, P. (1996). Temperamental and familial predictors of violent and nonviolent criminal convictions: Age 3 to age 18. *Developmental Psychology, 32*, 614-623.

Hepworth, D. H., Rooney, R .H. and Larsen, J. (2007). *Direct social work practice: Theory and skills,* (7th ed). Pacific Grove, CA: Brooks/Cole Publishing Company.

Herrenkohl, T.I., Huang, B., Kosterman, R., Hawkins, J.D., Catalano, R.F., and Smith, B.H. (2001). A comparison of social development processes leading to violent behavior in late adolescence for childhood initiators and adolescent initiators of violence. *Journal of Research in Crime and Delinquency, 38* (1), 45-63.

Herrenkohl, T.I. Maguin, E., Hill, K.G., Hawkins, D., Abbott, R.D., and Catalano, R.F. (2000). *Journal of Adolescent Health 26*, 176-186.

Hewitt, J.D. (1988). The victim-offender relationship in convicted homicide cases: 1960-1984. *Journal of Criminal Justice, 16*, 25-33.

Hiede, K.M. (1997). Juvenile homicide in America: How can we stop the killing? *Behavioral Sciences and the Law, 15*, 203-220.

Hiede, K.M. (1999). *Young killers: The challenge of juvenile homicide.* Thousand Oaks, CA: Sage Publications.

Hill, K.G., Howell, J.C., Hawkins, J.D., and Battin-Pearson, S.R. (1999). Childhood risk factors for adolescent gang membership: Results from the Seattle Social Development Project. *Journal of Research in Crime and Delinquency, 36* (3), 300-322.

Hinds, P.S., Vogel, R.J., and Clarke-Steffen, L. (1997). The possibilities and pitfalls of doing a secondary analysis of a qualitative data set. *Qualitative Health Research, 7* (3), 408-424.

Horowitz, M.A. (2000). Kids who kill: A critique of how the American legal system deals with juveniles who commit homicide. *Law and Contemporary Problems, 63* (3), 133-177.

Howell, J., Krisberg, B., Hawkins, J., and Wilson, J. (Eds). (1995). Serious, violent, and chronic juvenile offenders. Thousand Oaks, CA: Sage Publication.

Huang, B., White, H.R., Kosterman, R., Catalano, R.F., and Hawkins, J.D. (2001). Developmental association between alcohol and interpersonal aggression during adolescence. *Journal of Research in Crime and Delinquency, 38* (1), 64-83.

Huff, C.R. (1998, October). *Comparing the criminal behavior of youth gangs and at-risk youths.* Washington, DC: U.S. Department of Justice, National Institute of Justice.

Huizinga, D., Loeber, R., Thornberry, T.P., and Cothern, L. (2000). *Co-occurrence of delinquency and other problem behaviors.* Washington, DC: U.S. Department of Justice, Office of Juvenile Justice and Delinquency Prevention.

Inciardi, J.A., Horowitz, R., and Pottieger, A.E. (1993). *Street kids, street drugs, street crime: An examination of drug use and serious delinquency in Miami.* Belmont, CA: Wadsworth Publishing Company.

Ingram, A.L. (1993). Type of place, urbanisim, and delinquency: Further testing the determinist theory. *Journal of Research in Crime and Delinquency, 30* (2), 192-212.

Jang, S.J. and Smith, C.A. (1997). A test of reciprocal causal relationships among parental supervision, affective ties, and delinquency. *Journal of Research in Crime and Delinquency, 34* (3), 307-337.

Jenkins, P.H. and Welsh, W.N. (2003). Neighborhood-based prevention/intervention: A process evaluation of a risk-focused approach. *Children and Youth Services Review, 25* (4), 327-351.

Joe, S. and Kaplan, M.S. (2001). Suicide among African American men. *Suicide Life Threat Behavior, 31,* 106-121.

Juvenile Justice Bulletin (2000, June). Serious and violent offending by race and ethnicity. Retrieved July 11, 2005, from http://www.ncjrs.org/html/ojjdp/2000_6_1/page2.html.

Kandel, E. and Mednick, S.A. (1991). Perinatal complications predict violent offending. *Criminology, 29,* 519-529.

Kann, L, Kinchen, S., Williams, T., Ross, J., Lowry, R., Hill, C., et al. (1998). Youth risk behavior surveillance—United States, 1997. *Mortality Weekly Report, 47,* 1-89.

Katz, J. (1988). Seduction of crime: Moral and sensual attraction of doing evil. New York: Basic Books.

Kennedy, L.W. and Baron, S.W. (1993). Routine activities and a subculture of violence: A study of violence on the street. *Journal of Research in Crime and Delinquency, 30* (1), 88-112.

King, C.H. (1975). The ego and the integration of violence in homicidal youth. *American Journal of Orthopsychiatry 45* (1), 134-145.

Kleck, G. (1991). *Point blank: Guns and violence in America.* New York: Aldine de Gruyter.

Kleck, G. and McElrath, K. (1991). The effect of weaponry on human violence. *Social Forces, 69* (3), 669-692.

Kovandzic, T.V., Vieraitis, L.M., and Yeisley, M.R. (1998). The structural covariates of urban homicide: Reassessing the impact of income inequality and poverty in the post-Reagan era. *Criminology, 36* (3), 569-599.

Kracke, K. (2001). *Children's exposure to violence: The safe start initiative.* Washington, DC: U.S. Department of Justice.

Krienert, J.L. (2003). *Masculinity and crime: A quantitative exploration of Messerschmidt's hypothesis.* Retrieved May 9, 2005, from http://www.sociology.org/content/vol7.2/01_krienert.html.

Kubrin, C.E. and Hertig, J.R. (2003). Neighborhood correlates of homicide trends: An analysis using growth-curve modeling. *Sociological Quarterly, 44* (3), 329-350.

Kubrin, C.E. and Weitzer, R. (2003). Retaliatory homicide: concentrated disadvantage and neighborhood culture. *Social Problems, 50* (2), 157-180.

Kuhn, E.M., Nile, C.L., O'Brien, M.E., Withers, R.L., and Hargarten, S.W. (1999). Victim and perpetrator characteristics for firearm-related homicides of youth during 1991-1997. In P.H. Blackman, V.L. Leggett, B.L. Olsen, and J.P. Jarvis (Eds.), *The varieties of homicide and its research: Proceedings of the 1999 meeting of the Homicide Research Working Group* (pp. 117-130). Quantico, VA: FBI Academy.

Lee, M.R. and Ousey, G.C. (2005). Institutional access, residential segregation, and urban Black homicide. *Sociological Inquiry, 75* (1), 31-54.

Lennings, C.J. (2004). Young offenders who kill: A review of five Australian case studies. *International Journal of Forensic Psychology, 1* (2), 1-13.

Lennings, C.J., Copeland, J., and Howard, J. (2003). Substance use patterns of young offenders and violent crime. *Aggressive Behavior, 29*, 414-422.

Lennings, C.J. and Pritchard, M. (1999). Prevalence of drug use prior to detention among residents of youth detention centres in Queenslands. *Drug and Alcohol Review, 18*, 145- 152.

Levi, K. (1980). Homicide as conflict resolution. *Deviant Behavior: An Interdisciplinary Journal, 1*, 281-307.

Lewis, D.O., Moy, E., Jackson, L.D., Aaronson, R., Restifo, N., Serra, S., et al. (1985). Biopsychosocial characteristics of children who later murder: A prospective study. American *Journal of Psychiatry, 142* (10), 1161-1167.

Lewis, D.O., Pincus, J.G., Bard, B., Richardson, E., Prichep, L.S., Feldman, M., et al.(1988). Neuropsychiatric, psychoeducational, and family characteristics of 14 juveniles condemned to death in the United States. *American Journal of Psychiatry, 145* (5), 584-589.

Lewis, D.O., Shanok, S.S., Grant, M., and Ritvo, E.V. (1983). Homicidally aggressive young children: Neuropsychiatric and experiential correlates. *American Journal of Psychiatry, 140* (2), 148-153.

Lipsey, M.W. and Derzon, J.H. (1998). Predictors of violent and serious delinquency in adolescence and early adulthood: A synthesis of longitudinal research. In R. Loeber and

D.P. Farrington (Eds.), *Serious and violent juvenile offenders: Risk factors and successful interventions* (pp. 86-105). Thousand Oaks, CA: Sage Publication.

Lipsey, M.W., Wilson, D.B., and Cothern, L. (2000). *Effective intervention for serious juvenile offenders.* Washington, DC: U.S. Department of Justice, Office of Juvenile Justice and Delinquency Prevention.

Lizotte, A.J., Howard, G.J., Krohn, M.D., and Thornberry, T.P. (1997). Patterns of illegal gun carrying among young urban males. *Valparaiso University Law Review, Symposium, Juvenile Crime: Policy Proposals on Guns and Violence, Gangs and Drugs, 31* (2), 375-390.

Lizotte, A.J. and Sheppard, D. (2001, July). *Gun use by male juveniles: Research and prevention.* Washington, DC: U.S. Department of Justice, Office of Juvenile Justice and Delinquency Prevention.

Lorion, R.P. and Saltzman, W. (1993). Children's exposure to community violence: Following a path from concern to research to action. *Psychiatry, 56*, 55-65.

Luckenbill, D.F. (1977). Criminal homicide as a situated transaction. *Social Problems, 25* (2), 176-186.

Luckenbill, D.F. and Doyle, D.P. (1989). Structural position and violence: Developing a cultural explanation. *Criminology, 27* (3), 419-436.

Lundsgaarde, H.P. (1977). *Murder in Space City: A cultural analysis of Houston homicide patterns*. New York: Oxford University Press.

Marks, C. (1991). The urban underclass. *Annual Review of Sociology, 17*, 445-466.

Martinez, R. (1996). Latinos and lethal violence: The impact of poverty and inequality. *Social Problems, 43* (2), 131-146.

Martinez, R. (1997). Homicide among Miami's ethnic groups: Anglos, Blacks, and Latinos in the 1990s. *Homicide Studies, 1* (1), 17-34.

Martinez, R. and Lee, M.T. (1999). Extending ethnicity in homicide research: The case of Latinos. In N. D. Smith and M.A. Zahn (Eds.), *Studying and preventing homicide: issues and challenges*. Thousand Oaks, CA: Sage Publication.

Martinez, R. and Richters, F.E. (1993). The NIHM community violence project II: Children's distress symptoms associated with violence exposure. *Psychiatry, 56,* 22-35.

Massey, D.S. (2004). Segregation and stratification: A biosocial perspective. *Du Bois Review, 1* (1), 7-25.

Massey, D.S. (2005). The age of extremes: Concentrated affluence and poverty in the twenty-first century. *Demography, 33* (4), 395-412.

Massey, D.S. and Denton, N.A. (1993). American apartheid: Segregation and the making of the underclass: Cambridge, MA: Harvard University Press.

Massey, D.S. and Fischer, M.J. (1999). Does rising income bring integration? New results for Blacks, Hispanics, and Asians in 1990. *Social Science Research, 28*, 316-326.

Massey, D.S., Gross, A.B., and Eggers, M.L. (1991). Segregation, the concentration of poverty, and the life chance of individuals. *Social Science Research, 20* 397-420.

Matjasko, J.L., Needham, B.L., Grunden, L.N., and Farb, A. (2010). Violent victimization and perpetration during adolescence: Developmental stage dependent ecological models. *Journal of Youth and Adolescence, 39,* 1053-1066.

Maxson, C.L., Klein, M.W., and Sternheimer (2000, March). *Homicide in Los Angeles: An analysis of the differential character of adolescent and other homicides* (NCJRS No. 193812). Rockville, MD: National Criminal Justice Reference Service.

McCracken, G. (1988). *The long interview: Qualitative research methods series* (No. 13). Newbury Park, CA: Sage Publication.

McCurley, C. And Snyder, H.N. (2004). *Victims of violent juvenile crime.* Washington, DC: U.S. Department of Justice, Office of Juvenile Justice and Delinquency Prevention.

McDowall, D. (1991). Firearm availability and homicide rates in Detroit, 1951-1986. *Social Forces, 69* (4), 1085-1101.

McLaughlin, C.R., Daniel, J., Joost, T.F. (1999). The relationship between substance use, drug selling, and lethal violence in 25 juvenile murderers. *Journal of Forensic Sciences, 45* (2), 349-353.

Mears, D.P., Ploeger, M. and Marr, M. (1998). Explaining the gender gap in delinquency: Peer influences and moral evaluation of behavior. *Journal of Research in Crime and Delinquency, 35* (3), 251-266.

Merlo, A.V. and Benekos, P.J. (2010). Is punitive juvenile justice policy declining in the United States? A critique of emergent initiatives. *Youth Justice, 10* (1) 3-24.

Merton, R.K. (1968). *Social theory and social structure.* NY: Free Press.

Messerschmidt, J.W. (1993). *Masculinities and crime: Critiques and reconceptualization of theory.* Rowan and Littlefield Publishers, Inc.

Messerschmidt, J.W. (1997). *Crime as structured action: Gender, race, class, and crime in the making.* Thousand Oaks, CA: Sage Publications.

Messerschmidt, J.W. (2000). *Nine lives: Adolescent masculinities, the body, and violence.* Westview Press.

Messner, S.F. (1982). Poverty, inequality, and the urban homicide rate. *Criminology, 20* (1), 477-488.

Messner, S.F. (1983). Regional and racial effects on the urban homicide rate: The subculture of violence revisited. *American Journal of Sociology, 88* (5), 997-1007.

Messner, S.F. and Tardiff, K. (1986). Economic inequality and levels of homicide: An explanation of urban neighborhoods. *Criminology, 24* (2), 297-317.

Miethe, T.D. and Drass, K. A. (1999). Exploring the social context of instrumental and expressive homicides: An application of qualitative comparative analysis. *Journal of Quantitative Criminology, 15* (1), 1-21.

Miethe, T.D. and Regoeczi, W.C. (2004). *Rethinking homicide: Exploring the structure and process underlying deadly situations.* New York: Cambridge University Press.

Miller, W.B. (1958). *Lower-class culture as a generating milieu of gang delinquency.* Journal of Social Issues, 14, 5-19.

Miller, W.B. (1992). *Crime by youth gang and groups in the United States.* Washington, DC: U.S. Department of Justice, Office of Justice Programs, Office of Juvenile Justice and Delinquency Prevention.

Miller, D. and Looney, J. (1974). The prediction of adolescent homicide: Episodic dyscontrol and dehumanization. *The American Journal of Psychoanalysis, 34*, 187-198.

Mills, W.C. (1940). Situated actions and vocabularies of motive. *American Sociological Review, 5*, 904-913.

Moore, J. and Terrett, C. (1998). Highlights of the 1996 National Youth Gang Survey. Tallahassee, FL: National Youth Gang Center.

Myers, W.C. and Scott, K. (1998). Psychotic and conduct disorder symptoms in juvenile murderers. Homicide Studies, 2 (2), 160-175.

National Center for Injury Prevention and Control (2008). Retrieved March 1, 2008, from http:\\webappa.cdc.gov.

National Institute on Drug Abuse (2003). *Drug use among racial/ethnic minorities.* (NIH publication 03-3888). Bethesda, MD: U.S. Department of Health and Human Services, National Institutes of Health.

Nelson, R.C. (2000). Homicidal adolescents: Understanding kids who kill. *Dissertation Abstracts International* (UMI No. 9982779).

Nielsen, A.L., Martinez, R., and Rosenfeld, R. (2005). Firearm use, injury, and lethality in assaultive violence: An examination of ethnic differences. *Homicide Studies, 9* (2), 83-108.

Nofziger, S. and Kurtz, D. (2005). Violent lives: A lifestyle model linking exposure to violence to juvenile violent offending. *Journal of Research in Crime and Delinquency, 42* (1), 3-26.

O'Brien, R.M., Stockard, J. and Issacson, L. (1999). The enduring effects of cohort characteristics on age-specific homicide rates, 1960-1995. *American Journal of Sociology, 104* (4), 1061-1095.

Oberwittler, D. (2004, September). *Re-balancing routine activity and social disorganization theories in the explanation of urban violence: A new approach to the analysis of spatial crime patterns based on population at-risk.* Cambridge, UK: Institute of Criminology, University of Cambridge.

Office of National Drug Policy (2000, March). *Drug-related crime* (NCJ-181056). Rockville, MD: Drug Policy Information Clearinghouse/Fact sheet.

Oliver, W. (2001). *The violent social work of Black men.* San Francisco, CA: John Wiley and Sons, Inc.

Ousey, G.C. (1999). Homicide structural factors and racial invariance assumption. *Criminology, 37* (2), 405-425.

Ousey, G.C. (2000). Deindustrialization, female-headed families, and Black and White juvenile homicide rates, 1970-1990. *Sociological Inquiry, 70* (4), 391-419.

Pallone, N.J. and Hennessy, J. (1993). Tinderbox criminal violence: Neurogenic impulsivity, risk taking, and the phenomenology of rational choice. In R.V. Clarke and M. Felson (Eds.), *Advances in criminological theory*: Volume 5, Routine activity and rational choice. New Brunswick, NJ: Transaction.

Parker, K.F. and McCall, P.L. (1997). Adding another piece to the inequality-homicide puzzle: The impact of structural inequality on racially disaggregated homicide rates. *Homicide Studies, 1* (1), 35-60.

Parker, K.F. and Reckdenwald, A. (2008). Concentrated disadvantage, traditional male role modes, and African American juvenile violence. *Criminology, 46* (3), 711-735.

Payne, B.K. and Button, D.M.. (2009). Developing a citywide youth violence prevention plan: Perceptions of various stakeholders.

International Journal of Offender Therapy and Comparative Criminology, 53 (5), 517-534.

Pebley, A.R. and Sastry, N. (2003). *Neighborhoods, poverty and children's well-being: A review.* Retrieved January 30, 2006, from http://www.rand.org/labor/DRU/DRU3001-NICHD.pdf

Peterson, R.D. and Krivo, L.J. (1999). Residential segregation, the concentration of disadvantage, and Black and White homicide victimization. *Sociological Forum, 14* (3), 465-493.

Phillips, S. and Maume, M.O. (2007). Have gun will shoot?: Weapon instrumentality, intent, and the violent escalation of conflict. *Homicide Studies, 11*, 272-294.

Piquero, A.R. (2005). Reliable information and rational policy decisions: Does gun research fit the bill? *Criminology and Public Policy, 4* (4), 779-797.

Piquero, A.R. and Brame, R.W. (2008). Assessing the race-crime and ethnicity-crime relationship in a sample of serious adolescent delinquents. *Crime and Delinquency,* 1-33. doi: 10.1177/0011128707307219

Piquero, A.R. and Steinberg, L. (2010). Public preferences for rehabilitation versus incarceration of juvenile offenders. *Journal of Criminal Justice, 38,* 1-6.

Piquero, N.L. and Sealock, M.D. (2010). Race, crime, and general strain theory. *Youth Violence and Juvenile Justice, 8* (3), 170-186.

Pittman, D.J. and Handy, W. (1964). Patterns of criminal aggravated assault. *The Journal of Criminal Law, Criminology, and Police Science, 55* (4), 462-470.

Polk, K. (1993, May). *A scenario of masculine violence: Confrontational homicide.* Paper presented at the Australian Institute of Criminology Proceeding Conference, Australia.

Polk, K. (1994). *When men kill: Scenarios of masculine violence.* New York: Cambridge University Press.

Polk, K. (1997a). A re-examination of the concepts of victim-precipitated homicide. *Homicide Studies, 1*(2), 141-168.

Polk, K. (1997b, December). *When men kill: A comparison of everyday homicide with images of media violence.* Paper presented at the conference on Violence, Crime, and the Entertainment Media, Sydney, Australia.

Polk, K. (1998). Violence, masculinity and evolution: A comment on Wilson and Daly. *Theoretical Criminology, 2* (4), 461-469.

Polk, K. (1999). Males and honor contest violence. *Homicide Studies, 3* (1), 6-29.

Polk, K. and Ranson, D.L. (1989). *Homicide in Victoria,* report no. 41/88, Criminology Research Council, Canberra.

Porkorny, A. D. (1965). A comparison of homicide in two cities. *Journal of Criminal Law, Criminology and Police Science, 56,* 479–487.

Poussaint, A.F. and Alexander, A. (2000). *Lay my burden down: Unraveling suicide and the mental health crisis among African American men.* Boston, MA: Beacon Press.

Prothrow-Stith, D. (1991). *Deadly consequences: How violence is destroying our teenage population and a plan to begin resolving the problem.* New York: Harper Collins Publishers.

Prichard, J. and Payne, J. (2005). *Alcohol, drugs and crime: A study of juveniles in detention.* Research and Public Policy Series no. 67. Canberra: Australian Institute of Criminology.

Renzetti, C. and Lee, R. (1993). *Researching sensitive topics.* London: Sage Publications.

Rich, J.A. and Grey, C.M. (2005). Pathways to recurrent trauma among young Black men: Traumatic stress, substance use, and the "code of the street". *American Journal of Health 95* (5)*,* 816-824.

Richardson, J.D. (2003). Trauma care and the "lethality perspective". *The American Journal of Surgery, 186,* 97.

Riedel, M. (1987). Symposium in stranger violence: Perspectives, issues, and problems (special issue). *Journal of Criminal Law and Criminology, 78* (2).

Rohsenow, D.J. and Bachorowski, J. (1984). Effects of alcohol and expectancies on verbal aggression in men and women. *Journal of Abnormal Psychology, 93,* 418-433.

Rojek, D.G. (1999). Homicide and the drug connection. In P.H. Blackman, V.L. Leggett, B.L. Olson, and J.P. Jarvis (Eds.), *The varieties of homicide and its research: Proceedings of the 1999 meeting of the Homicide Research Working Group* (pp. 131-140). Quantico, VA: FBI Academy.

Ronel, N. (2010). Criminal behavior, criminal mind: Being caught in a "criminal spin". *International Journal of Offender Therapy and Comparative Criminology,* 1-26. doi: 10.1177/0306624X10384946

Rossow, I., Pape, H. and Wichstrom, L. (1999). Young, wet, and wild? Associations between alcohol intoxication and violent behavior in adolescence. *Addiction, 94* (7), 1017-1031.

Rubin, A. and Babbie, E.R. (2008). *Research methods for social work* (6th ed.). Belmont, CA: Thomson Brooks/Cole.

Russell, D.H. (1979). Ingredients of juvenile murder. *International Journal of Offender Therapy and Comparative Criminology, 23,* 64-72.

Russell, D.H. (1985). Girls who kill. *International Journal of Offender Therapy and Comparative Criminology, 29* (2), 171-176.

Rutter, M. (1985). Resilience in the face of adversity: Protective factors and resistance to psychiatric disorder. *British Journal of Psychiatry, 147,* 598-611.

Sales, E., Lichtenwalter, S., and Fevola, A. (2006). Secondary analysis in social work research education: Past, present, and future promise. *Journal of Social Work Education, 42* (3), 543-558/

Salfati, C. G. (1999). The nature of expressiveness and instrumentality in homicide and its implications for offender profiling. *Centre for Investigative Psychology,* 99 – 110.

Salfati, C.G. (2000). The nature of expressiveness and instrumentality in homicide: Implications for offender profiling. *Homicide Studies, 4,* 265-293.

Salfati, C.G. and Canter, D.V. (1999). Differentiating stranger murders: Profiling offender characteristics from behavioral styles. *Behavioral Sciences and the Law, 17,* 391-406.

Salfati, C. G. and Haratsis, E. (2001). Greek Homicide: A behavioral examination of offender crime- scene actions. *Homicide Studies, 5* (4), 335- 362.

Salts, C.J., Lindholm, B.W., Goddard, A.W., and Duncan, S. (1995). Predictive variables of violent behavior in adolescent males. *Youth and Society, 26* (3), 377-399.

Sampson, R.J. (1987a). Urban Black violence: The effect of male joblessness and family disruption. *American Journal of Sociology, 93,* 348-382.

Sampson, R.J. (1987b). Personal violence by strangers: an extension and test of the opportunity model of predatory victimization. *Journal of Criminal Law and Criminology, 78*, 327-356.

Sampson, R.J. (1997). The embeddedness of child and adolescent development: A community-level perspective on urban violence. In J. McCord (Ed.), *Violence and childhood in the inner city* (pp. 61-64). New York: Cambridge University Press.

Sampson, R.J. (2003). The neighborhood context of well-being. *Perspectives in Biology and Medicine, 46* (3), 53-66.

Sampson, R.J. and Lauritsen, J.L. (1990). Deviant lifestyles, proximity to crime, and the offender-victim link in personal violence. *Journal of Research in Crime and Delinquency, 27* 110-139.

Sampson, R.J., Morenoff, J.D., and Gannon-Rowley, T. (2002). Assessing neighborhood effects: Social processes and new directions in research. *Annual Review of Sociology, 28,* 443-478.

Sampon, R.J. and Wilson, W.J. (1995). Toward a theory of race, crime and urban inequality. In J. Hagan and R.D. Peterson (Eds.), *Crime and inequality.* Stanford, CA: Stanford University Press.

Sanders, W. (1994). *Gangbangs and drive-bys: Grounded culture and juvenile gang violence.* New York: Aldine de Gruyter.

Savitz, L.D., Kumar, K.S., and Zahn, M.A. (1991). Quantifying Luckenbill. *Deviant Behavior: An Interdisciplinary Journal, 12,* 19-29.

Schmideberg, M. (1973). Juvenile murderers. *International Journal of Offender Therapy and Comparative Criminology, 17,* 240-245.

Schmidt, A.E., Ryder, J.A., Crimmins, S.M., Spunt, B.J., and Brownstein, H.H. (1996). *Assessing hope among adolescents who commit violent crimes.* Paper presented at the meeting of the Academy of Criminal Justice Sciences, Las Vegas, NV.

Sendi, I.B. and Blomgren, P.G. (1975). A comparative study of predictive criteria in the predisposition of homicidal adolescents. *American Journal of Psychiatry, 132* (4), 423-427.

Sheley, J.F. and Wright, J.D. (1993). *Gun acquisition and possession in selected juvenile samples.* Research in Brief. Washington, DC: U.S. Department of Justice, Office of Justice Programs, National Institute of Justice.

Sherman, L.W. and Rogan, D.P. (1995). Effec*ts of gun seizures on gun violence: "Hot spots patrol in Kansas City.* Justice Quarterly, 12 (4), 673-694.

Shihadeh, E.S. and Maume, M.O. (1997). Segregation and crime: The relationship between Black centralization and urban Black homicide. *Homicide Studies, 1* (3), 254-280.

Short, J.F. (1997). *Poverty, ethnicity, and violent crime.* Boulder, CO: Westview.

Short, J.F. (1998). The level of explanation problem revisited–the American Society of Criminology 1997 Presidential Address. *Criminology, 36* (1), 3- 36.

Shumaker, D.M. and McKee, G.R. (2001). Characteristics of homicidal and violent juveniles. *Violence and Victims, 16* (4), 401-409.

Silverman, R. and Kennedy, L. (1993). *Deadly deeds: Murder in Canada.* Scarborough: Nelson Publishing.

Smith, M.D. and Feiler, S.M. (1995). Absolute and relative involvement in homicide offending: Contemporary youth and the baby boom cohorts. *Violence and Victims, 10* (4), 327-333.

Smith, M.D., and Parker, R.N. (1980). Type of homicide and variation in regional rates. *Social Forces, 59,* 136-147.

Sobol, J.J. (1995, November). *Victim characteristics and behavior attributes in criminal homicide: A case study in Buffalo, 1992-1993.* Paper presented at the annual meeting of the American Society of Criminology, Boston.

Sobol, J.J. (1997). Behavioral characteristics and level of involvement for victims of homicide. *Homicide Studies, 1* (4), 359-376.

Sommers, I. and Baskins, D. (1992). Sex, race, age, and violent offending. *Violence and Victims, 7* (3), 191-201.

Sorrell, J.M. (1977, July). Kids who kill. *Crime and Delinquency,* 312-320.

Sorrell, J. (1980, April). What can be done about juvenile homicide? *Crime and Delinquency,* 152-161.

Spano, R. and Bolland, J.. (2010). Disentangling the effects of violent victimization, violent behavior, and gun carrying for minority inner-city youth living in extreme poverty. *Crime and Delinquency,* 1-23. doi: 10.1177/0011128710372196

Spano, R., Rivera, C., and Bolland, J.M. (2010). Are chronic exposure to violence and chronic violent behavior closely related developmental processes during adolescence? *Criminal Justice and Behavior, 37* (10), 1160-1179.

Spergel, I.A. (1995). *The youth gang problem.* New York: Oxford University Press.

Starbuck, D., Howell, J.C., and Lindquist, D.J. (2001, December). *Hybrid and other modern gangs.* Washington, DC: U.S. Department of Justice, Office of Juvenile Justice and Delinquency Prevention.

Staub, E. (1996). Cultural-societal roots of violence: The examples of genocidal violence and of contemporary youth violence in the United States. *American Psychologist, 51* (2), 117-132.

Stewart, E.A., Schreck, C.J., and Brunson, R.K. (2008). Lessons of the street code: Policy Implications for reducing violent victimization among disadvantage citizens. *Journal of Contemporary Criminal Justice, 24* (2), 137-147.

Stretesky, P.B. and Pogrebin, M.R. (2007). Gang-related gun violence: Socialization, identity, and self. *Journal of Contemporary Ethnography, 36* (1) 85-114.

Sutherland, E.H. (1924). *Criminology.* Philadephia: J.B. Lippincott.

Sutherland, E.H. (1937). *The professional thief.* Chicago: University of Chicago Press.

Swisher, R.R. and Latzman, R.D. (2008). Youth violence as adaptation? Introduction to the special issue. *Journal of Community Psychology, 36* (8), 959-968.

Taylor, T.J., Esbensen, F., Brick, B.T., and Freng, A. (2010). Exploring the measurement quality of an attitudinal scale of street code-related violence: Similarities and differences across groups and contexts. *Youth Violence and Juvenile Justice, 8* (3). 187-212.

Tedeschi, J.T. and Felson, R.B. (1994). *Violence, aggression, and coercive actions.* Washington, DC: American Psychological Association.

Thornberry, T.P., Huizinga, D., and Loeber, R. (1995). The prevention of serious delinquency and violence: Implications from the program of research on the causes and correlates of delinquency. In J.C. Howell, B. Krisberg, J.D. Hawkins and J.J. Wilson (Eds.),

Serious violent and chronic juvenile offenders (pp. 213-237). Thousand Oaks, CA: Sage Publications.

Thornberry, T.P., Krohn, M.D., Lizzotte, A.J., and Chard-Wierschem, D. (1993). The role of juvenile gangs in facilitating delinquent behavior. *Journal of Research in Crime and Delinquency, 30* (1), 55-87.

Teplin, L.A., McClelland, K.M., Abram, K.M., and Mileusnic, D. (2005). Early violent death among delinquent youth: A prospective longitudinal study. *Pediatrics, 115*, 1586-1593.

Toch, H. (1980). Evolving a "science of violence": A propaedeutic comment. *American Behavioral Scientist, 23* (5), 653-665.

Turner, J.H. (2003). *The structure of sociological theory* (7th ed.). Belmont, CA: Wadsworth Publishing.

Uniform Crime Report (2004, October). *Crime in the United States 2003.* Washington, DC: U.S. Department of Justice, Federal Bureau of Investigations.

Unnever, J.D. (2008). Two worlds far apart: Black-White differences in beliefs about why African-American men are disproportionately imprisoned. *Criminology, 46* (2).

Valdez, A. (2000). *Gangs: A guide to understanding street gangs*, (3rd ed.). San Clemente, CA: LawTech Publishing.

Van Dorn, R.A. and Williams, J.H. (2003). Correlates associated with escalation of delinquent behavior in incarcerated youths. *Social Work, 48* (4), 523-531.

Van Horn, F.B. (1992). Father-absent, dangerousness, and high psychopathic deviancy: Causes of juvenile homicide. *Dissertation Abstracts International* (UMI No. 9334504).

Vaughan, R.D., McCarthy, J.F., Armstrong, B., Walter, H.J., Waterman, P.D., Tiezzi, L. (1996). Carrying and using weapons: A survey of minority junior high school students in New York City. *American Journal of Public Health, 86*, 568-572.

von Hertig, H. (1948). *The criminal and his victim.* New Haven: Yale University Press.

Voss, H. and Hepburn, J.R. (1968). Patterns in criminal homicide in Chicago. *Journal of Criminal Law, Criminology, and Police Science, 59*, 499-508.

Warr, M. (1993). Age, peers, and delinquency. *Criminology, 31*, 17-40.

Weaver, G.S., Wittekind, J.E., Corzine, L.H., Corzine, J. Peete, T.A., and Jarvis, J.P. (2004). Violent encounters: A criminal event analysis of lethal and nonlethal outcomes. *Journal of Contemporary Criminal Justice, 20* (4), 348-368.

Weinbach, R. and Grinnell, R. (2001). *Statistics for social workers.* Boston, MA: Allyn and Bacon.

Wells, W. and Horney, J. (2002). Weapon effects and individual intent to do harm: influences on the escalation of violence. *Criminology, 40* (2), 265- 296.

Werner, E.E. and Smith, R.S. (1982). Vulnerable but invincible: A longitudinal study of resilient children and youth. New York: McGraw-Hill.

Werner, E.E. and Smith, R.S. (1992). *Overcoming the odds: High risk children from birth to adulthood.* Ithaca, NY: Cornell University Press.

Whitaker, D.J., Baker, C.K., and Arias, I. (2007). Interventions to prevent intimate partner violence. In L. Doll, S. Bonzo, D. Sleet, J. Mercy, and D. Hass (Eds.), *Handbook of injury and violence prevention* (pp. 183-201).

Wieczorek, W.F., Welte, J.W., and Abel, E.L. (1990). Alcohol, drugs, and murder: A study of convicted homicide offenders. *Journal of Criminal Justice, 18*, 217-327.

Wiley, J.A. and Weisner, C. (1995). Drinking in violent and nonviolent events leading to arrest: Evidence from a survey of arrestees. *Journal of Criminal Justice, 23*, 461-476.

Wilkinson, D.L. and Fagan, J. (1996). Role of firearms in violence "scripts": The dynamics of gun events among adolescent males. *Law and Contemporary Problems, 59* (1), 55-66.

Wilkinson, D.L., McBryde, M.S., Williams, B., Bloom, S., and Bell, Kerryn (2009). Peers and gun use among urban adolescent males: An examination of social embeddedness. *Journal of Contemporary Criminal Justice, 25 (1)*, 20-44.

Wilkstrom, P.H. (1991). Cross-national comparisons and context specific trends in criminal homicide. Journal of Crime and Justice, 14, 71-96.

Williams, K. (1984). Economic sources of homicide: Re-estimating the effects of poverty and inequality. *American Sociological Review, 49*, 283-289.

Williams, J.H., Ayers, C.D., Abbott, R.D., Hawkins, J.D., and Catalano, R.F.(1991). Racial differences in risk factors for delinquency and substance use among adolescents. *Social Work Research , 23* (4), 241-256.

William, K.R. and Flewelling, R.L. (1988). The social production of criminal homicide: A comparative study of disaggregated rates in American cities. *American Sociological Review, 53*, 421-431.

Williams, J.H., Stiffman, A.R., and O'Neal, J.L. (1998). Violence among urban African American youths: An analysis of environmental and the behavioral risk factors. *Social Work, 22* (1), 3-13.

Wilson, J.Q. (1997). Hostility in America. *New Republic, 271* (8).

Wilson, M. and Daly, M. (1985). Competitiveness, risk-taking, and violence: The young male syndrome. *Ethology and Sociobiology, 6*, 59-73.

Wilson, W.J., Aponte, R., Kirschenman, J., and Wacquant, L. (1988). The ghetto underclass and the changing structure of American poverty. In F. Harris and R.W. Wilkins (Eds.), *Quiet riots: Race and poverty in the United States* (pp. 123-154). New York, NY: Pantheon.

Wolfgang, M. E. (1958). *Patterns in criminal homicide.* NY: John Wiley and Sons Inc.

Wright, J.D., Rossi, P.H., and Daly, K. (1983). *Under the gun: Weapons, crime, and violence in America.* New York: Aldine de Gruyter.

Yegidis, B.L. and Weinbach, R.W. (2002). *Research methods for social workers* (4th ed.). Boston, MA: Allyn and Bacon.

Yonas, M.A., O'Campo, P.O., Burke, J.G., and Gielen, A.C. (2007). Neighborhood-level factors and youth violence: Giving voice to the perceptions of prominent neighborhood individuals. *Health Education and Behavior, 34* (4), 669-685.

Yonas, M.A., O'Campo, P.O., Burke, J.G., Peak, G., and Gielen, A.C. (2005). Urban youth violence: Do definitions and reasons for violence vary by gender? *Journal of Urban Health: Bulletin of the New York Academy of Medicine, 82* (4), 669-685.

Zagar, R., Arbit, J., Sylvies, R., Busch, K.G., and Hughes, J.R. (1990). Homicidal adolescents: A replication. *Psychological Reports, 67*, 1235-1242.

Zimring, F.E. (1968). Is gun control likely to reduce violent killing? *University of Chicago Law Review, 35*, 721-737.

Zimring, F.E. (1972). The medium is the message: Firearm caliber as a determinant of death from assault. *Journal of Criminal Justice, 1*, 97-123.

Zimring, F.E. (1984). Youth homicide in New York: A preliminary analysis. *Journal of Legal Studies, 13*, 81-99.

Zimring, E.F. (1996). Kids, guns, and homicide: Policy notes on an age-specific epidemic. *Law and Contemporary Problems, 59* (1), 25-37.

Zimring, F.E. (1997). Juvenile violence in policy context. *Juvenile crime: Policy proposal on guns and violence, gangs and drugs, 31* (1), 419.

Zimring, F.E. (1998). *American youth violence.* New York: Oxford University Press.

Zimring, F.E. and Hawkins, G. (1999). *Crime is not the problem: Lethal violence in America.* New York: Oxford University Press.

Index

strain theory, 21, 136

Supplementary Homicide Reports, 75, 151

symbolic interactionism, 14, 18, 45, 58

victim-precipitation, 99, 102, 118, 121, 122, 131

violence, lethal, 2

weapon compensation, 53, 66, 81, 141

weapon facilitation, 66, 71, 76, 81, 134, 152

weapon instrumentality, 73–77, 79, 99, 100, 117, 119, 134, 141

weapon instrumentality effect, 71, 98, 121

Wells, William, 50, 52, 53, 59, 77, 83, 84, 85, 87, 88, 92, 134, 152, 153

Wilkinson, Deanna, 2, 4, 5, 6, 7, 8, 12, 19, 20, 21, 23, 29, 30, 33, 34, 35, 37, 38, 39, 40, 42, 44, 47, 48, 49, 54, 57, 58, 59, 62, 63, 64, 69, 70, 87, 89, 127, 130, 132, 133, 134, 137, 138, 139, 140, 141, 142, 157

Wilson, Margo, 2, 22, 25, 26, 27, 30, 35, 45, 47, 53, 55, 56, 59, 62, 64, 65, 69, 70, 72, 76, 83, 87, 89, 98, 128, 131, 133, 134, 140, 164, 170, 173, 181, 186

Wolfgang, Marvin, 2, 6, 7, 22, 23, 25, 29, 31, 43, 47, 50, 52, 53, 54, 55, 57, 59, 64, 67, 68, 72, 76, 77, 79, 80, 83, 87, 89, 104, 128, 129, 132, 151, 152, 153

Zimring, Franklin, 2, 3, 4, 8, 37, 40, 43, 44, 53, 55, 64, 67, 68, 70, 71, 72, 73, 76, 100, 127, 132, 134, 151, 152